'Warren Fahey tells us what Australian food is like and what it used to be like. This is a great and fertile country with an ingenious population and, when it comes to what we eat, we really don't have to wish ourselves anywhere else. Read this book to find out how we got to be that way.'

Alan Saunders
(Columnist and presenter of ABC Radio National's 'The Comfort Zone')

'Warren Fahey knows his tucker and can take his readers back along some fascinating bush tracks where campfires burned brightly and country kitchens produced dishes that were uniquely Australian and as tasty as the best.'

Joan Campbell
(Former food director for *Vogue* and *Vogue Entertaining + Travel*)

'My mother was fifth-generation Australian, which will mean nothing to you unless you too are Australian. The family were mostly engineers, and my great-grandfather went to Gympie in Queensland for the gold. I was raised on kitchen stories now retold so splendidly by Warren Fahey in his books. Australia is a harsh continent and raises strong brave women, and I am proud of my maternal inheritance and the stories that surround it.'

Clarissa Dickson-Wright
(TV chef and one of the 'Two Fat Ladies')

the curious history of
food in Australia

tucker
track

Warren Fahey

ABC
Books

Published by ABC Books for the
AUSTRALIAN BROADCASTING CORPORATION
GPO Box 9994 Sydney NSW 2001

First published December 2005

Every effort has been made to trace the orginal sources for quoted material
contained in this book. Please contact the publisher in case of any omission.

ISBN 0 7333 17278

Designed and typeset by Ellie Exarchos
Illustrations by Alexandra Sturrock
Typeset in 10/14 pt Berkeley Book
Printed and bound in Hong Kong, China by Quality Printing

1 3 5 4 2

Acknowledgements

There is no love sincerer than the love of food.

(George Bernard Shaw, Irish playwright, 1856–1950)

This book grew out of my continuing interest in what makes us unique as Australians. I am not an expert in gastronomy, rather an enthusiastic cook, host and folklorist, so I must thank all those generous souls who dug deep into their memories to make this book possible. I thank the staff of the Mitchell Library, Sydney, who still go searching for me, often chasing the nigh impossible. Thanks also to the Music Board of the Australia Council for the Arts, the Council of the City of Sydney, the Folklore and Oral History Section of the National Library of Australia, and my best mate, Rebel Penfold Russell, who all support my ongoing explorations in folklore collection and documentation. As always, thank you to Angelo Loukakis and the team at ABC Books who share my passion for Australiana and folklore. Finally, thanks to Mark Cavanagh, Moses and all those who have joined me in laughter and song around the dining table.

Contents

Introduction

This is a book about the curious history of food and the folklore we have created around its cultivation, preparation and consumption. It is definitely not a book of brain-numbing facts and some of it will appear quite peculiar and out of step with today's presumably sophisticated society. If anything, it is a book about us as a community, both an Australian and international community. Being folklore, it is the work of every man, woman and child, and is a vital part of our cultural treasury. It is mostly the work of anonymous creators lost in time, some recent and some centuries old, boasting of that glorious tradition of adoption and adaptation. Above all, it is about the most important aspect of our lives from birth to death — sustenance.

In truth, *Tucker Track* started out to survey the folklore of food and eating at the Australian table; however, in such a multicultural nation as ours, it became all too obvious the book would need to move to a more 'worldly' table. In many ways, the book is a time capsule that was born when the First Fleet settled in Sydney Cove and, as it whirled on through the years (more than two centuries), it collected new customs, habits, superstitions and other folklore.

It is well known that the 'folk' have never allowed the truth to get in the way of a good story, and the folklore associated with eating and drinking — and the preparation of both — is steeped in superstition, custom and habit. Often we draw upon this lore unconsciously and at other times we guard it and use it as a very personal bank. To be honest, it doesn't matter two hoots if it is factual as long as it serves a purpose in our daily lives. However, lore often does carry wisdom; it is one of the key factors in its very survival.

Tucker Track surveys a wide span of our eating traditions, showing how and what we ate, both in the country and city, mainly over the past two centuries. It shows how customs and traditions move in and out of society to suit the needs of the population. Colonial Australia planted some dishes firmly on the table, as did imaginative bush cooks and, more recently, the various waves of immigration that spiced us up and down. Food is rich in tradition and it is one of the ways each culture distinguishes itself from others. As the old maxim says, 'We are what we eat.'

Steven Shapin, writing in the *London Review of Books*, summed up the meaning behind eating very succinctly.

> Food is polysaturated with culture. Indeed, one could put it much more strongly: the practices attending the production, preparation and ingestion of food make up much of the substance of moral and social order. We are, literally and fundamentally, what we eat. A temperate person is someone who eats temperately; a posh and powerful person is someone who gets an eight o'clock table at the best restaurant; respect for life is shown with vegetarianism; red-blooded machismo by the consumption of red meat; your friends eat with you at home; you have coffee with your colleagues; the High eat later than the Low, thus making a standard display of delayed gratification and acquiring the associated status of those who can wait an hour longer than others for their food. Self-nourishment and self-fashioning both happen at the table.

While the 'average' Australian sees himself or herself as 'middle class' it is important to realise that there has also been a rich class and, to a lesser extent, a low-income class. All groups in society create and carry folklore; however, money does define what is served and usually how it is prepared and consumed. Expensive restaurants also attract an affluent clientele and that affects the folklore created around such dining experiences. But, in the end, rich or poor, we all have to eat.

I grew up in an average Sydney suburban household. Both my parents were the eldest of exceptionally large families; my father's was Irish and my mother's Jewish. Having little money, we considered food not only a necessity but also a combination of entertainment and tradition. My father, a one-time rationalist, atheist, socialist and scrap-metal merchant, was of the old school in as much as he never entered the kitchen other than to do the washing up, which he seemed to enjoy. I would do the wiping up as Dad sang Irish songs he'd learned from his parents. My mother ruled the roost and kept an extremely tidy yet effective kitchen. Her adherence to cleanliness defied her productivity, for the compact kitchen churned out a litany of dishes including a weekly quota of biscuits, cakes and puddings. I was the kitchen slave, or so it appeared, while my sister, eight years older, was more interested in dressmaking and the latest dance craze. I remember scrubbing, mixing, peeling, scraping and, of course, tasting. I loved being in the kitchen and was just as happy drying up, shelling peas or playing sous chef.

My interest in folklore started early and, as an Irish Jew (I called myself an 'Irish Stew'), I had songs, stories, ditties, customs and superstitions coming from all sides. My mother's family were the real foodies and no family gathering — and we had them at every opportunity — was complete without the aunts arriving with enormous pies, trifles and sponge cakes. My mother's father, Sid Phillips, was the accepted cook of the family with his wife Polly content to knit, play piano, read tea leaves, deal cards and talk about her nine children. Sid cooked Jewish-style, although none of the family was particularly religious. He had been an army cook in World War I and that also contributed to his repertoire. I used to help him fry fish and cod roe fillets and I still remember the way he dipped the fillets in egg, then in his homemade breadcrumbs and then back into the egg mix before they hit the pan. He fried beautifully and when he had finished he always made extremely thin pancakes, folded into triangles covered in sugar and lemon juice. He also pickled his own dill cucumbers that he stored in humungous glass jars. I still remember the tears that went with grating horseradish to accompany the fish and I also remember the slice of potato I clenched in my teeth to stop those very tears. Sid always referred to his chicken soup as 'Jewish penicillin' and I can still savour its gentle flavour and pieces of white chicken flesh mixed with the fine vermicelli noodles and parsley. What I remember most was the fact he strained the soup through one of Polly's old stockings!

My mother, Deborah, loved to read cookery columns, especially Margaret Fulton in the *Women's Weekly* (when it was a weekly). I loved to look at the usually out-of-register colour images of wobbling jellies, tiered cakes and new dishes with unpronounceable names like stroganoff or cacciatore. She maintained a scrapbook where she pasted favourite recipes carefully scissored out of magazines or written down by friends. She loved to experiment and we loved being guinea pigs. We had fondues, stir fries, casseroles and slow-cooked foods alongside the usual silverside, roasted lamb, beef stews and fish pies. It didn't take me long to realise there was a subtle difference between a casserole and a stew. Deborah was equally adventurous with spices. Curry for us changed from bright yellow to rich and creamy when we threw out the 'English' curry powder and replaced it with chilli and Indian spices. Another favourite was pickled-walnut beef casserole.

Although I grew up in the city, I ended up spending a great slice of my twenties and thirties travelling bush roads collecting old songs, poems and other lore. At one stage, in the early seventies, I lived in a kombi for a year travelling up and down the east coast, tape-recording and noting down folklore. This provided me with an opportunity to compare the city kitchen with the country kitchen and, not surprisingly, there was little difference. Country women, like their city counterparts, read the cookery pages of the *Women's Weekly* and *Woman's Day*, they held to a rigorous baking day regime, and cooked up a storm of stews and puddings, using whatever fresh ingredients were available. Coastal cooks favoured seafood while further inland saw a greater reliance on beef and lamb. Over time I saw an increase in the popularity of rice and other grains and also a growing interest in more exotic spices, especially Asian. Our foodways continue to change in the city and country and are influenced by everything from the increasing availability of fresh foods, the popularity of television food programs and the adventurous nature of the average Australian.

It is in childhood that folklore plays such an important role. Food is the one thread that takes us from the cradle to the grave. Many lullabies are designed to act as a soothing encouragement during breast-feeding; however, it is in the important formative years when the child starts to speak that folklore really kicks in. We hear of Georgie Porgie with his puddings and pies; that silly, fragile egg Humpty Dumpty; little Miss Muffett with her curds and whey, and, of course, that little girls are made of sugar and spice and everything nice. Sad about the boys! A few years later we delight in stories like Goldilocks and the three bears and their obsession with porridge, the three little piggies who went to market, Snow White and that apple, Pooh and his honey pot, and, under our very own gum tree, the amazing story of the Magic Pudding. These are just a few examples from the culinary folklore common to most of us. Some, like the nursery rhymes are straight out of tradition, anonymous creations handed down from family to family, while others like Snow White and Pooh officially belong to a commercial world. However, in most cases, the stories have twisted and turned to become part of the same family despite the continuing claims of their copyright owners.

Once in the schoolyard folklore cranks into high gear as it skips, hops, claps and generally goes on the ran-tan. Food is one of the major elements of any playground insult or taunt, perhaps in the guise of a custard pie in the face (as in 'One, two, three, four … out you go!'). Gwenda Davey and June Factor, two Melbourne folklorists, have specialised in collecting and analysing children's folklore and a check through their books reveals food as the dominant subject matter, even if quite scatological.

We need to consider what role food plays in children's folklore for it is far more than just entertainment. There is definitely traditional wisdom to be found and that is most probably the key factor in its perseverance in the tradition. The little songs, sayings and ditties prepare us, educate us, and show us values that we use in our lives.

Some may appear to be pure nonsense but often there is an underlying value, even if only familiarity. They also play a role in our appreciation of words, sentences and rhythms of language. In its most basic sense, children's folklore is a vibrant expression of the genre as a whole in as much as it is learned directly from oral transmission.

We congregate when someone dies, marries, celebrates a birthday or anniversary, graduates, etc — all with the common cry of, 'Let's eat!' The importance of food in our lives as we celebrate, congregate, worship, work and play tends to be overlooked because it is thought of as a necessity. There is also the fact that traditional knowledge, in most of its expressions, is poorly documented. The act of sharing food at a table is now regarded as an act of confirmation, as if to seal an event or action. It is interesting to note that communal eating and drinking was seen by the Ancient Greeks to be a sign of equality — a distinct social group sharing the same values, political power and food. Today we even see business and politics staging 'power lunches' at which issues are discussed and often resolved as if the table is neutral territory. This is not an entirely new idea for it was the eighteenth-century Scottish author James Boswell who remarked, 'A dinner lubricates business.'

Home entertaining, like the business lunch, continues to change with regard to what we eat, how much we eat and where we eat it. In the nineteenth century a formal dinner party could involve over a dozen courses, from canapés and soup through to desserts and cheeses. By the latter half of the twentieth century a more realistic three-course meal had become the norm. In the health-conscious twenty-first century we are looking at not only what we eat, but also *how much* we eat. Three hefty courses are, of course, too much for the average stomach, however this depends on what is actually served. A small salad followed by the main dish and then a small sweet or cheese would solicit a polite nod. However, a heavier entrée, like a soup, or a cream- or cheese-based dish, followed by a main and then a heavy pudding (and most are fairly heavy) would definitely get a dietician's frown. Dégustation menus, however enticing, would also be a big no-no. We are what we eat but we are also how much we eat and we all know the result of carrying too much weight. We often create folklore around our approach to eating, reflecting the influence of dietary change, current urban myths, superstitions, fashion and peer pressure.

Despite a natural scepticism, Australians are still quite superstitious. One only needs to look at how popular astrology and horoscopes are in the daily rags. We usually don't like to admit to being superstitious, since it implies a certain weakness, yet we are slaves to those quaint customs and habits formed in our youth. Given a choice we will avoid walking under a ladder and, in the kitchen, if we happen to spill the salt we will more likely than not, throw some over our left shoulder. Better to be safe than sorry!

Our language is peppered with food references (and I have just used one) and few countries could claim a language as expressive as ours. We have a knack of abbreviating words, using rhyming slang and changing the meaning. So we 'light the barbie', 'chuck on the snags, chook or spuds', 'burn the bastards and hoe in'. We also pass on words of wisdom as if we were Hippocrates or Pliny: 'feed a cold, starve a fever', 'an apple a day keeps the doctor away', 'eat your crusts if you want your hair curly'. In most cases we have absolutely no idea what these old sayings mean or where they originated, other than 'Mum [or Dad] used to say that.' There is some truth in the adage, 'Say it often enough and you will believe it.'

Sayings such as 'born with a silver spoon in the mouth' passed into popular circulation as part of the evolution of our language. We like to describe things colourfully and shared metaphors allow us to converse in a popular tongue. Linguists are always tracking our language and, in truth, even language is a member of the folklore family as it is passed on down through the years by popular ownership and oral transmission. We employ and pass on folk sayings because they are understood by a wide section of the community. The Australian language is particularly expressive, especially the slanguage we use to describe certain foods: 'snags' (sausages) and 'dog's eyes' (pies) are consumed with bottles of 'piss' (alcohol). The Bible has also been the source of some of our well-known food sayings: 'Eat, drink and be merry' sounds Shakespearean but is straight from Ecclesiastes in the Old Testament, 'sour grapes' is from Ezekiel, 'living off the fat of the land' is from Genesis, and 'salt of the earth' is from Matthew.

So called 'old wives' tales' abound in the Australian tradition. It makes sense that new mums would find comfort in such tales and superstitions because most are the product of their own family upbringing and, 'If it was good enough for Mum, it's good enough for me.' They also recognise that Mum or Grandmother was right about a number of things in the home so a general acceptance is better than individual doubt. Pregnancy is a major event in any household and anything reassuring is seen as a positive. Belief in the healing powers of a particular plant, for example, is likely to be carried down from family to family even if not actually used. Again, it is not difficult to believe in the recuperative power of chicken soup, the 'Jewish penicillin' usually prescribed for those suffering from a cold. The heat of the soup probably does a little good but that's about its total contribution. It is important to realise there is a blurry line between some folklore and reality. At this point, it's probably also wise to point out that foods and herbs are natural partners in medicine; however, they can also be based on myth and none of the contents of this book should be construed as an alternative to professional medical care or advice.

Organised religion has also played a role in popularising some folklore when it happened to suit the church's needs: it's easier to incorporate some superstitions rather than fight their acceptance. Christianity, for example, inherited from Judaic tradition the practice of regulating what and when people ate. Fish on Fridays was nothing more than a folklore custom that tickled the church and popular sense of obligation. Special fasting, during Lent or the Muslim Ramadan, is another example. The Christian Last Supper with its shared meal and table has special significance, as does the transmogrification of bread to the body of Christ. Believers identify these as fact and sceptics view them as myth. Many Asian religions also use food as a sacrificial offering both in religious celebration or during the actual ceremony.

Food has always been used as religious folkloric symbolism:

Adam and Eve's apple, the fatted calf sacrificed for the return of the prodigal son, the sacrifice of Cain and Abel, Lot's wife turning to salt, and the various church calendars of fasting and feasting. Stewart Lee Allen summed it up perfectly in his book *In The Devil's Garden* when he noted: 'If you deconstruct most religious ceremonies, you wind up with a man dressed suspiciously like a chef serving some kind of snack.'

Thankfully, the average Australian eats three meals a day and has rarely experienced lean times. Those who have experienced starvation will tell you they dream of food, inventing elaborate stories of full tables offering dishes of extraordinary expanse. The old-time bush workers experienced these dreams regularly and tell of them in poems and songs. This is the basis of the utopian worlds of Cockaigne, Schlaraffenland and the Big Rock Candy Mountain where delicious foods are free and flowing:

In the Big Rock Candy Mountain, you never change your socks,
And the little streams of alcohol come trickling down the rocks.
The brakemen have to tip their hats and the railroad bulls are blind.
There's a lake of stew and of whiskey, too.
You can paddle all around them in a big canoe
In the Big Rock Candy Mountain.

(Written by Harry 'Haywire' McClintock)

Health food and diets attract folklore too and are often referred to as 'fads', implying they are viewed with a cyclical eye. We've all heard of the Israeli Army diet, the apple cider vinegar diet, the eat-as-much-fat-as-you-like diet, the Atkins diet, the grapefruit diet and, my favourite, the alcohol diet. Fad diets tend to encourage disciples who spread the 'word' as if a miracle will encourage the faithful to listen up. They often create stories, usually 'wonder' stories, to reinforce their claims. These stories sometimes enter the folk tradition but usually get a bit twisted in the process. The marketing of the Sydney-based Unique Water brand is a good example of how these stories spread. This bottled mineral water has been hailed as a cure for just about anything from Alzheimer's to Parkinson's disease and is often described as a 'miracle cure'. The main sales outlet is via the Internet alongside testimonials where consumers swear black and blue it has cleared their eczema, arthritis and even eased multiple sclerosis. It has been shown to be nothing more than bottled water but this has not stopped a flow of orders from across the world. Obviously there are people who want to believe miracle stories and, just like the circulation of urban myths, they are ready to relate a story 'that I heard from a friend of a friend…'

Then there is the folklore surrounding the failure of a particular diet or 'remedy' and the dreadful consequences. The Internet has emerged as a major carrier for this type of folklore. I have always been interested in natural health and, in the eighties, operated a natural grocery and health store in Paddington, Sydney, called Grandma Was Right! It was an interesting learning curve and one that further opened my eyes to the potential of natural remedies and the intelligent intake of natural foods. Health, and that includes healthy eating, is a personal journey and one needs to find the combination that best suits, and that includes dismissing the quackery and faddish. During this time I was continually presented with new 'wonder' products and amazing testimonials. These products covered everything from yoghurt being used to treat thrush to the healing powers of New Zealand's green-lipped mussels. One learnt to distinguish fact from fiction and also the position of folklore in such stories.

We are naturally wary of technology and folklore has a role to play in allowing us to express and share our fears. In the 1950s aluminum was a target and thousands of Australians were unnecessarily warned off cooking in pots made from the metal. In the 1970s it was the microwave oven and we spread urban myths about exploding cats that had been placed in the cookers, supposedly to dry their coats. We were eager to pass these stories on because they fed our fear of technology. We are now developing, and rightly so, a fear of food additives and especially genetically altered foods. Stories abound of two-headed chickens and three-yolk eggs and, recently, we had the scare associated with the distinctive red colouring additive common to many Indian recipes: it was found to be extremely toxic. The current debate surrounding the value and danger of eating too much soy is another example. Fear is often the result of misinformation, however, and in our twenty-first century kitchen we need to be wary of how misinformation is sent to us. Particular note should be taken of the role of the spin-doctors of the public relations industry, who provide us with information based on economic rationalism and commercial manipulation rather than good old common sense.

Food festivals have become an important part of our national arts calendar. These annual events are usually born of a tourist or outright commercial program, however they still tend to be community driven. Some of these events tend to seem phoney as they sit under the shadow of the Big Banana, the Giant Potato or the Big Pineapple, but in a real world they celebrate a community's local produce and are perhaps not that far removed from similar celebrations from centuries back when festivals celebrated a good harvest and implored the gods for the coming year to be more fruitful. Some early festivals even went so far as offering human sacrifice, so the odd Big Banana is a small price to pay!

Australians have defined the art of eating outdoors, especially the barbecue and picnic. The word 'barbecue', although originally indicating a Caribbean cooking style, has become synonymous with Australia especially its ocker diminutive, 'barbie'. If we were to have any definable food rituals the barbecue would be the high altar and its sacrificial food burnt offerings. So much lore surrounds the barbecue — and the picnic, to a lesser degree — including word usage, slanguage, cooking 'secrets', recipes, stories and jokes. We have also been inventive in designing and making barbecue units out of the most surprising things: old lawn mowers, sides of cars, etc, and often decorating them in a folk art style.

Australia, of course, is a giant stew pot where some of the world's most tasty cultures come together. It took us quite a time to appreciate the indigenous approach to bush foods but we readily accepted the myriad flavours, spices and foodstuffs that came with various waves of migration. Our palate has been spiced up by the Chinese who came for the gold rush; the Afghans who hawked camel-led caravans across our sun-baked plains; refugees who came from war-torn Europe; and a flow of new arrivals from South America, Asia and all points north. Our lives and our palates continue to be enriched by immigration as exotic meats, seafood, vegetables, fruits, nuts and spices combine with the early stew pot of English, Scots, Irish and Welsh pioneers — a tasty dish indeed. In *Tucker Track* you will find a wide survey of folklore; however, understandably, I have concentrated on the lore familiar to my own 'average' cultural background of Anglo–Celtic–European. A whole book could be written just about Chinese folklore in Australia and similarly all other imported cultures. I have offered a smattering of what has come across my table. How we cook and what we like are very closely related to family history and traditions. Food traditions are things that we inherit and carry on with determination. Sometimes nationality and religion disappear but not the upkeep of family food traditions. Even if language is long forgotten and there are no other ties to the homeland, the food traditions and recipes most often live on.

Our attitudes to food continually change and, as with most things in our everyday lives, we are manipulated by the media. We are told we can now judge a food by how guilty we feel about eating it. If it is not considered naughty we find it less appealing and this message is fired at us from all quarters. Much is related to sex. Freud suggested that we humans experience our first sexual and culinary thrill simultaneously when we suckle at our mother's breast.

Then there's the food of love. Our lust for aphrodisiac foods has led to the extermination of entire species and it is only lately that governments are taking firm action to prevent this unnecessary slaughter. Folklore has played a devil's role in the popularisation of such foods. In this book you will find references to many natural foods and recipes that supposedly have a sexual connection.

Of late we have seen the emergence of the gastronome, whose whole purpose in life appears to be to delight in the joys of the table. Bookstores are bursting at the seams with food-related publications and especially books by celebrity chefs. This is not new, for early Greek literature gives strong evidence of a keen interest in gastronomy including the relationship of food to health and the right way to prepare and cook food. The Greeks were also among the first to recognise cooking as an art and one of life's basic skills.

Folklore enables us to look at ourselves as a community and as a culture. In some ways it is emotional history far more relevant and important to our lives than all the facts and figures of library historians for it enables us to see who and what we are. Food history has generally been the result of paid social historians, often contracted to multinational food processing and marketing companies, and their results are usually tainted by their engagement. Hopefully, this survey will show how Australian food folklore has travelled and its relevance in the twenty-first century.

Cookbooks only became popular in the period 1880–1900. Before this, recipes were a form of lore passed down in oral tradition, usually from family to family. Over the years many of these family recipes found their way into local and even national cookbooks and some ended up with blue ribbons at the local agricultural show. A quick glance through any of the Country Women's Association cookbooks will give evidence of our inventiveness in the Australian kitchen. Some cooks jealously guard their recipes and some see giving away a favourite recipe as the ultimate bonding experience: it makes friends for life. It is a standard joke that, even in the best cookbooks, ingredients are left out so nobody will be able to recreate exactly the art of a famous chef.

Cooking has recently emerged as a major leisure activity for many Australians who assiduously hunt down unusual ingredients to produce meals to compete with the likes of Tony Bilson, Stefano Manfredi, Bill Granger, Nigella Lawson, Christine Manfield, Jamie Oliver, Neil Perry, Lyndey Milan, and countless other television chefs. Most are excellent, some good and some woeful. We have television programs exploring every area of food and wine and even a dedicated cable channel for the food obsessed. Reality television is also right up there, with food taking a large slice of *Queer Eye for the Straight Guy* and all of *My Restaurant Rules!* There are food reviews and columns in every newspaper and most magazines and, of course, magazines devoted solely to food and wine. One wonders how these 'celebrity chefs' get time to scratch themselves let alone actually cook. We've come a long way from campfire to designer kitchen!

The folklore in this book comes from an extraordinarily wide field and has been collected over the past thirty years of fieldwork. It has been recalled from family reminiscence, diaries, magazines and newspapers, and from scraps of paper scribbled down over many kitchen and restaurant tables. The old sayings, herbal wisdom, poems, songs, jokes, nursery and schoolyard rhymes are vibrant examples of folklore in action in today's society. It's not possible to give sources for many of these sayings, yarns, ditties and reminiscences, as their origins have often been lost in the mists of time. However, I'm sure you'll find much to press your nostalgia buttons — especially among the many familiar children's skipping, clapping and singing rhymes.

Food folklore celebrates our diversity and originality as a people and for that reason it is a valuable insight into our unique culture. This book is not the definitive survey of our foodways but it hopefully offers a hearty and tasty bite.

One word's as good as ten

Grace

Australia, born of a rough and tumble childhood, has never been a particularly God-fearing country. We tend to call a spade a spade and have a roll-up-the-sleeves approach to everything from work and war to romance and eating. Maybe our peculiar attitude stems from the reality of facing God-given tests of drought, flood, pestilence and bushfire, where determination and the occasional bush curse offers the only salvation. We appear to begrudgingly acknowledge the powers above for our bountiful tucker. As they say, a wink is as good as a nod.

I was brought up in a much stricter era where a child would not dare leave the table without an almost whimpering, 'Please may I leave the table?' Certain manners were expected including keeping 'those darned elbows off the table', using the cutlery properly (none of that lazy American fork business), maintaining an acceptable voice level, never ever talking with your mouth full and, above all, only speaking when spoken to. Playing with your food was not at all acceptable and it was expected that you would finish all if not most of the main meal. If you didn't the dessert would instantly disappear! It sounds like boot camp but somehow it worked. It may not have been quite as strict as I make out but we definitely knew the parameters of table conduct and what was expected of us. Of course times have changed — in the early 1950s we had no television, however the radio was probably just as much of a temptation, and there was always a mountain of homework to be completed. I now look back and think how eager I was to leave the table and can't help but compare myself to young European children, especially French and Italian, who appear almost reluctant to leave the ambience of the family table. I can't recall my family ever saying grace, other than for my occasional offering of 'Five, six, seven, eight — bog in, don't wait!' The real 'grace' in our family was inevitably led by my father — I can't recall him ever leaving the table without praising my mother's cooking skills and the meal itself.

APPETITE

Rise from dinner with an appetite, and you will not be in danger of sitting down without one.

ETIQUETTE

Where the guest of honour is a man, he should take the hostess's arm when entering the dining room. If the hostess is very far gone, another gentleman may take the other arm, a third gentleman going in front with the legs. (Lennie Lower)

GRACE

One word's as good as ten
All bog in, Amen

Heavenly Father bless us,
And keep us all alive;
There's ten of us for dinner
And not enough for five.

See my finger
See my thumb
Look out tummy
Here it comes.

Hail Mary, full of grace
All her knickers made of lace

One word's as good as ten
Bog in, Amen

Roll your eyes around the table
Fill your belly while you're able.

Eat away, chew away,
Munch, bolt and guzzle,
Never leave the table 'till
You're full up to the muzzle.

> (The Magic Pudding)

Not for my sake
Not for your sake,
But for Gawd's sake —
I give this bread to you.
But for my sake
And for good's sake —
Put some butter on it.

> (Swagman's prayer)

Porridge for one
Porridge for two
I shall be finished
Long before you.

'Never eat more than you can lift.'

> (Miss Piggy)

And, on those occasions where one burps:
Pardon me for being so rude
It was not me it was my food
It just came up to say hello
And now it's gone back down below.

Distinctly Australian

Iconic foods

There was a time, not so long ago, when Australian cuisine was seen as a joke, an oxymoron. If anything, it was a meat pie with tomato sauce or, just as scary, a badly barbecued sausage slapped between two slices of tasteless white bread and, you guessed it, dripping with tomato sauce. The national drink was beer and good manners didn't exist. Times have changed and so too the stereotyped image inherited from the male-dominated nineteenth century and the awkward theatrical interpretations of the twentieth century. George Wallace senior, followed by Chips Rafferty, followed by Bazza McKenzie, then Paul Hogan, all reinforced the uncomfortable image of the pie-eating, beer-drinking, loud Australian. However, Australian cuisine is now considered to be up there with the best. Not only do we successfully export our beef, lamb and wheat but also our chefs who continue to be hailed as international culinary stars. At restaurants, and at home, we eat dishes that would make a drover's eyes pop out as we drizzle our plates with virgin olive oil, truffle oil and balsamic vinegar. We still enjoy a cold beer but if wine sales are anything to go by we are popping the corks off everything from Jacob's Creek to Penfolds Grange. To top this off we are among the world's largest consumers of cookbooks and cookery television programs.

We may have become sophisticated in our dining and wining; however, the average Australian will still step forward to the barbecue or be just as content shelling prawns on the beach as he or she would be in a top restaurant. It has a lot to do with our climate and the fact that so many of us live on the coast. We are a relaxed people blessed with some of the world's best produce, and we know it. This doesn't stop us getting nostalgic about certain food brands that have travelled down the years with us and have become what we refer to as 'iconic'. To be classed as iconic, a product — usually a commercial, branded product — must have time on its side, or universal recognition. The Hills Hoist that once twirled in most Australian backyards is rarely seen these days, however it is always at the top of the list of Australian icons. Some food has also disappeared into history but is often still remembered as an icon. An example of this would be the Sundowner Apricot and Pineapple Jam and, for that matter, the distinctively plain IXL jam wrappers that once graced most Australian tables. The meat pie must still be at the top of such iconic food lists and, by all accounts, doesn't show any sign of disappearing. Most of us still believe a meat pie and sauce can be a bloody great meal.

AEROPLANE JELLY

First manufactured in Melbourne in 1928 these jelly crystals became a household name when in 1939 the 'Aeroplane Jelly' song, written by one of the company's partners, Albert Lenertz, was released to radio. Five-year-old Joy King first sang the commercial jingle and it is still used today.

> I've got a song that won't take very long,
> Quite a good sort of note if I strike it…
> It is something we eat, and I think it's quite sweet,
> And I know you are going to like it.
>
> I like Aeroplane Jelly… Aeroplane Jelly for me,
> I like it for dinner; I like it for tea,
> A little each day is a good recipe.
> The quality's high, as the name will imply,
> And it's made from pure fruits, one more good reason why
> I like Aeroplane Jelly, Aeroplane Jelly for me.

ANZAC BISCUITS

There is some dispute whether the Anzac biscuit was created in New Zealand or Australia; however, no one could dismiss the enduring popularity of this round, flat biscuit that first appeared during World War I. Folklore has it that women wanted to send something nutritious and sweet to the boys at the front, and the Anzac biscuit with its long-lasting ingredients was ideal. They were sometimes called 'Soldier's Biscuits' and were packed in tins, often billy cans, sealed with greaseproof paper. The binding ingredient is none other than good old golden syrup or treacle. Anzac biscuits are still cooked and are the pride and joy of the Country Women's Association.

RECIPE FOR ANZAC BISCUITS

125 grams (4 ½ ounces) of butter
1 tablespoon golden syrup
1 teaspoon baking soda
1 cup shredded coconut
¾ cup flour
¾ cup sugar
1 cup oats
a pinch of salt

Melt the butter and add the syrup and then add the soda, which should be dissolved in two tablespoons of boiling water. Beat mixture for one minute and then add remaining ingredients. Pour flat round discs of the mixture onto a cold greased slide and bake till nice and brown. The biscuits should be crisp.   (Mrs Wendy Henderson, Heathcote, NSW)

BARCOO SANDWICH

Anything in the bush thought to be inedible — for example, 'a goanna between two sheets of bark' or 'a couple of gibber stones marinated in port'. Also known as a Borroloola sandwich.

BILLY TEA

Although one could be forgiven for thinking that any tea boiled in a billy could be iconic, it is actually the Inglis & Co., tea merchants of Sydney, branded Billy Tea that Australians hold dear. This could be for two reasons; firstly because of their distinctive advertisement showing the swagman leaning against a gum tree in earnest discussion with a kangaroo carrying a swag, and, secondly, because this company was the first to use Banjo Paterson's 'Waltzing Matilda' for a marketing campaign, in 1903. Incidentally, the popular music to which we now sing 'Waltzing Matilda' was set by the wife of the manager of Inglis & Co., one Marie Cowan.

COCKY'S JOY
The bush name for golden syrup, that sticky relative of treacle, which became the favourite sweetener on damper and in puddings in the nineteenth century.

COTTEE'S PASSIONA
This sweet soft drink was once an Australian favourite. Along with the brilliantly coloured green GI, it was delivered by local licensed cordial bottlers. We used to joke that GI stood for green ink. We also made soda drinks by plonking a knob of ice-cream into a glass full of these cordials.

LAMINGTON
Lord Lamington was the Governor of Queensland for a time and his lordship and good wife were touring the outback in the late 1890s and decided to visit an average household. The sturdy country woman of the house, showing necessity to be the mother of invention, chopped up a stale sponge cake, then dipped it in chocolate and shredded coconut — and the rest is food history.

A popular school fundraising custom is to sell lamingtons. This is called a 'lamington drive'.

LOLLIES
The first recorded 'lolly shop' appeared in 1854 and lolly became the accepted Australian term for sweets, especially boiled sweets and toffees. In the early twentieth century picture theatres employed 'lolly boys' to carry trays of sweets to customers. Who could forget the

sound of chocolate Jaffas rolling down the cinema aisle, the taste of black and white humbugs, the mess one made with a Choo Choo Bar or the excitement of sharing a box of Fantales?

MEAT PIE

For far too many years Australian 'cuisine' was said to be the meat pie with tomato sauce. Round or square it was considered a suitable icon and the consumption of steak pies — complete with gristle and guts — was part of the Australian identity of the first half of the twentieth century. It was Bazza McKenzie's favourite food and the ideal partner to a schooner of beer. This, thankfully, has changed and, although we still consume millions of pies every year, our national cuisine has moved on and is now more definable as seafood and chardonnay.

That said, the meat pie is still alive in our folklore and the subject of songs, poetry, jokes and urban myth. One of our most famous commercial brands, Four 'N Twenty, draws upon children's folklore ('Sing a Song of Sixpence') for its brand name. As if to differentiate our pie from the French-style pie, the *real* Aussie pie needs to be doused in tomato sauce or, if you are a Crow-eater from South Australia, it will be a 'pie floater', complete with mashed peas and gravy.

Originally, pies were created as a way of preserving meat. The fat and aspic jelly encased in pastry will keep meat for over a week in warm weather. It was not unusual for people to eat the contents and throw the pastry casing to the dogs.

NATIONAL DRINK

The German likes his beer.
The Pommy likes his half and half.
Because it brings good cheer,
The Scotsman likes his whisky,
The Irishman his hot,
The Aussie has no national drink,
So he drinks the bloody lot.

26

PAVLOVA

Essentially a soft-centred meringue filled with cream and fruit, this iconic dessert reputedly got its name when described to be as 'light as Pavlova' (the ballet dancer) when she toured Australia in 1929. Much to the horror of most red-blooded Australians the dessert was actually invented in New Zealand where it won a prize in a newspaper competition. It was greatly improved and made internationally famous by Chef Herbert Sachse of the Hotel Esplanade, Perth, Western Australia, who served it at the hotel's afternoon tea. It is the national dessert of both Australia and New Zealand.

PMG

A popular brand of black, fruit-based sauce similar to House of Parliament and Father's Favourite. Kids delighted in calling it 'PMG — Pig's Meat & Gravy'.

SAO

This dry water biscuit was made by William Arnott, the pioneer biscuit makers, and, according to folklore, took its name from the acronym of Salvation Army Officers. One of the Arnott family was very active in the Salvation Army, especially in composing songs and music. For a time in the 1950s the Sao was used to make vanilla slices: a slab of solidified custard wedged between two biscuits with the top Sao covered in pink icing. They weren't that good!

TOMATO SAUCE

What Australian icon list could avoid including tomato sauce? Rosella, one of the most popular brands, was established in 1894 when Horacio McCracken and Thomas Peel started boiling up fruits and vegetables in a copper pot in their Carlton, Melbourne, backyard. Folklore has it that the name came from the family members Rose and Ella; however, it could also have been because of the large flocks of eastern rosellas that would have flown over the area. It is interesting to note that the company's website opens with the line, 'One of Australia's favourite icon foods'.

VEGEMITE

Created in Melbourne in 1922, this black spreadable yeast goo is recognised as Australia's national health spread. Its United Kingdom cousin is Marmite, the invention of one Baron Liebig who also created Extract of Beef. At one stage it looked as if our home-grown spread was to be permanently renamed Parwill. This marketing move resulted in a popular saying, 'If Marmite, then Parwill!' Alan Weeks saved the day with his clever advertising commercial that put a rose in every cheek.

> We're happy little Vegemites, as bright as bright can be,
> We all enjoy our Vegemite for breakfast, lunch and tea.
> Our Mommy says we're growing stronger every single week,
> Because we love our Vegemite, we all adore our Vegemite —
> It puts a rose in every cheek.

WEET-BIX

In what is probably another example of advertising campaigns reinforcing a food myth, whenever most people think about this breakfast cereal they are reminded of the jingle, 'Aussie kids are weet-bix kids'. I remember as a kid we not only ate these brick-like compressed cereal cakes but also tried making sandwiches out of them by coating the biscuits with peanut butter or honey.

The staff of life
Bread

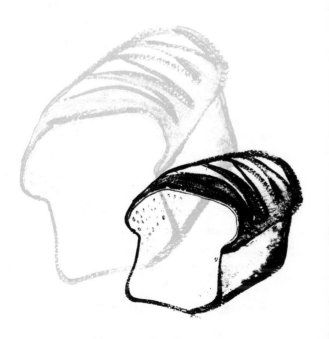

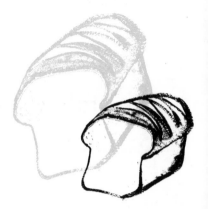

Bread is significant in many religious ceremonies, most notably the Christian transmogrification from bread to body of Christ. Unleavened bread is also an integral part of Jewish religious ceremony, especially Passover observance. To this day many French people trace the sign of the cross on their loaves before slicing.

Universally, bread is known as 'the staff of life' — signifying its role as the major element at the table. Bread has also long been seen as indicative of social status, with the coarse brown breads being seen fit for the lower classes and the fine white bread for the rich. This custom seems to date back to Roman times when the landed gentry viewed being offered brown bread as a hideous insult. Caesar even made the serving of brown or black bread a punishable crime.

In Australia we have gone from home-baked loaves to an industry that churns out new varieties every month. In the early 1950s there were tank loaves — so called because they resembled a water tank with corrugated sides — high-hatted Vienna loaves and a standard loaf, and many a kid got into trouble for gnawing at the fresh crusts as they carried the loaves home. A few years later storekeepers offered to slice the loaves with a special slicing machine. With the move away from corner stores to supermarkets in the 1960s, the range of bread started to expand introducing rye, wholemeal, pumpernickel and multi-grain; then, with the 1980s, all hell broke loose as the industry introduced designer breads, fancy rolls and loaves of every description.

There's just one bit of eating
Which I hold supremely great
An' that's good old bread and gravy
When I've finished up my plate.

If thou tastest a crust of bread, thou tastest all the stars and all the heavens.
(Robert Browning, English poet, 1812–1889)

How can a nation be great if its bread tastes like Kleenex?
(Julia Child, American food writer)

BAGUETTE

The thin, approximately two-foot long baguette — the French word for 'wand' — is as recognisable a symbol of France as any tourist attraction. This bread stick is hugely popular and in France it is not uncommon to see a line of twenty people or more queuing for a favoured baker's bread. The baguette has been popular in Australia for around thirty years, however the consistency varies dramatically. In France the flour for baguettes is highly controlled and, in the best shops, they're baked fresh twice a day. The best baguettes balance a crispy exterior with a light interior. Here, however, some baguettes are less like wands and more like wooden clubs.

There is a belief that the baguette was popularised by Napoleon Bonaparte who didn't want the old heavy country loaves weighing down his army's knapsacks. He designed the baguette to go down the legs of the soldiers' trousers!

BAKER'S DOZEN

The baker's dozen dates back to the twelfth or thirteenth century. European bakers caught selling less-than-law-weight loaves were liable to be nailed to their bakery doors through their ears. An extra loaf avoided that fate and a baker's dozen became thirteen loaves.

BAKING BREAD

Without a doubt baking, and especially bread baking, produced a huge body of folklore, much of it bound to religion and ceremony.

Bread baked on Christmas Eve will never go mouldy.

If you find a hole inside your bread this is a warning that someone's grave is ready.

Burning a loaf of bread is unlucky.

If you sing before baking bread you will cry before it is eaten.

If a loaf taken from the oven breaks apart, expect a stranger.

BREAD AND DRIPPING

Earlier generations were brought up with parents threatening to replace uneaten food with 'bread and dripping, just like we had to eat during the Great Depression years.' When children wouldn't eat their food, parents would also say, 'There are children in India who would love that.' To which the inevitable response would be, 'Name one!'

BREAD LORE FROM THE PLAYGROUNDS

Q: When is bread most wanted?
A: When it's kneaded

Q: Why is the sun like a good loaf?
A: Because it's light when it rises

BREAD SPEAK

We use bread as a metaphor in much of our Australian speech.

What does he do for a crust?

He earned his crust.

She likes her bread buttered on both sides.

You need to know which side your bread's buttered.

It's the greatest thing since sliced bread.

The term 'upper crust' refers to the rich and privileged and in fact comes to us from the sixteenth century when King Henry would only eat the top half of his morning white bread roll — the upper crust.

BREAD SUPERSTITION

When two people reach for the same slice, expect company.

Cutting bread from both ends is considered to be unlucky.

Bread falling on the ground butter-side up means you will have a visitor.

To drop bread butter side down is bad luck.

Dreaming of bread is considered lucky.

It is bad luck to break bread in someone's hand.

To take the very last piece of bread is bad luck.

Never give away the heel (the end) of the loaf to a stranger because they will take your luck with them.

CRUMBS

If you brush crumbs off the table onto the floor you will always be poor.

CRUSTS

I must not throw upon the floor
The crust I cannot eat
For many a hungry little child
Would think it quite a treat.

A widespread folk belief is that eating crusts produces curly hair.

SLICED BREAD

Otto Frederick Rohwedder invented the bread slicer, which he started working on in 1912. At first, he came up with the idea of a device that held the slices together with hatpins (not surprisingly, it was a failure). In 1928, Rohwedder designed a machine that sliced and wrapped the bread to prevent the sliced bread from going stale. Pre-sliced bread was popularised by the American Wonder Bread Company in 1930, and appeared in Australia in the 1940s.

TOAST

Toast is grilled sliced bread. The word comes from the Latin *tostus*, meaning 'roasted' or 'parched', and toast's origins lie in the Roman practice of dipping a piece of burnt bread into the wine. Roman wine varied considerably and was often of dubious quality and taste. The burnt bread was said to absorb some of the bad flavour — the charcoal reduced the acidity of soured wines making them more palatable.

Toasting bread was also seen as a method of prolonging its life. The first electric toaster was invented in 1893 in Great Britain by Crompton and Co (UK) and re-invented in 1909 in the United States. It only toasted one side of the bread at a time and it required a person to stand by and turn it off manually when the toast looked done. Charles Strite invented the modern timer, pop-up toaster in 1919.

In 2004, a piece of grilled toast said to be carrying the face of the Virgin Mary was sold over eBay. With a starting price of $7 it finally went to a man in Florida who paid $35,814.79 for it. Apparently the slice of toast even had a bite out of it!

YEAST

In 1860, Louis Pasteur proved that fermentation is caused by living organisms and asserted that the agents responsible for the reaction were connected with the yeast cell. Yeast is used in bread making and beer brewing and has a noble history that dates back to Ancient Babylon.

If a man dreams of yeast his wife or lover will fall pregnant.

Yeast should never be carried over water, as it will result in bad luck.

Down in the dairy

Milk, cream, cheese and yoghurt

I t is not surprising that, as our first nourishment, milk was believed to possess magical powers. Be it from cow, sheep, camel or goat, milk has become an important part of our diet. We drink it by the glassful; we make milkshakes by adding syrups and malts; and we turn it into butter, yoghurt, buttermilk, quark, cream cheese and, of course, ice-cream.

It will probably surprise many readers to learn that two brothers, Norman and Clarence Burt, opened the first milk bar in the world in 1930 at Manly, a beachside suburb of Sydney. It was an instant success with a trade of hamburgers, saveloys and, of course, milk-based, iced flavoured drinks. There was also a mysterious concoction called 'The Girvana Sling' that cost ten pence. In 1935 Hugh McIntosh, an Australian entrepreneur, opened a similar milk bar in London and, as they say, the rest is history.

Cheese and other dairy products were made in Australia from the early days of the penal settlement, mainly from goat's milk. The major problem, of course, was keeping the products fresh in such a hot climate. Most houses had an insulated cool room or below-ground storage. In the 1950s, most Australian households depended on ice-chests and a twice-weekly delivery of large ice blocks for refrigeration. The 'ice man' delivered right to the kitchen and most had a familiar street 'cry', a drawn out or musical 'iccccce maaan' that would ring out through the suburbs.

Dairy products, like all foods, attract folklore. The most persistent dairy lore is that milk is essential for healthy bone formation, especially in children. This is a myth and no other species, apart from some domesticated animals, drinks milk beyond infancy. Osteoporosis is less common in Asia where people consume fewer dairy products and where most of their calcium intake is derived from nuts, pulses and other plant sources. It is not uncommon for commercial interests to maintain myths for their products and the dairy industry is just one example of this, repeatedly urging the market to drink milk to build strong bones. A recent campaign used the catchphrase 'Milk — The Food for Life'.

BUTTER

Eat butter first, and eat it last, and live till a hundred years be past.

(Old Dutch proverb)

Butter was known in ancient times and was introduced to the Greeks by the Scythians. Herodotus spoke of the Scythians who 'poked out the eyes of their slaves so that nothing could distract them from churning their milk'.

Butter is heavy in fats and an old saying offered wisdom:

Gold in the morning,
Silver at noon,
Lead at night.

Butter speak: 'To land with one's arse in the butter' means to be born lucky.

There was a time in history when the European rich had their kitchens prepare elaborate carvings out of butter for display purposes.

In colonial Australia the preparation of butter and other dairy products was almost exclusively the domain of women and children. This must have been difficult in a climate where extreme heat and cold play havoc with making butter and cheese. After refrigeration came in, Australian butter became a major export product.

BUTTERFINGERS

Anyone who has played ball games in the schoolyard will recall the shouts of 'Butterfingers!' if they continually dropped the ball. We are not sure where this reference originated other than the fact that butter has a history of being used as a lubricant.

BUTTERMILK

To remove mildew from garments, put sour buttermilk on the spots and then leave in the sun to bleach. People also used buttermilk to clean corrosion from brass.

CHEDDAR

An English cow's milk cheese originally from Somerset, cheddar was one of the earliest commercial cheeses to be eaten in Australia where it was, for no definable reason, referred to as Coon cheese.

A giant 500-kilogram cheddar was given to Queen Victoria on the occasion of her marriage. Maybe this is where the term 'big cheese' came from?

If we want to express displeasure we say, 'stiff cheddar' or 'stiff cheese'.

CHEESE

After cheese comes nothing!

Cheese is a peevish elf
It digests all by itself.

How can you be expected to govern a country that has 246 kinds of cheese?   (Charles de Gaulle, 1890–1970)

A dinner which ends without cheese is like a beautiful woman with only one eye.   (Jean-Anthelme Brillat-Savarin, 1755–1826)

There is a legend that cheese was invented by accident. An Arab merchant was setting off on his journey and put his fresh milk in a pouch made from a sheep's stomach. He rode away on his camel and by nightfall discovered his milk had interacted with the rennet and, agitated by the camel's continual movement, had turned to whey and curds.

Cheese has been called the 'food of the gods' and 'the first fast food'.

CHEESECAKE

The cheesecake was one of those food fads, like lasagne, that never went away. This will probably come as a surprise but cheesecake is believed to have originated in Ancient Greece. History records that cheesecake was served to the athletes during the first Olympic Games held in 776 BC.

American James L. Kraft invented pasteurised cheese in 1912, and that led to the development of pasteurised Philadelphia cream cheese, the most popular cheese used in Australia for making cheesecake today.

CREAM

It is said that 'cream rises to the top', which it does; however, this saying has also come to mean that excellence will eventually show itself.

Because of its changing character, cream became associated with many colloquial sayings such as 'he was a cream puff', implying a lightweight, or 'she was cream of the crop', implying the best.

An old custom aimed at ridiculing bachelors required cream to be put into a glass vessel and then placed in a bachelor's bosom, where it was said it would freeze. This implied bachelors had no warmth or even a heart.

ICE-CREAM

Folklore has it that ice-cream was invented for Charles I of England— his cook prepared it with snow as a surprise dessert for a banquet. Unfortunately there is no evidence to support this tale or other legends concerning Marco Polo bringing it back from China or Catherine de Medici taking it to France. More likely it is a nineteenth-century creation coinciding with the invention of the hand-cranked ice-cream freezing machine in 1846, by a New Jersey woman named Nancy Johnson. Whatever its history, ice-cream has become a major confectionery throughout the world — even in Alaska.

I scream
You scream
We all scream
For ice-cream

Ice-cream and jelly, a punch in the belly,
Fruit and nuts, a punch in the guts.

MILK

As kids we were always told drinking milk was vital for building strong bones. In 1953 the Commonwealth Government introduced a free milk scheme to Australian schools. Delivered in a third of a pint glass bottles the milk was consumed by primary students in the mid-morning at what was called 'play lunch'. Often the bottles were warm from sitting in the sun and tasted quite disgusting. The aluminium tops were used for decoration. Special tops, sometimes coloured, were created for celebrations like Empire Day and the Queen's birthday — these are now a valued collector's item. Many schools collected the standard silver tops and made Christmas decorations by stringing them together. The government-funded milk deliveries ended in the 1980s. When Margaret Thatcher ended the British scheme she was dubbed 'Margaret Thatcher — Milk Snatcher'.

Since the year 2000, 29 September is designated by the dairy industry as World School Milk Day.

Whether it is custom or habit many Australian tea drinkers will argue forcibly to extol the merit of putting the milk in the cup before the tea. Others will swear black and blue it must be added after the tea has been poured.

It was common for children to refer to milk as 'moo juice'.

Milk is for babies. When you grow up you have to drink beer.

(Arnold Schwarzenegger, 1975)

Hast thou not poured me out as milk, and curdled me like cheese?

(Job, speaking to God)

Never cry over spilt milk.

If you stir milk with a fork the cow will go dry.

It is bad luck to allow milk to boil over.

When breast-feeding a baby one should never offer the left breast first, as it will result in a left-handed child.

Milk spilling is unlucky, except in Ireland where milk is the favourite drink of fairies.

Drink a glass of milk before alcohol to prevent the alcohol absorbing into the system.

MILK SUBSTITUTE

When there is no milk, soak half a pound of oatmeal in a quart of cold water for twelve hours. Strain, and the mock milk is ready to be used in tea, coffee or cooking.

(Sara McCrea, Gawler, SA)

YOGHURT

Q: what is the difference between yoghurt and Australia?
A: Yoghurt has a culture. (Ouch!)

Yoghurt has been used as a beauty product for over 1500 years and, in particular, as a face cream and cleanser. It is now eaten all over the world and recognised for its healthful qualities.

According to Persian tradition and Biblical records, Abraham once served a bowl of yoghurt to three angels. He believed he owed his fertility and longevity to daily consumption of yoghurt. It was also mentioned that King David kept his soldiers strong and healthy on a diet of yoghurt.

Buddhist history tells of the Buddha meditating under fasting conditions. He lost consciousness and was near death when a woman came along and offered him a bowl of yoghurt. After Buddha consumed this, he regained consciousness. According to the Buddhist Holy Scriptures (*nyet pan*), yoghurt was said to be the highest quality of food able to be derived from the fermentation of cow's milk.

The great Mongol Emperor, Genghis Khan was said to have issued a military command that all soldiers carry yoghurt with them when out in the battlefields. These soldiers consumed yoghurt as part of their daily diet to keep healthy, strong and powerful.

Koranic records points to many instances where the Prophet Mohammed referred to yoghurt as 'food from God and an elixir for all illnesses'. He carried a goatskin of yoghurt with him at all times and would feed some of it to any disciple who was sick.

Yoghurt probably originated in the Balkans ('yoghurt' is derived from the Turkish word *jugurt*), but its popularity spread from the Middle East where milk production was seasonal and the nomadic people who produced the milk lived a long way from the coastal markets where they could sell their produce. High temperatures soured or fermented the milk quickly, so lactic acid and bacteria — which turned the milk into a soft curd — were encouraged by heating the milk over a fire. This mixture was then hung in animal skins where it cooled to form curd or whey.

Europeans discovered a taste for yoghurt around the fourteenth century.

The history of yoghurt in Australia dates back to the 1930s when it was mostly associated with the Seventh Day Adventists. In the 1960s it was still considered a 'hippy' health food and has only gained mainstream popularity since the 1980s.

Baking day

Pies, tarts, biscuits and cakes

There is nothing quite like the aroma of a kitchen on baking day. Up to the mid-1960s, almost everybody's mum baked cakes and biscuits, and store-bought biscuits were a treat. Baking was done on a Saturday and family members were often recruited to help with the mixing and pouring and especially the washing up. There were real pleasures to be earned by joining in, not the least being the opportunity to take a giant spoonful of the moist cake batter that always tasted so heavenly. Cakes came in all shapes and sizes and flavours, including orange cake, marble and rainbow cake, sponge cake, caraway seed cake, poppy seed cake and those little cup cakes that were ever so popular. We also bestowed fancy names like Vanilla Snow Cake, Angel Cake, Fairy Cake and Butterfly Cake. Icing was part of the ritual and the creative cook gave free rein to her favourite flavourings and decorations. On Saturday afternoons, we mowed the lawn, washed the car and then sat down to afternoon tea and cake.

Baking was traditionally an art taught to the girls of the house and passed on down through the family. Smacking of 'secret women's business' the kitchen emerged as the room in the house where idle gossip was acceptable and folklore thrived. Old sayings were trawled out time and time again, half-remembered rhymes recited and songs sung. It was also a place where superstition ruled supreme and woe betide anyone who broke with tradition. After all, why not place a horseshoe in the oven to guarantee success in baking? It was in the kitchen that tea leaves would be read, the petals of flowers plucked to find a lover's name, and where herbal knowledge, prized recipes and cooking tricks were passed on. Titbits were repeated and if Aunty Maude said that to throw away baking scraps was unlucky then, over time, it came to be regarded as truth. Of course one of the main reasons for all this is that cooking, especially baking, needs preparation and attentive watching. Time in the kitchen was time well spent.

Many cakes have a ceremonial or symbolic significance linked to Christian religious feasts such as Christmas, Easter, Epiphany and Candlemas. Asian and other religions also use cake in a similar way. In addition, cakes have an important role in anniversaries, birthdays, engagements and weddings.

A number of foreign cakes are well known in Australia including the Black Forest, cheesecake, carrot, strudel, baklava, linzer-torte, devil's chocolate and panetone.

AUSTRALIAN GEMS
Gem scones appear to be an Australian creation made with light dough baked into dainty balls and served with butter or cream and jam

BAKED ALASKA
The baked Alaska doesn't appear to have much to do with Alaska and seems to be a very old dessert. Prosper Montagne in *Larousse Gastronomique* suggests it was invented in 1720 by a Swiss pastry cook called Gasparini. Whatever the history, this dish was all the rage in swanky Australian restaurants in the 1970s and still surfaces, mostly at festive occasions. It is usually made with ice-cream and sponge encased in a meringue. It is also known as omelette surprise.

BISCUITS
In the first half of the twentieth century no self-respecting housewife would dare have a half-empty biscuit tin. Saturday was usually baking day for two cakes, a pudding and several types of biscuit. The

biscuits were always on hand in case friends or neighbours dropped in — an empty tin was a major embarrassment. Popular biscuits included sultana biscuits, Anzacs and treacle drops.

After World War I biscuits were made commercially and sold in bulk by the weight. Up to the 1950s most corner stores offered Arnott's biscuits out of a large distinctively designed tin and, if you weren't fussy, you could also buy broken biscuits at a discounted price. We never called them cookies!

BROWN BETTY

An old-fashioned dessert made with sliced apples, cinnamon, sugar, lemon juice and breadcrumbs. Served hot with fresh cream. As they say, 'a moment on the lips and a lifetime on the hips!'

BROWNIE

To a standard recipe for damper add sugar, currants or raisins and a goodly whollop of fat. The standing joke is that if you have no currants then use dead flies, as no one will know the difference! Some suggest you should add cocoa to give the brownie the right taste and colour. A 'whitey' is a brownie made without fat.

BUN IN THE OVEN

A colloquial Australian reference to someone being pregnant — 'She's definitely got a bun in the oven.'

CAKE

Cake making and decorating hold a special place in Australian household lore. Sixty years ago most women spent half a day baking cakes, puddings and biscuits and many took extreme pride in their specialities.

A menstruating woman cannot make a good cake.

A cake baked in the afternoon will fall by sunset.

A cake will fall if two or more persons stir it.

You can't eat your cake and keep it.

CARAWAY SEED CAKE

The shearer had earned a spree in town and headed down to Adelaide where he decided to hit the high spots. His first stop was a swish restaurant where he ordered tea and cake. The waitress delivered the tea and a lovely fresh caraway-seed cake. The shearer looked at the cake, 'I see the mouse plague has hit down here too.'

EMERGENCY CAKE

A cake made from all manner of ingredients that are available. A case of necessity being the mother of invention.

FARMER'S CAKE

A cake made with cooking apples, golden syrup, cinnamon, cloves, flour, butter, sugar, egg and sour milk.

FRUIT CAKE

Australians appear to be great fruit cake cooks and there was a time when most women wouldn't dream of not having one in the cupboard — in case friends dropped in. The abundance of fruit and nuts in Australia helped popularise this cake and, above all other recipes, the fruit cake recipe was prized and preserved. Some women freely surrendered their family recipe only to leave out one important step or ingredient so the cake would never be as good as theirs!

People can also be 'mad as a fruitcake'.

POUND CAKE

So named because it used to be made it with a pound of butter.

SCRIPTURE CAKE

The ingredients of this cake are all mentioned in the relevant Bible passages.

225 grams (½ pound) butter	Judges 5:25
1 cup sugar	Jeremiah 6:20

1 cup warm pumpkin	Psalms 63:5
1½ cups self-raising flour	1 Kings 4:22
1½ cup plain flour	1 Kings 4:22
3 eggs	Isaiah 10:14
2 cups figs	1 Samuel 30:12
2 cups raisins	1 Samuel 30:12
a pinch of salt	Leviticus 2:13
spices to taste	1 Kings 10:10

Follow Solomon's rule for making good boys (Proverbs 23:14) and the cake will be perfect.

SPONGE CAKE

Farmer Sandy, a canny Scot, was always proud of his wife's ability to make a meal out of just about anything.

'What are we having for afternoon tea?' the canny Scot asked.

'Sponge cake, dear,' replied Sandy's proud wife. 'I sponged the eggs off Mrs Doughty, the flour off Mrs Robinson and the milk off Mrs O'Malley.'

The typical sponge cake is made using many whole eggs and no shortening or leavening. It is the pride and joy of the country kitchen. It is usually sliced into two with a layer of fresh whipped cream and jam — a sponge sandwich.

CURRANTY BUNS

These buns, obviously made with currants, were extremely popular in colonial Australia along with drop scones, rye and treacle bread, date rings, treacle scones and drought buns.

MAIDS OF HONOUR

Maids of Honour were small raspberry and lemon tarts. Although popular in Australia, their origin dates back to the sixteenth century where folklore has it they received their name from King Henry VIII. Apparently the king observed his royal maids eating these tiny lemon curd tarts and asked what they were called. They said that the tart had no name so he replied, 'They are Maids of Honour.'

MARGARINE

Margarine was discovered in 1869 by Hippolyte Mège Mouriès, a French food research chemist, in response to Napoleon III's request for a wholesome butter alternative. It is not entirely clear whether the primary aim was the betterment of the working classes or economics in the supply of food to the French army. Margarine became popular in Australia in the 1970s.

PARKIN

Parkin belongs to the economical family of tea breads sometimes called 'cut-and-come-again' cakes. Made with little fat and no eggs, the texture depends on treacle or golden syrup which, during baking, caramelises and makes the cake hard outside yet moist inside. Parkin originated in Britain and was associated with Guy Fawkes Night festivities. In Australia it was served on Bonfire Night, and, one assumes, a few nights after that!

PASTRY COOKS

One bush worker remembered a famous cook who turned up at the Speewah Station one year. Apparently this cove had been the chief pastry cook at the Australia Hotel in Sydney but had been fired for hitting the booze. The cook had been sent to the bush to dry out. 'He was a marvellous cook. The only problem we had was that his pastries were so unbelievably light that if you didn't keep the mess hut windows shut they would just float out and off into the clear blue sky.'

PIKELETS

Pikelets are Australian, but belong to the international pancake family together with the Chinese egg roll, French crêpe, Swedish platter, Jewish blintzes, American griddle or hotcakes, Hungarian palacsinta and Welsh crempog, to name but a few.

RECIPE FOR PIKELETS

1 egg
2 tablespoons sugar
1½ cups of flour

1 teaspoon golden syrup

½ teaspoon baking powder

1 teaspoon cream of tartar

1 small cup milk

1 tablespoon butter

Beat the egg and sugar till light and frothy then add the remaining ingredients, except for the butter. Melt the butter in 4 tablespoons of boiling water — hot water and butter is the secret ingredient for successful pikelets — and then add to mixture. Use a hot, slightly greased griddle or pan and pour small pikelet drops with a spoon. Cook till nicely brown. Eat with jam.

SCONES

The scone is said to have taken its name from the Scottish Stone of Destiny (or Scone), the place where Scottish kings were once crowned. The original triangular-shaped scone was made with oats and griddle-baked. Today's versions are more often flour-based and baked in the oven. They come in various shapes, including triangles, rounds, squares and diamonds, and are usually served with butter or cream and jam. There was a time, not so long ago, when every Australian woman — and some men — could dish up a rack of scones at the mere sound of a doorbell.

PUMPKIN SCONES

Pumpkin scones are associated with the state of Queensland as Australia's favourite pumpkin — the Queensland Blue — is, not surprisingly, readily available there. It is like a giant-sized buttercup winter squash. The Queensland Blue has hard, bluish-green skin; inside is firm, orange flesh. The pumpkin scone came to national attention through its association with Lady Flo Bjelke-Peterson, wife of the former Premier of Queensland.

55 grams (2 ounces) softened butter

¼ cup sugar

1 egg

1 cup mashed, cooked pumpkin

¼ cup milk

2 ¾ cups self-raising flour

Preheat oven to 200°C (400°F). Lightly grease two baking trays. Cream softened butter and sugar. Add egg and beat well. Add mashed pumpkin and milk. Fold in flour using a fork, and mix well. Place mixture on a well-floured board or pastry sheet and gently press out to approximately 1 to 2 centimetre (½ to ¾ inch) thickness. Cut into scone shapes using a round cutter with a 5 centimetre (2 inch) diameter. Place rounds on greased baking trays and brush tops with milk. Bake for 10–15 minutes or until golden brown. Remove from oven, turn out onto a clean dishtowel, wrap and allow to cool slightly. Serve warm, split open and spread with butter. Makes approximately 24 scones.

Magic potions
Food and health

The history of food is a fascinating study and much of what we know started with the Ancient Greeks, Romans and Chinese. Much is tied to religion and some to famous healers, theologians and even witches. Most foods have a traditional association born of suggestion, experimentation or muddled belief. Many have come to us after centuries of use, especially the medicinal herbs. It is difficult to weed out fact from fiction and even now we are continuing to discover hidden benefits as well as debunk long-held beliefs. Today, we describe as 'natural remedies' what, in some cases, were previously the stock-in-trade of herbalists and witches.

For most people herbs have a stereotyped image. They are thought to be usually green and often bitter to the taste. The average person will also acknowledge that many herbs have medicinal powers along with properties of flavour, decoration and scent, and that some are edible. Magical qualities are often attributed to herbs and we become quite superstitious about their use. The same could be said of edible roots, bark, stems, leaves, fungi, seaweed, fruits, nuts and flowers that are used as both food and medicine. Some of these beliefs are based on fact and others on hearsay.

Some come with a promise that they will make the consumer 'feel better' and this is half the battle with many illnesses. It is common to see pharmaceutical and alternative medicine proclaiming 'feel better faster' and similar and, once again, seeing or hearing is believing.

One would imagine that old lore, sometimes referred to as 'old wives' tales', has little place in today's world where fact and figures rule our lives. This is far from true and the more we speed towards globalisation and computer-driven lifestyles the more valued the old ways seem. They have a role to play in stabilising us, reassuring us and passing on wisdom.

ACORN

The mighty oak tree is recognised as the king of all trees — 'as staunch as a mighty oak'. The tree's roots go deep and the tree itself shoots tall. This might possibly explain why acorn nuts were placed on windowsills to protect the house from lightning. Like much folklore this has been adapted and adopted for modern-day life and you will still find acorns, usually plastic, as the decorative toggle at the end of commercial window blinds manufactured in Australia.

Acorns are considered to be a symbol of prolonged effort preceding perfection, and are still used as lucky charms and can also be found as key-ring ornamentation.

One should note here that close proximity to the tree did not stop Chicken Licken from being hit on the head by an acorn and then declaring to her fairyland friends Henny Penny and Goosey Loosey, 'The sky is falling.'

If a woman dreams of eating acorns she will do well in life.

Great oaks from little acorns grow.
(Or as our grandparents sometimes offered:
'Great aches from little toe corns grow.')

ANGELICA

Familiar as a bright green, candied cake decoration, angelica is also the major ingredient in Chartreuse, Vermouth, gin, and that priestly drop Benedictine. It originally came from Scandinavia to central Russia and then to France and the rest of the world. The Chinese have a variant of angelica called *dang fui*.

The folk believed angelica aided digestion, circulation and

respiration. It is said to give a warm sensation when eaten. Angelica was also taken to prevent plague, and folklore has it that its remedial powers were revealed in a dream when an angel appeared with a sprig in its hand — hence the name angelica.

Another version of the origin of the name comes from the United Kingdom where the herb comes into bloom around the feast of St Michael the Archangel (8 May in the old calendar) — angelica was seen as a gift from the archangel. It was widely used against the powers of witchcraft.

APHRODISIACS

Aphrodite, the Greek goddess of love, sprang forth from the sea on an oyster shell and proceeded to give birth to Eros and, eventually, the word aphrodisiac.

The folk have eclectic taste in erotic foods, historically favouring artichoke, figs, asparagus, celery, cabbage, leek, lettuce, parsnip, turnips, caviar, clams, oysters and chocolate. (One would certainly have to think hard about the sexual powers of turnips and cabbage). Such foods were supposed to provide the consumer with special sexual powers, usually of exaggerated capacity; however, there is no reasoning behind most associations.

I had a dozen oysters last night but only three of them worked!

ARROWROOT

Q: What is the hardest job in the bush?
A: Milk arrowroot biscuits!

Arrowroot is the starch extracted from the underground stems of several tropical plants. Its name originated with the American Indians who attributed the roots with a healing power, especially in the treatment of arrow wounds.

BASIL

Basil has been used successfully for centuries to treat mild nervous disorders. The most common use was as an infusion tea to treat colds.

Hindus often start their day with a reverential walk around their *tulsi*, or basil plant, believing it to be the sacred hair of the goddess Virendra. Legend has it that when Virendra discovered her husband had been killed she leapt on his funeral pyre and was burnt alive. The Hindu gods commemorated this act by turning her charred hair into the sweet-smelling plant that we know as basil.

Basil is used in many recipes but is best known as the main ingredient in pesto.

You should plant basil on both sides of your doorstep to encourage luck into your home.

BAY
The aromatic leaves of the bay tree were used in Ancient Rome to fashion laurel crowns for noted poets. The bay was sacred to the god Apollo.

BORAGE
There is an old saying — 'borage for courage' — implying that the herb fortified the spirit. We now know that borage encourages the release of adrenaline in the body when stressed. It was also believed to be uplifting for people in an emotional crisis. Pliny tells of adding it to wine to 'increase the exhilarating effect'.

CARAWAY
Europeans believed the seeds sharpened the appetite while others believed it was an effective cure for hiccups.

Caraway seeds are good for a gargle to clear a throat infection.

Place caraway seeds in your lover's pocket to find out if they are being faithful.

Add carraway seeds to pigeon seed to ensure the bird will always return to the same coop.

CLOVES

The sun-dried bud of the clove tree has been used from ancient times as a spice. At one stage in about the fourth century cloves were as popular as pepper, particularly as a meat preserver. They were also believed to possess secret powers and were studded into oranges to ward off the plague.

A simple way to give a light perfume to clothes is to place a few cloves in each drawer. This also deters cockroaches and silverfish.

CORIANDER

One of the bitter herbs of the Jewish Passover ceremony, coriander is also the most used green herb in the world (although never popular in middle Europe because of its pungent smell). It grows wild in South-east Asia and Europe, and has been cultivated in Egypt, India and China for thousands of years. It is mentioned in Sanskrit text and the Bible. Spanish conquistadors introduced it to Mexico and some parts of South America where it is now commonly paired with chilli, chicken and vegetable dishes. Coriander has also become an important addition to Australian cuisine and is available at supermarkets and greengrocers.

The herb is believed to take its name from *koris*, the Greek word for 'bedbug', as it was said they both emitted a similar odour.

The Chinese used it in love potions believing it provided immortality.

Coriander is thought to have aphrodisiac qualities. The fabled book *The Arabian Nights* tells of a merchant who had been childless for forty years, but was cured by a brew that included coriander.

CUMIN

Cumin is the second most used spice in the world after pepper.

Cumin is one of the main ingredients in curry powders, and the combination of cumin and coriander leaves gives a characteristic smell to much Indian food.

Cumin sprinkled on food was thought to keep husbands faithful. Cleopatra, cunning girl that she was, brewed a pot of cumin tea every evening for Mark Anthony.

DILL

The name comes from the Old Norse *dylle*, meaning 'lull', as dill was commonly used to pacify babies suffering colic.

Witches favoured dill in love potions and also used it to ward off the evil eye. Ironically, it was also widely believed that a bunch of dill would repel witchcraft and enchantments in particular.

The Ancient Greek herbalists knew the plant as *anethon* and recognised its usefulness in aiding digestion.

There is a school of thought that suggests it might also have been the 'anise' mentioned in the Bible (Matthew 23:23).

EUCALYPTUS

The oil from the eucalyptus tree has been used as a household and campsite substitute for everything from an antiseptic to a throat gargle. Bushmen used it on ulcers and post-World War II children were given a spoonful of sugar laced with the bitter-tasting oil to treat a sore throat. It tasted disgusting but was a notch up from cod liver oil, which tasted much worse.

FENNEL

Socrates advised that a stalk of fennel and a glass of water was the only cure for a night of culinary excess.

Fennel was thought of as one of the good 'magical' herbs that counteracted evil. Legend has it that Prometheus concealed the fire of the sun in the hollow stalk and presented fire to the human race.

Greeks and Indians chew on fennel seeds to improve their breath.

GALANGAL

The German nun, healer and musician Hildegard of Bingen (1098–1179) mentions galangal in her work: 'Whoever has heart pain and is weak in the heart, should instantly eat enough galangal, and he or she will be well again.'

GARLIC

Garlic is a herb and a member of the lily family. It has a very long history including being mentioned in Chinese Sanskrit writings dating back to 3000 BC. We also know the King of Babylon had a garlic garden. Herodotus tells us that it was mixed with onions and fed to the workers on the Great Pyramid at Giza, and it also gets a plug in the Bible. The Romans believed garlic had magical powers so they fed it to the imperial soldiers to give them courage, but it was the Elizabethan English who decided it had aphrodisiacal powers — Lord knows what they were thinking!

Garlic is one of the world's oldest and most respected medicinal herbs. There are references of it being used in Ancient Babylon some 5000 years ago. It does have anti-histamine qualities useful in the treatment of allergies but people have consumed it for a wide range of medical reasons. The Prophet Mohammed extolled its use for the treatment of scorpion and snakebites and it is also reputed to ward off fleas and most insects. In addition, garlic has been used to ward off or cure sickness — everything from worms to the shakes, from the common cold to insanity. Finally, yes, it has been suggested it can cure baldness and remove freckles.

Ask most people about the mysterious qualities of garlic and they will tell you how it supposedly wards off vampires and witches; apparently neither beastie can bear to smell the herb and immediately rushes in the opposite direction. Those Dracula stories have a lot to answer for, however the bulb's magical powers go back a great deal further than Bram Stoker's books.

Maybe it was the overpowering strength of the garlic that encouraged the folk to attribute it with strong magical powers. Europeans certainly took up the lore and wreaths of garlic bulbs were openly displayed over doors and near windows. Some people even took to carrying cloves in their clothing or around their neck.

Taking garlic with you on a sea voyage is said to prevent you from drowning and intrepid mountain climbers have been known to slip a clove into their rucksack to ensure good weather.

Spanish bullfighters often wear a clove of garlic around their neck to prevent a goring from their bovine opponent.

If you dreamed of garlic you will have good fortune.

Another article of cuisine that offends the bowels of unused Britons is garlic. Not uncommonly in southern climes an egg with a shell on is the only procurable animal food without garlic in it. Flatulence and looseness are the frequent results.

(Dr. T. K. Chambers, *A Manuel of Diet in Health and Disease*, 1875)

Shallots are for babies; onions are for men; garlic is for heroes.

GINGER

East Indian and Chinese cultures have used ginger as a digestive aid for centuries. The Chinese consider ginger a yang, or hot, food that balances the cooling ying foods to create harmony. Ancient Greeks and Romans also utilised it for this purpose.

In Australia, ginger became very popular for the making of homemade ginger beer.

For many years ginger was regarded as a cure for toothache with the ginger being ground to a paste and spread on gums.

You will also find it as an additive in 'power' drinks popular with young clubbers. The ginger supposedly provides extra 'zing'.

HERBS

Long the provenance of witches and healers, herbs do have special qualities acknowledged by the medical profession.

Edwardian and Victorian England liked to bestow special attributes to herbs, flowers and vegetables. The following is a list of herbs and their associated sentiments.

Allspice – compassion
Basil – hatred
Bay leaves – loyalty and honour
Chamomile – energy in adversity
Chervil – sincerity
Cloves – dignity
Coriander – concealed merit
Fennel – strength
Marjoram – blushes
Mint – virtue

Parsley – knowledge
Rosemary – revival
Sage – esteem
Sorrel – parental affection
Thyme – activity

MIXED HERBS
An awful combination of commercially prepared, dry, confused herbs that will usurp and destroy most flavours. Avoid it!

HORSERADISH
Taking its name from the German for 'sea root', horseradish actually has nothing to do with horses or the sea. German settlers, especially in South Australia and rural Victoria, planted the horseradish in Australian soil.

Frying fish in breadcrumbs and grated horseradish is popular, and it's also commonly used as a meat accompaniment.

Horseradish is said to be one of the five 'bitter herbs' — together with coriander, horehound, lettuce and nettle — which Jews were required to eat during Passover.

Hold a pin in your mouth while grating horseradish and you will not cry.
If the pin doesn't work try a fork.

Horseradish applied to the breast prevents excessive lactation.

LIQUORICE
Known to the Ancient Greeks as Sythian root, liquorice was a popular treatment for asthma and coughs. It is still found in health food stores as a herbal curative tea.

The Chinese refer to liquorice as the 'great detoxifier'.

MARJORAM
This gentle herb was a favourite of the goddess Aphrodite. It was believed anointing oneself with it would cause dreams of a future spouse, while planting it on a grave would comfort the dead.

MINT

Mint was named after the nymph Menthe, who was the illicit lover of Pluto. Ovid tells the story that when Persephone came upon the guilty pair, she threw Menthe to the ground to trample her — thus mint is always crushed to release the flavour.

Never give mint to the ill. If a wounded man eats mint he might never recover.

MUSHROOMS

The Irish believed that the mushroom sprang from where St Patrick spat breadcrumbs. (I have no idea why the good saint had a mouthful of breadcrumbs!) Toadstools, on the other hand, were where the devil spat.

Many cultures believed the mushroom, especially when found in so-called 'fairy rings', was a direct gift from the gods and some believed it to be the very flesh of the gods. There was also a belief that mushrooms were the aftermath of lightning or the result of lunar cycles.

The shiitake mushroom is a relatively new edible fungus but it has already been hailed as a cure for everything from HIV to cancer. The Chinese have been using it in traditional medicine for over 2000 years.

PARSLEY

Parsley has a long association with death and disaster. The Romans decorated graves with parsley to drive the devils away. They also fed parsley to their chariot horses before they raced or went to war.

Hercules wove garlands out of parsley.

The Ancient Greeks believed parsley encouraged appetite, which might explain why so many restaurants use a sprig as decoration on dishes. It has also been used for centuries as a natural breath freshener.

It is said that parsley seeds take a long time to sprout, as they have to go down to hell and back before they can grow. One belief was that the seeds had to go down to hell thirteen times before germination but only once if planted on Good Friday.

One early folk belief suggested babies miraculously came from parsley beds.

You should never eat parsley when you are in love — it is unlucky.

Chewing parsley three times a day for three weeks can terminate pregnancy.

Never transplant parsley from one garden to another — transplant parsley, transplant death.

Never give away parsley seeds for you will give away luck.

Parsley is better if sown by a woman.

It's bad luck to replant parsley.

The milk of pregnant women will dry up if they eat parsley.

PEPPER

Pepper is the world's most used spice and the table partner for salt.

Native to India, pepper has played an important role throughout history and has been one of the most prized spices. Since Ancient Greece, pepper has held such high prestige that it was not only used as a seasoning but as a currency and a sacred offering.

Pepper, like salt, was used to pay taxes and ransoms as well as in temple offerings. During the fall of Rome, the invading barbarians were even honoured by being given black pepper.

In the Middle Ages the wealth of a man was often measured by his stockpile of pepper.

ROSEMARY

Rosemary or, as it was known, Mary's Rose, was believed to keep nightmares away, ward off evil and protect against moths. One belief was that the name came into being when Mary, Mother of God, hung her robes over a bush and the flowers turned blue.

Ancient Romans carried sprigs of rosemary as a symbol of love and life.

The herb was also made into an infusion mixed with borax and boiling water and then used externally as an astringent to prevent premature balding.

We wear rosemary sprigs on Anzac day as a sign of remembrance.

SAFFRON

'Saffron' comes from the Arab word *assfar,* meaning yellow, and was mentioned as far back as 1500 BC in many classical writings, as well as in the Bible.

According to Greek myth, handsome mortal Crocos fell in love with the beautiful nymph Smilax. But sadly, his favours were rebuffed by Smilax, and he was turned into a beautiful purple crocus flower — the saffron.

Saffron is harvested from the fall-flowering plant *Crocus sativus*, a member of the iris family. It is native to Asia Minor, where it has been cultivated for thousands of years for use in medicines, perfumes, dyes, and as a wonderful flavouring for foods and beverages. It is very expensive but, fortunately, a little goes a long way.

SAGE

Sage has traditionally been associated with longevity. An English proverb offers: 'He who would live for aye must eat sage in May.' Similarly, an Arab proverb states: 'Why should a man die who has sage in his garden?'

The word sage comes from the Latin *salvere*, meaning 'to save'.

Q: What man is a vegetable?

A: A sage

SPEARMINT

The herb oil from the spearmint was used to make an infusion: 25 grams (1 ounce) of spearmint was added to 4 cups of boiling water sweetened with honey. Small doses were suggested for heartburn.

THYME

The name thyme is thought to come from the Greek word *thymon*, which means 'to fumigate'. In fact, Ancient Egyptians used thyme oil in their embalming process.

Thyme is rich in lore. According to legend, thyme was one of the fragrant herbs used for the bed of the Virgin Mary.

In medieval days, thyme was said to be a great source of invigoration, inspiring courage. It was an emblem of activity, bravery and energy.

TRUFFLES

Considered 'the jewel in the crown of French cooking', these black devils have been delighting palates for over 3000 years. Even Pope Gregory IV boosted his mettle with a meal of truffles before setting out to do battle with the Saracens.

In the Middle Ages *tartufi* (or truffles) were closely associated with witches.

It is said Lord Byron kept a black truffle on his desk to stimulate his imagination.

Truffles are rare and subsequently very expensive. Traditionally the truffles are 'hunted' by a pig or dog—now that's a job worth considering!

Black Truffles are now grown in Australia with the Perigord Truffle Company of Tasmania (established in 1992) operating a dozen *truffières* (groups of truffle sites).

In 2005 a giant truffle, possibly the world's largest, was found in West Australia.

Over the shoulder
Salt

S alt has a noble place in history and folklore and this probably stems from its use as a preserving agent in many foods. (Salt was also a popular preserving agent for embalming Egyptian mummies.) It has shaped history, inspired artists and storytellers, and added zest to our taste buds, yet we are so used to seeing salt on our tables that we take it for granted. It has often been described as the 'fifth element' of life, along with air, earth, water and fire. It is essential for humans and animals, and even some plants. It also has unlimited uses in industry, especially as an absorption agent. Our body contains approximately 115 grams (4 ounces) of salt and without it our blood would not flow, muscles would not work, and our heart would not beat. Known as sodium chloride, salt literally gives us life.

Salt was so valuable in Ancient Rome that soldiers were paid in sacks of it; those who didn't measure up were said to be 'not worth their salt'. This method of payment was known as *sal* and it is from this that we get the word 'salary'.

It is difficult to imagine life without salt and it was certainly a valued commodity in early Australia where every traveller carried a small salt bag, and riverboats transported small mountains of the stuff up to the outback. All salt was imported and used for food preservation as well as flavouring. These days we still import salt; however, locally mined salt is becoming a growing industry and, of late, specialist Australian salt is being marketed and even exported.

SALT LORE

Salt, excuse the pun, peppers our language and lore as well as being a welcome addition to any table. There is little doubt that the singularly most widespread kitchen folklore is associated with salt and particularly what to do if you accidentally spill it. If you should spill salt, throw it over your left shoulder without looking (remember Lot's wife!). Some informants suggest that it should be thrown three times. The most widespread belief is that when you throw salt over your left shoulder you throw it in the devil's eye (because, according to popular belief, the devil is always behind you).

Old-timers used to delight in telling youngsters that the best way to catch a bird is to quietly sneak up behind it and pour salt on the bird's tail—the bird will not be able to fly away. Mind you, I suspect this is related to similar questions such as 'How do you catch an Eskimo?' The answer, of course, is to creep up on him and kick him in the ice-hole (arsehole).

Salt is sometimes sprinkled on the front steps of a new house for luck and to ward off evil spirits. Similarly, the first thing taken into a new house should be salt. Some people bring salt as a gift to new house dwellers.

Many people placed salt on a baby's tongue after the baptism ceremony and, once again, this was to ward off the evil eye.

Salt is born of the purest of parents: the sun and the sea.

(Pythagoras, 580–500 BC)

With all thine offerings thou shalt offer salt.

(Moses, Book of Leviticus)

Salt is what makes things taste bad when it isn't in them.

(Anonymous)

You should never pass salt to another person: 'pass the salt and pass the sorrow'.

You should sprinkle salt on yourself when returning from a funeral so that the dead won't follow you.

If you take away the salt throw the meat to the dogs. (This old saying implies that salt was considered a necessity for flavouring meat.)

Always put salt on the table first to preserve friendship.

Salt placed on the table in front of a guest is a sign of goodwill from host.

A tear will flow for every grain spilt.

Never borrow salt.

Always fill salt shakers on New Year's Eve.

Never return borrowed salt.

Never place two salt cellars in front of the same person.

Sprinkle salt between planks of a new boat to guarantee luck. (Greeks did this believing salt was what gave the sea life.)

Pour salt down the chimney for a better smoke flow.

A salt shaker that overturns between two friends means they will quarrel. (One of the best examples of this belief is Leonardo da Vinci's famous painting 'The Last Supper' where Judas is portrayed with a spilt salt shaker.)

The sweet life
Sugar and desserts

The first record of sugar cane in the Western world was in 327 BC. Sugar cane is mentioned in Chinese and Russian records between AD 200 and 600, and it is believed that it was introduced into Spain and Egypt around the eighth century.

It was in 1493 that Columbus, on his second voyage from Spain, transported a single variety of sugar cane to Santo Domingo where it spread to Brazil, Mexico, Peru, Cuba and Puerto Rico and, later, to the rest of the tropical world.

Sugar cane was introduced to Australia by the First Fleet in 1788. However, early attempts to grow sugar cane around Sydney Cove, Port Macquarie and Norfolk Island were unsuccessful. It wasn't until the 1860s that a viable sugar cane plantation and raw sugar mill was established at Ormiston, near Brisbane, by Captain Louis Hope.

By the 1880s, cane lands were being developed further along Queensland's tropical coast and along the northern coast of New South Wales. However, the high cost of wages for Australian workers made it difficult for the industry to compete successfully with overseas sugar producers such as Fiji, Java (Indonesia) and South Africa. To overcome this problem, cheap 'contract' labour was brought in from the South Pacific islands. Between 1863 and 1904, more than 60,000 Kanakas (as they were called) were brought to Queensland to work on sugar plantations, some illegally through a process known as 'blackbirding'. This involved Europeans luring islanders onto ships by pretending they wanted to trade with them. Instead, they would kidnap the Kanakas and ship them to Australia where they were forced to work on the sugar cane plantations and live under very poor conditions.

In the late 1880s regulations were introduced to control the recruitment of Kanakas, and by 1908 many of the Kanakas had been returned to their homelands although some stayed in Australia. However, the need for labour on the cane fields continued and in the early 1900s a new type of cane cutter entered the industry. These were young European migrants who came to Australia to 'make their fortune' on the cane fields. Italians in particular contributed to the growth of the Australian sugar industry with large numbers being brought to Australia as cane cutters in the mid-1950s.

During the 1950s, the sugar industry boomed and dramatic changes took place within Queensland. In 1954, bulk handling of raw sugar was introduced into Australia replacing bagged sugar, and mechanical cane harvesters gradually began to replace manual labour in the fields. By the late 1960s, more than 85 per cent of Australian sugar crops were mechanically harvested. In 1979, Australia achieved 100 per cent conversion to mechanical cane harvesting.

Today, the Australian sugar industry is internationally regarded as one of the most efficient sugar producers in the world and a leader in mechanical cane harvesting and bulk handling of raw sugar.

Australians have a sweet tooth. We eat sugar in many foods and not only so-called sweet foods and confectioneries. In many cases the sugar is used to disguise less palatable flavours — in medicines, for example — but, above all, it is ever present because we have been conditioned to expect the flavour.

Bushmen used a spoonful of sugar to revive the dying embers of a campfire.

Andy Pandy, sugar and candy
French almond, raisin, rock.

(children's skipping rhyme)

BULLOCKY'S JOY

Bullocky's joy is treacle or golden syrup, a byproduct of the sugar industry. It is honey-like and extremely sticky. It was also widely known as cocky's joy and was a favoured spread on damper.

CHOCOLATE

Chocolate has a long history as a potent 'love gift' and it is endowed with powerful symbolism. It remains a popular gift for wedding anniversaries and many seasonal holidays, especially in the form of an Easter egg or rabbit. Recently we have seen the chocolate bilby make an annual appearance as a local Easter gift.

Chocolate fish are a popular gift in confectionery stores. These relate to the French tradition of April Fool's Day where the person tricked is known as a *poisson d'avril* or 'April fish'.

Chocolate has been called 'the food of the gods' and the Aztecs believed the cocoa tree was a gift from the god Quetzalcoatl who brought the seeds with him from heaven.

Q: What do geese get if they eat too much chocolate?

A: Goose pimples

COCONUT ICE

Coconut ice is a perennial favourite on the Australian fête stall table, alongside the stick-jaw toffees, toffee apples, chocolate crackles and cupcakes. Usually made in slabs, it gets its name from the desiccated coconut top layer, which, presumably, resembles snow. No one has a clue what the sweet, pink cochineal base is supposed to represent!

RECIPE FOR COCONUT ICE

125 grams (4 ½ ounces) butter

½ cup sugar

1 cup flour

1 teaspoon baking powder

1 egg

Topping

½ cup milk

2 small cups sugar

1 teaspoon butter

½ cup desiccated coconut

a few drops vanilla essence

a few drops cochineal

Mix the butter, sugar, flour, baking powder and egg together. Press the mixture into a baking tray and bake for twenty minutes. Set aside to cool. To prepare the topping, boil the milk, sugar and butter for about four minutes. Set aside to cool. Once cool, mix in the coconut, vanilla essence, and the cochineal for colour. Beat until fairly thick and then spread on the base mixture. Cut into slice

(Mrs Fotheringham, Sans Souci, NSW)

CUSTARD

Custard played a large part in sweetening up the early Australian festive palate. The best-known brand was undoubtedly Foster Clark's Custard Powder, advertised with the message: 'Many Australian homes appreciate this economical luxury.' Keeping an eye on the custard was a tough job for any kid and the temptation to take a wee spoonful was too great to withstand. Personally I preferred my custard a day old and straight from the refrigerator and, if I was lucky, complete with a few hefty lumps! There was only one thing that beat it — the rubbery bit at the bottom of the jelly bowl.

HONEY

Honey has been collected and used for some 9000 years. Bees were a favourite symbol of the Ancient Egyptians and appear in many tombs.

The heavy sweet fluid has long been used as an antiseptic on open wounds and it does have a proven inhibitory effect on around sixty species of bacteria. The Ancient Egyptians used honey in many cures and especially for impotence and sterility. In the Australian bush, honey was mixed with a little warm water and used as an antiseptic eyewash.

Mead made from honey was drunk to celebrate and sweeten marriages and this is possibly the origin of the word 'honeymoon'.

Jewish people eat apples dipped in honey at the beginning of their New Year. Rosh Hashana is the beginning of the Jewish High Holiday leading up to Yom Kippur. Apples and honey are symbolic foods for a sweet and blessed New Year.

> Pass the honey, Honey.
> Pass the sugar, Sugar.
> Pass the tea — Bag!

> The only reason for being a bee that I know of is making honey … and the only reason for making honey is so I can eat it.
>> (Winnie the Pooh in A.A. Milne's *The House at Pooh Corner*)

> Plant thyme near beehives to improve the taste of honey.

> Dreaming of honey means you will make money.

JAMS

Jams and jellies are centuries old and were first popularised by the returning Crusaders who had no doubt spied the delicacies in the Middle East. By the late Middle Ages, because of the availability of sugar, both preserved jams and jellies were extremely popular throughout Europe. In the first half of the last century home preserving was all the go in Australia, and especially with the Fowler's Vacola system with its large boiler, myriad bottles, screw tops and rubber seals. We pickled, sugared and preserved and bottled everything from native quandongs to pickled cucumbers, from pears and pineapples to oranges and apples. Green tomato pickles, with a touch of curry, were at the top of the list.

JELLY

Jelly comes from the French word *gelé* meaning 'to solidify or congeal'.

As kids we were told that jelly (and chewing gum) was made out of the hooves of dead horses. A favourite part of the jelly for many was the rubbery hard layer at the base of the bowl.

> Jelly belly custard, pizza pie,
> All mixed together with a dead-dog's eye.
> Slam it on a pancake, nice and thick,
> Then eat it all up with a cup of sick.

> Jelly made on a rainy day will be cloudy.

JUNKET

Junket always seems to get a bad rap and be thought of as 'invalid food'. Mind you, it doesn't take much effort to eat junket. As a child we are always told junket (and gelatin) was made from horse's hooves from the knackery, but it's actually made with milk, sugar and flavourings and thickened with rennet. The sweet, mild dessert appears to have originated with a rennet maker in Denmark.

MARMALADE

Marmalade is believed to have been created in 1561 by the physician to Mary, Queen of Scots, when he blended orange and crushed sugar as a tonic for her health. *Marie est malade* does translate into 'Mary is sick'; however, there is also a belief that the word comes from the Portuguese *marmelo* for 'quince'. Whatever the case, the confectionery jam spread was extremely popular in Australia.

MARZIPAN

The Egyptians are reported to have made marzipan from crushed almonds and honey as early as 1800 BC. According to legend, marzipan was so valued in the early Nile River villages that it was used for trade as coins called *marchpans*. Thus it spread throughout the civilised world. It was prized by the emperors of Rome and became an important part of Italy's culinary heritage.

It is traditionally associated with Christmas; especially the giving of small sculptured animals made of marzipan. This started with the Swiss who made commercially produced little pink marzipan pigs.

MOLASSES

Blackstrap molasses, a heavy raw sugar processing extract, was a popular tonic and usually taken in a small glass of warm water first thing in the morning.

MOLASSES CRINKLES

A thin crisp biscuit with cracked sugar topping, molasses crinkle is made with flour, baking soda, salt, brown sugar, egg and molasses, with the hot liquid being poured thin for baking. Ginger is a popular flavouring. These biscuits seem to have originated in Scotland and are usually made at Christmas.

PEACH MELBA

When the famous opera singer Nellie Melba was performing in *Lohengrin* at Covent Garden in 1892 the Savoy Hotel celebrated her performance with a dinner. Auguste Escoffier presented the Dame with a large iced swan filled with peaches and ice-cream. Later, in 1900, he added some raspberry purée. In Australia, we have made it with tinned peaches and condensed cream.

PUDDING

There are so many types of pudding. Some light as a feather and others heavy as lead. My favourite has always been the traditional milk pudding with nutmeg sprinkled on top. The art of cooking this pudding is to never let the milk boil.

Milk puddings cannot be cooked too slowly — 'if the milk boils the pudding spoils'.

SUGAR BAGS

Before commercially packaged sugar products came onto the market, sugar was supplied to shops in large hessian sugar bags. When selling the sugar, the shopkeeper would use a scoop and fill whatever size paper-bag weight you required. In the bush these hessian sugar bags had many uses, including being sewn together as rough blankets, window drops, doormats, etc.

SUGAR PLUMS

A confectionery fondant made with chopped nuts and dried fruit and supposedly the favourite food of the sugar plum fairy.

TIRAMISU

The tiramisu has become one of Australia's most popular desserts and is made by lacing a sponge cake or finger biscuits with a liqueur then covering with grated chocolate and rich custard or, more recently, mascarpone cheese. Essentially it is an Italian trifle with the word translating as 'carry me up' — possibly because after a few of these you certainly won't be able to walk upstairs! In Australia, it is more commonly translated as 'pick me up', because it does just that, lifting the spirits and livening you up! It is a relatively new sweet with its first Australian sighting being in the 1970s.

TRIFLE

This sweet dish was once very popular in Australia because of the abundance of fresh fruit and dairy. The 1930s appear to have been the trifle heydays. Usual ingredients included a Swiss sponge roll, port wine jelly, sherry, port, lemon juice and fruit. (Sponge-makers go to great lengths to create the perfect sponge and often regard their recipes as top secret.)

Trifle is sometimes known as 'tipsy cake' because of the alcohol. From the mid-nineteenth century onwards, non-alcoholic versions— sometimes called 'chapel trifles' — were popular with the teetotaller brigade.

The English word trifle appears to originate with the mid-European word *trufle*, meaning 'whimsical' or 'of little consequence'.

Colonial cuisine
Food in the colonies

Our early settlers never really understood the hunter–gatherer diet of the indigenous Australians. The fact that we built our townships on the riverbanks, the main food gathering areas of the native people, shows our insensitivity and ignorance or, worse still, our colonial intolerance. So-called 'bush foods' have only become recognised over the last twenty-five years and wattle-seed, native berries and vegetables, and yams have gained respect along with Aboriginal bush remedies made from native plants and herbs. The first settlers looked on the Aboriginal diet as scant and uninteresting. In reality, the indigenous people enjoyed a wide range of foods, including poultry, wild rice, grains, nuts and tubers. The Australian bush is a bountiful kitchen but one best left for the experts. This section tells of the colonial kitchen of the European settlers.

Prices in the early days of the colony — especially at the beginning of the gold rush — were extremely high, being dependent on unpredictable demand and highly erratic supply. Settlers could only compare the prices paid in England and shudder at the reality of living in such a seller's market. There was a general feeling that locally made goods—in this case 'a needle made of Australian lead' and 'a cabbage from an Australian garden' — were of inferior quality and grossly overpriced. Disgruntled settlers returning to England further inflated these prices often to legitimise their return. One song, found in the Mitchell library broadside collection, and captioned 'I've

Been To Australia-O', tells of these high prices. It appears that this anonymous songwriter was a contender for the title of our first 'whinging Pom' and, it seems, with good reason.

A pound of steak is seven bob, twelve shillings for a mop,
And two and twopence-halfpenny for a pound of mutton chops;
Ten and sixpence for an ounce of tea, oh, dear! such nobby stuff,
And three and sevenpence-farthing for half an ounce of snuff.

Two shillings for a glass of gin, and ninepence for a leek,
And if old ladies want to buy a bit of pussy's meat
The rogues will charge them half a crown, how cruel is not that,
And scarcely give them half enough to satisfy a cat.

There, table beer I do declare, is thirteen bob a pot,
And they'll charge you half a guinea for a bottle of ginger pop;
Two and ninepence for a baked sheep's head, a shilling for a pipe,
And six and threepence—farthing for half a pound of tripe.

Sixpence-halfpenny for a lollipop, and ninepence for a lemon,
One and twopence-halfpenny for a little pickled herring;
Tenpence for a cabbage small, from an Australian garden;
For a bit of soap to wash your shirt, thirteen and threepence-farthing.

Fifty-seven pounds a year for a house that's got no windows,
Two and tenpence-halfpenny for a nightcap full of cinders,
Sixpence for a needle, made of Australian lead,
And one and eightpence-halfpenny for a dirty skein of thread.

They'll charge you seven shillings for a pint of mouldy peas,
Six and ninepence-farthing for a pound of rotten cheese.
Of going a-gold-digging, friends, I think I've had my full,
May the devil take Australia, I'll live with Old John Bull.

All them that like to emigrate, across the seas may go,
They'll never catch me again going to Australia-oh.

The country kitchens of the nineteenth century were basic yet inventive. Bread was baked daily, butter and cheese made weekly and the wood-burning ovens churned out stews, pies, tarts, baked meats and whatever else came with the territory. Native animals were cooked to emulate the foods of old England, so many was the baked wombat, bush turkey and slice of roo meat served in the style of English beef, pheasant or lamb. Very little was wasted including the offal, and dishes like lamb or cow tongue, oxtail soup, tripe and fried liver were the norm. Even Mrs Beeton, in her 1930 edition, provided recipes for kangaroo, wallaby and native parrot. It has often been said that the only part of the pig not eaten was the oink. Bush work was hungry work and the women and men who did the cooking worked equally long and hard days. Supplies came irregularly by inland riverboat or travelling road hawkers. It was these hawkers, many of them Afghans or Chinese, who introduced exotic herbs and spices into our cuisine.

Inventive bush cookery very much depended on where people lived. River folk ate codfish and mullet, while isolated station owners were forced to eat, among other things, native fruits, wild pig and kangaroo. The coastal people had the full fruits of the sea and those 'in transit' up country fed on salted and dried meats and other dried foods. With the gold rush came better roads and more frequent supply, especially by the efficient riverboat system, unless, of course, the river was in flood or drought.

Native animals were common fare in our colonial cities. In the 1870s Melbourne and Sydney street hawkers regularly offered wild duck at 7s 6d, swans for 2s 6d, rabbits at 6d a pair, bush turkeys for 3s each, as well as wild pig, koala and kangaroo meat.

Restaurants of every size and style were also built to cater for the hungry hordes, especially the newly rich citizens. In the 1850s, a chain of fourpenny and sixpenny restaurants was established in Melbourne by David Way, an English emigrant. By all accounts one was likely to find 'more flies in the dishes than refined prejudices might fancy'. For the more affluent, particularly Melburnians, there were Langlois Luncheon Rooms and the Scots Pie Shop in Royal Arcade, where the diners could eat for a shilling, with a glass of colonial port wine for an additional threepenny. There were also fancy restaurants serving quality foods aimed at would be gourmands.

This extract from *The New Chum in Australia* by Percy Clarke, London, 1886, tells of a visit to a city dining establishment.

In most colonial towns you may find out restaurants where for 'a square meal' you may have the melancholic pleasure of 'bang went sixpence'. For the curious Epicurean here is the menu presented to me by the beaming proprietor of one of these enterprising restaurants. The dining saloon, which really deserved its name, was occupied by large tables covered in spotless cloths, on which were spread in readiness for dinner the usual appointments. The display of flowers and plated forks and spoons and the notes of an orchestra playing popular tunes were sufficient to make one wish one's own dinner hour was at hand. A man, woman, or child might have each and all of —

Pea soup

Steak and onions

Roast beef and mutton

Boiled mutton and parsley sauce

Corned beef and carrots

Stewed rabbit

Stewed veal and pork

Boiled and baked potatoes

Cabbage

Jam roll and rice pudding

Tea ad-lib.

The only bargain made by the proprietor being that the diner should be able to remove himself from his seat by his own unaided muscular exertions.

CABBAGE PATCH

'The cabbage patch' was a derogatory New South Wales' reference to colonial Victoria, along with its inhabitants who were 'cabbage patchers'.

COLONIAL GOOSE

This was a boned leg of mutton stuffed with sage, onions and breadcrumbs and baked. There was also a 'colonial duck' which was a boned shoulder prepared in exactly the same fashion. Both recipes have been in circulation for well over a century and a half.

CORNSTALK

New South Welshmen and women were called 'cornstalks' for most of the nineteenth century. I assume the name came from the fact that Europeans actually did seem to sprout, grow taller, in the Australian climate and with hard work and good food. They also wore a floppy hat, known as a 'cabbage tree', that would have made them look like corn!

A colonial recipe for 'cornstalk sandwiches' called for the cook to beat four eggs and three-quarters of a pound (250 grams) of sugar together for about twenty minutes, and then add one-and-a-quarter cups of self-raising flour and bake for ten minutes. It was a type of flat cake bread.

FARMER'S DINNER

It was not uncommon for Australian farmers to hold a 'farmer's dinner' at the end of a successful season and also on completion of a new building. This was the equivalent of the British 'Harvest Home' and served as a thank you to the workforce. It was also held, one suspects, with an eye on thanking the 'gods' for a successful season. Reports show that the group would sit down to a feast of kangaroo soup, huge meat pies, boiled leg of mutton, peas and suet puddings with beer and porter to wash it all down.

FILLERS

This term seems to come from the old days when the man of the house would eat most of the meat and leave the rest of the family to 'fill up' on dumplings or potatoes. These foods were also called 'swimmers' because they were usually swimming in gravy.

FLYING PIEMAN

The Flying Pieman was undoubtedly Sydney's best-known hawker with a reputation for extraordinary feats of endurance and eccentricity. Once he walked, with his tray of pies, from Parramatta to Circular Quay and met the Sydney-to-Parramatta ferry as it pulled into the wharf. The Flying Pieman wore an old frock coat of different coloured patches, his hat was covered with tickets and placards, and his legs and feet were wrapped in hessian bags.

A newspaper report on 11 February 1841 reported:

A man named King tried to walk from Smith's public house Parramatta to the Commercial Wharf Sydney in less time than it took the steamer *Australia* to do the run. King completed the distance in two hours twenty-five minutes. The steamer arrived three minutes before.

FOLK CHARACTERS

Pumpkin Paddy sowed pumpkin seeds as he travelled the country and particularly along the Warrego River and Condamine River areas.

Quandong Joe travelled throughout west New South Wales and supposedly used quandong seeds for everything—buttons, rosary beads, novelties, necklaces, etc.

Reverend Selwyn sowed citrus seeds while riding from station to station along the Richmond River. Lemon trees in unusual places are still known as 'parson's lemons'.

GALAH

We were camped on a lonely part of the Darling River, and as our meat supply had been exhausted, we decided to try cooking some galahs that we managed to trap. After boiling all the afternoon they were still as tough as old boot leather so we boiled them another hour or so, and drank the soup, throwing the bodies to the dog. Later, I asked a bushman the correct way to cook a galah, as I had been told it was a common item on the bush menu. This bushman told me that the only successful way is to get a farrier's rasp and file the galahs to a fine powder. Mix with water and make a soup.

(From *The World News*, circa mid-nineteenth century)

GRABBEN GULLEN PIE

This was also known as possum and pumpkin pie. One suspects in the nineteenth century one 'grabbed' whatever tucker was available, including native animals. It could possibly have been created in the small hamlet of the same name in the Goulburn Valley.

> In the early days, possums were caught, cleaned and cut up, put into a hollowed out pumpkin which was then roasted until the meat was cooked — a very tasty pie it was too.
>
> (Quoted in the wonderful *Bill Harney's Cook Book*, Melbourne, 1960)

GRANDFATHER PUDDING

This was made from stale damper soaked in black tea and sprinkled with sugar. This improvised recipe is typical of hard times cookery and representative of Australia's recognisable 'dry' humour. A bushworker most probably spied an old hand making such a dish and immediately declared the dish 'grandfather's pudding'.

KANGAROO TAIL SOUP

Two possible recipes for this staple colonial dish are given here, but every bushman had his own preferred method, while 'city cooks' would make use of more 'sophisticated' methods and ingredients.

RECIPE FOR 'INDIGO' KANGAROO TAIL SOUP

Remove the hair and clean the tail then cut into strips to fit your cooking pan. Bake for about two hours with a little salt and fat. Peel off the skin and cut into pieces then roll each piece in flour. Put the meat into a pot with water to cover, adding salt, pepper and available herbs. Some chopped bacon is always good in this soup. Halfway through the cooking add some chopped carrots, onions and potatoes then simmer for one and a half hours.

A SLIGHTLY 'POSHER' VERSION

In order to make this satisfactorily, the meat must have been killed for some time or it will possess no distinguishing flavour, yet care must be taken not to use any portion of the meat tainted. If in the bush where kangaroo is plentiful, the stock may be made from the kangaroo instead of beef or veal. Cut up the meat into proper sized pieces and place into a saucepan with about 3 or 4 pounds [1.3 or 1.8 kilograms] of the meat from the leg or any other part, a slice of ham or lean bacon, two blades of mace, two onions, celery, marjoram and seasoning. Add 4 quarts [4.5 litres] of light stock, place on fire and cook gently until the tail is thoroughly done. Drain liquid and thicken it with brown roux to the proper consistence, cook gently for half an hour, take off all the scum or fat, pour in a large glass of madeira or similar wine. A large tablespoon of red currant jelly and the juice of a lemon and pieces of the tail. Boil and serve. (*Australian Journal*, 1879)

The Aborigines had a far simpler method for cooking roo tail. They placed the entire tail directly on the ashes and turned it every fifteen minutes until the meat sizzled. It was then peeled and eaten.

TAILING A KANGAROO

(attributed to Tom Tallfern, *Australian Journal*, 1877)

Bill Swiggen and myself were bushed up in the mallee scrub,
For two long days and two long nights we had not tasted grub,
And on the third, my blessed word, affairs looked rather blue,
When Bill descried, with joyful pride, an old man kangaroo.

This old man quite majestically sat upright on his tail,
He looked at us contemptuously, nor did he shake nor quail,
He seemed to say, 'To come this way, what business friend had you?'
'By Jove!' cried Bill, 'I'd like to kill, that old man kangaroo.'

Without another word he rushed with waddy in his hand,
To where the old man kangaroo undauntedly did stand,
He aimed a blow but this hairy foe upon poor William flew,
And grabbed my mate, as sure as fate, this old man kangaroo.

He clasped him tightly in his arms and Bill began to roar,
A struggle so terrific, I had ne'er beheld before,

'Oh Tom, why blow my eyes, you know he'll break my back in two,
Come hither quick and fetch a stick, oh cuss the kangaroo.'

At my approach the kangaroo made ready for a bolt,
But still he clung to William tight, he would not loose his holt,
But Bill you see, was twelve stone three, flesh, bones and muscle too,
That's overweight, the truth I state, for any kangaroo.

Then stealing up behind the brute, my bag I opened wide,
And pulling it down over his ears, I then securely tied,
It 'round his neck, this seemed to check his progress so I drew,
My dover out and with a shout, I tailed that old man kangaroo.

A kangaroo without a tail can't run we all well know,
So finding his appendage gone, he let poor Willie go,
He gave a shout, a gory tail I tell you but it's true,
Then with a jump he sunk, a lump of lifeless kangaroo.

My mate was slightly bruised about but scarcely he was freed,
When turning round to me he says, 'By George, we'll have a feed.'
Then Billy got the billy pot and cooked a splendid stew,
The sweetest meal I ever ate was that old man kangaroo.

MURRUMBIDGEE SANDWICH

This was a slice of white bread dipped in cold tea and sprinkled with sugar, preferably brown sugar. The brown sugar and cold tea mix was also known as 'Murrumbidgee jam'.

MUTTON PIES

Not surprisingly, considering the abundance of sheep and the popularity of pie-making, the mutton pie was widely consumed in early Australia. As this song suggests, the probability of getting a bad one ran high.

TWO BAD MUTTON PIES
(Air: 'My Nellie's Blue Eyes')

Take a careful look at me,
And you certainly will see
One that's full of misery.
Tears flow from my eyes,
Through some pies I bought last night,
But I only took one bite
Of two bad mutton pies.

Chorus
Two bad mutton pies,
Chock full of blow-flies,
Pieces of rat, and remains of tom cat,
Of two bad mutton pies.

First I took a bite of one,
Then the other I did shun,
Lifted up the crust for fun,
When, oh! What a surprise!
In the place of meat I saw
Nothing but a tom cat's paw
And a nasty goose's claw.
Oh! Two bad mutton pies.

(Australian Melodist Songster, circa 1880)

PEASE PUDDING

Pease pudding hot
Pease pudding cold
Pease pudding in the pot
Nine days old.

The old nursery rhyme explains how pease pudding needs to age.
Our First Fleeters prepared this dish, which is essentially dried peas
reconstituted, boiled in a cloth and then boiled again and again.

PLUM CRAZY

It has been suggested that the term 'plum crazy' could be related to the thought of finding (or not finding) a gold nugget in a plum duff.

PLUM DUFF

Surprisingly the Christmas plum duff did not contain any plum but gained its name from plum porridge. During the gold rush days of the 1860s and 70s the plum duff often contained small nuggets of gold and the finder was encouraged to make small pins, rings and brooches out of the metal. It was also known as plumb duff.

PORKATO SANDWICH

Take two cooked pig's ears and place a cooked whole potato between them. Add pepper and salt to taste and squash ears to make a sandwich. Said to have been particularly popular in the potato-growing Bungaree district of Victoria.

PROFESSIONAL HUMS

To 'hum' meant to be on the cadge for rations, to be a bum. This song, 'Two Professional Hums', is from the singing of Harry Chapin, Broken Hill, collected in 1974. It is an old song, dating around the 1870s.

TWO PROFESSIONAL HUMS

Come all you jovial fellows and listen to me chums,
And I'll relate to you the story of two professional hums,
Who travelled England, Ireland; all over Scotland too,
And took an oath in Bendigo, no more work they would do.

No more work they would do boys, troll old army dough boys,
Humming a drink where 'ere we go, sing fol the righty-o,
For we are hums and jolly good chums, we live like Royal Turks,
And if we've luck we'll hum our cheques and shoot the man who works.

We asked a lady, the other day, for something for to eat,
A little bit of chicken or a little bit of meat,

A little bit of turkey or a little bit of ham,
A half-a-dozen loaves of bread and a bucket full of jam.

Or anything at all, Mam, for we're nearly starving,
Anything to help a poor joker on his way,
For we are hums and jolly good chums, we live like Royal Turks,
And if we've luck we'll hum our cheques and shoot the man who works.

A farmer asked me the other day, 'If I would go to graft?'
Says I, 'What is the work ?', says he, 'A-cutting of some chaff.'
Says I, 'What is the payment?'—'A dollar and a half's the sum.'
Says I, 'Why don't you go shoot yourself! For we would rather hum

Than work upon the harvest and let the cockles starve us.'
Humming a drink where 'ere we go, sing fol the righty-o,
For we are hums and jolly good chums, we live like Royal Turks,
And if we've luck we'll hum our cheques and shoot the man who works.

So to conclude and finish, the remainder of my song,
The song that was proposed, me boys, by two professional hums.
Who travelled England, Ireland; all over Scotland too,
And took an oath in Bendigo, no more work they would do.

No more work they would do boys, troll old army dough boys,
Humming a drink where 'ere they, sing fol the righty-o
For we are hums and jolly good chums, we live like Royal Turks,
And if we've luck we'll hum our cheques and shoot the man who works.

QUANDONG

This fruit is only found on the inland plains of Australia. Early colonial settlers used it to make quandong jam. Remove the kernels and add about three-times the bulk of the fruit in brown sugar. Allow to boil at a low heat for as long as it likes. Leave to cool.

If you need to keep the quandong fruit for a long time you can bury them in sand and they will ripen very slowly.

A 'quandong' is also an expression for a disreputable person.

QUEEN'S NIGHTCAP

Caroline Chisholm, writing in the mid-1800s offered this dish for hard times. Stew small pieces of salt beef in water, drain, and then cook gently for a little longer with a sprinkling of flour. This was then served on a base of a pancake made with flour and water, and fried. The origins of the dish's name have been lost in time, however it probably has more to do with the hair net that fashionable women wore to bed in the eighteenth century (men wore a similar net on their beards) than a nip of brandy. The reference could be to the thin pancake base, which might have resembled the hair net.

SHEARER'S JOY

Colonial beer was sometimes known as 'shearer's joy' and also 'jerrawicke'. The ale was dark and often tainted by tobacco juice or ale slops in the more dubious shanties.

STEAMER

A popular early bush dish was a stew made from pieces of kangaroo meat, some roo tail and a few slices of salty pork. This stew was slow-cooked in a little water in a sealed camp oven.

STREET CRIES

Way before Mr Whippy's 'Greensleaves' ruined our peaceful Sundays in the 1960s, music was part of urban life. The following street cries were reported in the *Australian Journal* of 1868.

Fish alive-oh, fish alive.
All alive and kickin'
Come an try and buy and try —
Anything under a bushel for sixpence —
Alive-o, alive-o, fish alive.

Mullet-o, mullet-o, fresh whitin'
Feel 'em and try 'em,
Taste 'em and buy 'em.

Oysters 6d a plate
Don't be late
Oysters!

Ripe strawberries, turn and try the strawberries.
Rollup and buy the strawberries —
Fit for pies, jams and all sorts!
Fine ripe strawberries.

TEN-POUND NOTE SANDWICH

Successful diggers on the Victorian gold fields were known to hit Melbourne's finest restaurants, order two slices of bread and then proceed to place a ten-pound note between the slices and eat it. They reputedly washed this delight down with a bucket of champagne.

THROAT CUTTERS

A nickname given to Australian saveloy sellers. The sellers carried around a portable stove and would slit the saveloy and sprinkle it with vinegar. Supposedly the slit saveloy resembled a cut throat!

TUCKER

Tucker has been used in Australia since the gold rush days of the 1850s and is a derivation of the English word 'tuck', meaning food or appetite. We eagerly adopted the word, putting it to use as 'tucker bill', 'tucker box', 'bush tucker', 'tucker time' and 'tuck shop'. Tucker box probably stuck in our folklore because of its association with that damned dog that sat on, and sometimes shat in, the tucker box at Gundagai — as told in the popular Jack Moses poem — *The Dog Sits on the Tuckerbox* — and its traditional song variants.

Bush tucker
Outback

Much of the folklore in this collection comes to us from an earlier Australia where necessity really was the mother of invention. The pioneers went out back with the bare essentials: a shovel, pick, blankets and a few cooking pots. Some brought seeds of herbs and healing plants that they had treasured back home in the northern hemisphere. As they settled they bought the occasional kettle and tongs from travelling Afghan hawkers and made do with what they could make in the back shed. It was a rough and tumble life and usually lonely. Dreams of 'back home' in England, Ireland, Scotland or wherever, were important and so were the little bits of remembered and treasured lore. Ditties, rhymes and other lore provided a link to friends and good memories and were passed on as a sharing of wellbeing. Some of the words we used back then have disappeared from our vocabulary, especially the names of pots and pans and how we cooked food. So many things have changed and the quart pot of yesteryear is a long way removed from today's fondue set.

The mess huts of pastoral stations were often huge affairs and one such outback shed was reputedly so large it had forty cooks just to cook for the cooks! In truth many of the outback cooks were trained chefs who had found themselves in the bush to 'dry out' from their time in the big smoke. Many songs, yarns, poems and associated folklore grew out of this colourful era and still contribute to our national mythology and how we see ourselves.

The great art of bush cookery consists in giving a variety out of salt beef and flour.

(Caroline Chisholm, quoted in
The Emigrant's Guide to Australia, London, 1852)

BABBLING BROOK

Popular rhyming slang for 'cook'. It was popular in British army slang but was used here way before World War I. Cooks had a hard time in the outback, faced with sparse rations and enormous appetites, but they were mostly a sorry lot and 'Greasy' was another popular nickname. 'He was so greasy you couldn't look at him — yer eyes would slide right off him. He was that greasy!'

Only a fool argues with a snake, a woman or a cook.

(Old bush saying)

The missus on Wallandamper Station was widely regarded as a tough operator. One morning, she comes bawling and whining into the men's quarters and obviously upset about something or other. She eyed the new cook with one of those looks that could kill.

'Who was it?' she demanded. 'Who left the soap to disintegrate in the dishwater? It was you, wasn't it, Cookie?'

All eyes turned to the new cook.

'Nar, missus, t'wasn't me and I can prove it. I've only been here a week and I definitely haven't washed me hands yet!'

BAGMAN'S TOAST

The 'bagman' was the swagman who carried several bags rather than the conventional swag. During the lean times of the 1890s depression it was common for station owners to provide the travellers with basic rations, usually in exchange for light farm labour like chopping wood.

The bagmen and swagmen, and sometimes women, who arrived at dusk, hopefully to avoid work, were known as 'sundowners' (because they arrived as the sun went down). The rations were 8 pounds of flour, 10 pounds of meat, 2 pounds of sugar and ¼ pound of tea. It was universally known as the 'eight, ten, two and a quarter'.

After the turn of the century they reckoned you could still count on the eight, ten, two and a quarter — eight reasons why you could be held up for trespassing, ten reasons why you didn't deserve handouts, only two chances to explain yourself, and a quarter yard start on the dog.

Me and me dog,
We travel the bush,
In weather cold and hot,
Me and me dog,
We don't give a stuff,
If we get any work or not.

BANJO
A leg of lamb was known as a 'banjo' because its shape was reminiscent of the musical instrument.

BACHELOR'S TART
A popular name for any improvised bush cooking, as in 'Sid's making a bachelor's tart.'

BILLY
The most popular cooking utensil in the Australian bush was the billy can. Stories have been written about it, songs have been sung in praise of it. It is cheap, light and a burden to no one. It originated during the late gold-rush days of the 1870s when miners consumed a popular French soup known as *bouilli*. As containers were scarce, the old *bouilli* cans were reused as carrying and cooking containers.

I have humped my bluey in all the states,
With my old black billy, the best of mates;
For years I've camped and toiled and tramped
On roads that are rough and hilly,
With my plain and sensible,
Indispensable. Old black billy.

My old black billy, my old black billy,
Whether the wind be warm or chilly,
I always find, when the shadows fall,
That my old black billy's the best mate of all.

> (Words by Ted Harrington and from the Australian theatre musical
> *Reedy River* as presented by New Theatre.)

Old Billy — battered brown and black,
With many years of camping,
Companion of the bulging sack,
And friend in all our tramping;
How often on a Friday night —
Your cubic measure testing —
With jam and tea we stuffed you tight,
Before we started nesting.

BOILED BEEF

As the colony grew and ships began to make the crossing faster, Australia started to send produce back to England. Tinned boiled beef was particularly sought after. This parody circulated around the 1870s.

THE BOILED BEEF OF AUSTRALIA
(Air: 'The Roast Beef of Old England')

Hurrah for the meat now our own's got too dear
They're bringing preserved from Australia to here
The workmen can add to his bread and his beer
The tender boiled beef of Australia,
Oh, the Australian boiled beef.

The butchers will shake in their shoes I'll be bound
With their chops and their steaks at a shilling a pound
A joint for poor folks that are touch'd and unsound,
For now we've the beef of Australia,
The tender boiled beef of Australia,
Oh, the Australian boiled beef.

When juicy boiled beef is the artisan's fare,

He'll find it at once inexpensive and good;

At fivepence a pound, fat and bones will exclude,

For now we've the beef of Australia,

The tender boiled beef of Australia,

Oh, the Australian boiled beef.

So let us from all the stale rubbish refrain,

Some butchers oft sell for exorbitant gain,

And stick to the beef that's brought over the main,

For now we've the beef of Australia,

The tender boiled beef of Australia,

Oh, the Australian boiled beef.

BOXTY

A pancake-type concoction made from grated potato, flour, salt and milk. A bush version of Jewish latke cakes, but here they were typically eaten with butter and sugar.

Boxty on the griddle

Boxty on the pan

The wee one in the middle

Is for Mary Ann:

If you don't eat boxty

You'll never get your man

BUGGERS ON THE COALS

These were small, scone-like doughboys cooked on the coal ash and popular with bushmen.

Now I'm living in retirement, and I live a life of ease,

Catching up on all my hobbies just exactly as I please,

But when my thoughts they wander to my droving days of old

I can't say that I hanker for those buggers on the coals.

(From Cec Cory, collected by Wendy Lowenstein, 1972)

BUSH COOKS

There is a standard joke in the outback that a man cannot be considered a good bush cook until he's made an edible soup out of an old pair of socks.

Most bush cooks, especially station cooks, were given nicknames like 'Old Bait Layer', 'Bowel Twister', 'The Magician', 'Belly-Whinger', 'Grub Pusher', 'Dough Puncher' or simply 'Pierre'. The latter is particularly interesting since many of the station cooks were Chinese. Bad-tempered cooks fared much worse, copping 'Hot Bum' the curry-maker, 'Grizzle Guts', 'Stone Face' and the 'Silent Knight' because 'he never uttered a word'.

A bush cook's life was hard, rising before the crew to make tea and damper and providing breakfast, morning tea, lunch and dinner.

Traditionally the camp cook was the one who was too old or ill to keep up with the hard yakka of blade shearing or cattle mustering. At most camps the men would take a vote to see who would be elected cook for the season. Since the cook was paid on performance they usually tried hard.

Q: What sort of cook was he?
A: Just.

Q: Who called the cook a bastard?
A: Who called the bastard a cook?

BUSHMAN'S BREAKFAST

A fart, a yawn and a good look 'round.

BUSHMAN'S CHUTNEY

Chutney was important in the bush and one suspects it flavoured and saved many a tough station meal. Native fruits were used; however, more likely than not, tinned plum jam ruled the roost. (In the city, fancy boarding houses used to line the large IXL Henry Jones jam tins with crêpe paper. Very posh!)

Bush recipe: Take a quarter of a tin of dark plum jam and two tablespoons of Worcestershire sauce. Mix together and serve.

BUSHMAN'S DINNER

Mutton, tea and damper.

BUSHMAN'S HOT DINNER

Damper and mustard.

BUSHMAN'S LUNCH CAN

This was about the size of a three-quart billy, made in two parts that fitted together in the middle. The bottom section usually held the hot meat and vegetables; the top held the pudding. At the very bottom of the can was a hollow for a red-hot iron that was popularly used to toast cheese.

BUSH OYSTERS

Sometimes referred to as 'prairie oysters' or 'mountain oysters', these are lamb or cattle testicles. Folklore has it that they should be eaten raw and in one swallow — and chewing is not advisable — although they were also popular fried.

Australians are not the only people to eat testicles and in 2004 cooks from all over the world gathered in Serbia for the World Testicle Cooking Championship. The Serbian daily, *Glas Javnosti*, reported that the championship was won by Dejan Willovanovic of Belgrade. He said: 'The best cooked balls come from Serbia and we wanted to stage this contest to show the world what great dishes can be cooked using testicles, which are known locally here as "white kidneys".'

BUSHTESHIRE SAUCE

Early Australians missed the taste of English condiments and sauces so they made their own. This is a version of Worcestershire sauce gone bush.

RECIPE FOR BUSHTERSHIRE SAUCE

- 3 pounds (1.3 kilograms) treacle
- 1 gallon (4.5 litres) vinegar
- 1 bottle anchovy sauce

2 ounces (50 grams) cloves

1 ounce (25 grams) cayenne pepper

2 ounces (50 grams) garlic

salt to taste

Boil all the ingredients together for about half an hour then allow to cool.

BUSH TUCKER

Bill Harney, the great bushman of yesteryear, had a favourite saying about native food: 'If it moves, catch it — it might be good bush tucker.' In his classic *Bill Harney's Cook Book* he mentions many bush tucker recipes, including crocodile, emu egg dishes, possum pumpkin pie, baked bandicoot, roasted goanna and witchetty grubs — all cooked in the bush style. He also passed on a great piece of Aboriginal wisdom: 'If you want food to go further, eat less.'

Bush tucker has come to mean game, fowl, native vegetables or seafood gathered by one who is living off the country. There was also an expression 'gin tucker' denoting snakes, goannas and other foods eaten by wild Aborigines, and so called because its gathering was the usual task of the womenfolk, while the men hunted larger game.

CAMP PIE

This was traditionally made with minced meat, gelatine and whatever else was hanging around, and then cooked in the billy. The tinned commercial version tasted just as dreadful as the original.

CAMP MAST

To cook the perfect camp oven roast, place a small roast and a big roast together in a camp oven. When the small roast is burnt the big roast is ready to eat!

CANECUTTER'S LAMENT

The Maltese and Italians who took work in the Queensland cane industry must have been taken aback by the thought of a Chinese cook, let alone the just-as-strange local diet.

How we suffered, grief and pain,
Up in Queensland cutting cane.
We sweated blood, we were as black as sin,
And the ganger, he drove the spurs right in.

The first six weeks, so help me Christ,
We lived on cheese and half-boiled rice,
Doughy bread and cat's-meat stew,
And corned beef that the flies had blew.

The Chinese cook with his cross-eyed look,
Filled our guts with his corn-beef hashes.
Damned our souls with his half-baked rolls,
That'd poison snakes with their greasy ashes.

The cane was bad, the cutters were mad,
And the cook, he had shit on the liver,
And never again will I cut cane,
On the banks of the Queensland river.

CANNED DOG

Tinned meat in the bush was given this nickname. It most probably comes from a reference in *The Bulletin* in 1895, which mentioned how the men ate 'tinned dorg'.

CHINESE COOKS

According to *My Experiences in Australia* by 'A Lady', London, 1860, 'They [Chinese cooks] are generally considered very quarrelsome, are easily offended, and so terribly revengeful and treacherous.' In truth, Chinese cooks were popular in the outback, as they were considered careful, sober and non-talkative.

He was lazy, he was cheeky, he was dirty, he was sly,
But he had a single virtue and its name was rabbit pie.

DAMPER

Damper is the foundation of bush cuisine. The word was first used in 1827 and strictly speaking referred to bread baked in the ashes of a campfire or in a camp oven. It is not always unleavened as many cooks added bicarbonate of soda or baking powder. Some cooks also used Eno's Fruit Salts, which were readily available as a liver tonic. The salts had the approximate ingredients to make the bread rise.

RECIPE FOR DAMPER

Take about 3 pounds [1.3 kilograms] of flour and put it in a dish, adding a good pinch of salt and a combination of 2 parts cream of tartar to 1 part bicarbonate of soda. Pour some water into the dish and mix into a light dough. Sprinkle some flour over the bottom of the camp oven to prevent the damper from sticking, then put in the dough and put the lid on top. The best way to cook the damper is in a hole in the ground and, covering the pot with hot ashes. It must be completely covered or it will burn. It will take about half an hour to cook and the best way to test it is to scrape off the ashes, lift the lid and tap the damper with a stick. If it gives a hollow sound it's ready to eat. The best way to eat damper is with cocky's joy.

(Joe Watson memoirs, 1973)

While travelling once I came upon a man in a tent who was very anxious for me to stay to dinner. Said he would have damper bread cooked in a jiffy; pulled off his shirt, poured some flour on it, added water and started to mix the dough. Have myself used a corner of a tent, and even a saddle cloth, when nothing better was to be had; but that dirty shirt made me suddenly remember that I was in a great hurry.

(*The Bulletin*, September 1898)

We used to call our cook Jesus 'cause he could turn bread into stone.

With a pint of flour and a sheet of bark,
We wallop up a damper in the dark,
With a ru-da-ma-rah, and a rub- a-dub-dub,
Drive me back to the limejuice-tub.

(Old bush song)

BUCK'S DINNER
Nothing to eat but water.

DUST
Bush cooks usually referred to flour as 'dust' in the same way they called baking powder 'dynamite', honey was 'bee-jam', fried eggs were 'bulls-eyes', boiled sago was 'frog's eyes' and any tinned fish was called 'goldfish'.

JACK JUMPERS
A heavier version of a traditional damper, usually made with lard. It was said, 'If you eat a Jack Jumper for breakfast your horse will never throw you.' It must have been heavy on the gut.

JACKSHEA OR JACK SHAY
This was another name for the popular bush cooking and food storage can, the indispensable quart pot. The quart pot's history dates back to 1844, while 'billy' was not used in print until 1850.

JOHNNY CAKES
Johnny cakes, or doughboys, are best baked on ashes — first one side and then the other.

RECIPE FOR JOHNNY CAKES
You need flour, water, salt and a bit of baking powder. It's pointless giving quantities as it all depends on the state of your ration bags. Cut a sheet of bark from an available tree and use the clean side as a mixing dish. Build a good fire and let it settle as hot coals. If your best water is full of mosquitoes and flies then skim with a spoon, stick or rim of your hat to remove the foreign bodies. If your water is muddy and you have plenty of time you can clean it with wood ashes. Mix the ingredients into a stiff dough and make into cake sizes — about eight to ten inches [20 to 25 centimetres] in diameter by about an inch [2.5 centimetres] thick. Cook on both sides and eat with whatever you have.

(Quoted in *The Bulletin*, 1884)

FOUR LITTLE JOHNNY CAKES

Hurrah for the Lachlan, boys, and join me in a cheer,
That's the place to go to make a good cheque each year,
With a toad-skin in my pocket I borrowed off a friend,
Oh, isn't it nice and cosy to be camping in the bend.

With my little round flour-bag sitting on a stump,
My little tea-and-sugar bag looking nice and plump,
A little fat codfish just off the hook,
And four little Johnny cakes, a credit to the cook.

(Traditional song. A 'toad-skin' is a ten-pound note.)

LEATHER JACKET

A Johnny cake-shaped small damper that is fried in whatever is available — be it lard, goanna oil or corned-beef fat. These were seen by old-time bushmen as a welcome change from the plain damper eaten when there was no butter, suet or fat available.

MIXUM GATHERUM PIE

A popular colonial description for pies made with leftovers. Put the remains of 'this' with 'those' and add 'these' and 'that' (or milk will do if you have run out of 'that'). Season to taste. Put into a standard pie dish, sprinkle with crumbs made from old bread, dot with butter and bake until golden brown.

PADDY MELON

A small marsupial and a favoured 'last resort' meal for many the early settler and bush traveller.

PANNIKIN

A bush cooking and food storage can. Most popular for drinking tea or coffee.

PAROO SANDWICH

A meal of wine and beer. As travellers knew, the 'parched Paroo' of western Queensland offered very few pleasures for the bushman.

PUFTALOON

Also called 'puftaloonies', this was essentially damper made with sugar, fried in a generous amount of fat then spread with jam, sugar or treacle. It's another example of how Australians created a culinary art form out of flour.

QUART POT

A bush cooking and food storage can. Along with the billy can, the quart pot was the bushman's favourite cooking pot. It's celebrated in traditional verse and yarns, and songs like Edward Harrington's 'My Old Black Billy' as featured in the 1950s Australian musical 'Reedy River', and bush songs such as 'Four Little Johnny Cakes'.

SHOVEL COOKERY

Bushmen, and especially prospectors, were known to cook on their shovels when proper cooking pots were unavailable. The shovel was simply cleaned and greased ready for the mutton chops, Murray cod or even wild bird.

SINKERS

Small dampers that were boiled in the billy as a dumpling, either in water or placed directly in the stew, were called sinkers. Sometimes these tennis ball-shaped dumplings were eaten with golden syrup.

STATION COOKS

They used to say the old station cooks worked when they weren't sleeping and slept when they weren't working. I found this song, dated 1877, in the *Evening Star* newspaper, Adelaide.

THE SHEARER'S HARDSHIPS
(Air: 'Knickerbocker Line')

Oh dear, I feel so queer, I don't know what to do
The thought of leaving Fowler's Bay, it breaks my heart in two.
If I only meet that slushy, I'll make him rue the day,
That he destroyed my constitution, at that station — Fowler's Bay.

Oh dear, I feel so queer, I don't know what to do
The thought of leaving Fowler's Bay, it breaks my heart in two.

Our cook he is a baker and confectioner by trade
And many a batch of sour bread and brownie he has made
He turns out in the morning and gives us plenty of stewed tea
So don't forget when shearing's done to pay the cook his fees.

Oh, you ought to see his plum duffs, doughboys and meat pies
I swear by long Maloney it would open shearers' eyes
He says, 'Take your time good fellows,' and stares up with a glance
'I will dish you up much better if you give me but the chance.'

Won't I have some news to tell my friends in Adelaide?
How much I did improve in health while in Fowler's Bay I staid;
Our cook is so kind, and sweet, and obliging to us all,
That every time I look at him he reminds me of St Paul.

Spoken
Now, gentlemen when I say St Paul, I beg to be excused. I don't wish to distinguish that inferior individual as a representative of that good saint to whom we are all taught to believe in according to Scripture. No, gentlemen shearers and brother bushmen, I am only comparing him to that Boolcoomatta blackfellow, who assumes the name of St Paul owing to his religious style of corroboree, but a more tender-hearted fellow than our insignificant cook. So it's…

Chorus
Oh dear, I feel so queer, etc.

STATION JACK

Caroline Chisholm mentioned 'station jack' while writing in the 1850s when there was often nothing more than salted beef and flour in the station rations. She suggested soaking and beating the salted meat, then rolling it in a paste of flour and water, and boiling it.

STEW

The mainstay of most outback cookhouses, the stew, would run from wonderful to frightful depending on ingredients and cookery skills. The outback workers demanded stew that would 'stick to your ribs'. Legend has many tales of stews, including the one about the cook who was suspected of continually adding new ingredients and never bothering to wash the bottom of the pot. One day a disgruntled shearer decided to put a stop to this particular stew so he popped in a Reckitt's Blue bag (which was used in washing). The cook delivered the pot that night with a broad smile and 'I've a special tonight — blue stew!'

Stews were also known as 'mulligan' or 'mullinga stew' and 'fly-swisher stew'. Mullinga could possibly be from the tramp slang mulligan stew or even influenced by the mulga. 'Fly-swisher', of course, was oxtail stew.

I remember a cookie we had up on a Queensland station. He was a big, ugly brute named Fighting Foley. We all thought that his nickname was in honour of the great boxer Larry Foley, but we were wrong. He was a terrible cook and every day we'd leave the hut whinging loudly so he could hear us. Well, one night he came in with his usual pot of stew and plonked it down saying, 'This here is stew and any man who disagrees can meet me outside!' One of the shearers, a big burly fellow, thought he'd try it on and went outside. Ten minutes later he comes in with blood on his face and sat down quietly muttering, 'It's bloody stew alright!'

(Rad Dawson, Forresters Beach, NSW, 1973)

Australian soldiers also needed something heavy to eat too, since 'an army marches on its stomach'.

All soldiers live on bread and jam
They like it better than eggs and ham
Early in the morning, you'll hear the corporal say:
Stew, stew, stew, stew,
Stew for dinner today.

STICK-UP MEAT

Meat that had been skewered and roasted over a campfire on a forked stick was called 'stick-up'.

WALLAPALABRAZA FLOUR

The late Russell Ward, an historian, explained that 'Wallapalabraza flour' is singular = (abo.) for "Valparaiso flour", a synonym for cheap and nasty flour cum ground-rice cum sand, etc.' The term was quoted in *Bushmen All* in 1908, by H. J. Driscoll in his popular bush verse 'Gow of Mount Gambee':

> I've lived on beef and pigweed in the drought of sixty-three,
> I've starved on yowah and munyeroo adown the St-relec-kee,
> But the hardest patch I ever struck was Gow of Mount Gam-bee.
> He fed his blacks on 'roos and rats and 'wallapalabraza-flours'.
> His stagy meat was lively, and his sodden damper sour,
> And weevils big as bull-ants played leap-frog in the flours.

WHITELY KING

Many outback travellers made their own billy cans out of empty jam tins with a bit of a handle made from fencing wire. This crude billy was known as the 'Whitely King', from the disgraced name of the secretary of the Pastoralists' Union who used scab labour during the great shearers strikes. All bushmen despised this billy.

Tea time
Drinks hot and cold

Australians delight in abbreviating many words but 'cuppa' must be up the top somewhere as it has been in circulation for well over a century as a description of a cup of tea or coffee. We have always consumed a large quantity of hot drinks, particularly tea, and this inevitably led to a flow of folklore surrounding the brews, including song, yarn, word usage, custom and that great ongoing debate whether the milk should be added before or after the tea. In colonial days the station or camp cook had to rise at sparrow-fart to ensure that plenty of strong, hot tea was ready to get the men off on the right foot. More tea was demanded mid-morning, at lunch, in the mid-afternoon and, of course, when they knocked off at day's end. They referred to it as their 'darling', 'sweetie' and 'lifesaver'. An old saying offered: 'a hot drink is as good as an overcoat'.

In the city, workers in factories also broke regularly to take tea from massive urns of boiling water in what became recognised as a 'smoko' because of the popularity of cigarettes. In city offices the tea was wheeled through on tea trolleys and dished out by tea ladies. In the early 1970s self-serve café machines became popular and rattling tea trolleys started to disappear.

Over the past fifty years coffee has become very popular, possibly due to the large post-World War II European immigration programs or the determined television advertising by corporate brands like

Nescafé and Maxwell House. The last few years have also seen coffee retail chains like Starbucks enter the market offering a startling range of hot drinks in a 'club' atmosphere where patrons are invited to plug in their laptops and even download their favourite music onto their iPods. I'm a traditionalist when it comes to coffee so I am little nervous at some of the Starbucks offerings like Gingerbread Latte, Toffee Nut Latte, Peppermint Mocha and, for the Yuletide season, Eggnog Latte.

It was the Dutch, in 1610, who introduced tea to Europe and also the name by which it has been known ever since. It became immediately popular — if not expensive — and shipments from China, India and Korea enticed the European tastebuds and changed society forever. Around the time the First Fleet was preparing to set sail to Australia the average Englishman was consuming two and a half pounds of tea per capita and tea imports for 1770 totalled £9 million. William Gladstone summed up the national craving for tea: 'If you are cold, tea will warm you. If you are heated, it will cool you down. If you are depressed it will cheer you. If you are excited, it will calm you.'

It was the Victorians who really fashioned our tea drinking and the custom of afternoon tea became the main testing ground for fashionable ladies. If your manners passed the afternoon tea test you might be considered acceptable for other events. Lord help the wench who tried to sip her tea out of a saucer! Afternoon tea ranged from two to over one hundred people and leading hotels started to introduce daily afternoon tea with light entertainment, a pianist or guest vocalist. At home tea was often followed by card games. Before World War I afternoon tea was combined with the latest craze for dancing and this continued until the 1920s when some bright spark introduced cocktails and the tea trolley rattled away.

BEEF TEA

A tea made from extracted beef and popularised in the nineteenth century for its nourishing benefits. Its main use appears to have been in gravies and it predates the Oxo cube. In Australia we also consumed mutton tea.

In *The Doctor in the Kitchen*, published in the 1930s, Mrs Arthur Webb insisted that these teas 'must not boil or even approach boiling point'. Mind you, she also recommended a 'Liver Cocktail' that consisted of half-cooked liver passed through a sieve and mixed with the juice of an orange and lemon with a pinch of sugar. I can't think of anything as scary as this hideous concoction. The good woman also added, 'It is helpful to drink water after each dose, to remove any aftertaste.'

Florence Nightingale was dubious of the beef tea's nourishing benefits, 'Give a pint of beef tea and you have given scarcely a teaspoon of nourishment.'

BILLY TEA

Traditionally the bushman made tea by boiling clean (with any luck) water in a billy can and throwing in a generous handful of tea leaves when the water came to the boil. The next step was to make the tea leaves sink to the bottom and several methods were employed. Some added a couple of gum leaves, claiming that they made the tea leaves sink, others insisted that the leaves would always sink when the sides of the billy can were given several short, sharp taps with a stick. Some bushies stirred the tea with a twig while others recommended swinging the billy can around with a circular motion so that the law of gravity would force the leaves to the bottom.

THE BILLY OF TEA

You may talk of your whisky or talk of your beer,
I've something far better awaiting me here;
It stands on the fire beneath the gum tree,
And you cannot much lick it — a billy of tea.
So fill up your tumbler as high as you can,
You'll never persuade me it's not the best plan,
To let all the beer and the spirits go free
And stick to my darling old billy of tea.

I wake in the morning as soon as it's light,
And go to the nosebag to see it's all right,

That the ants on the sugar no mortgage has got,
And immediately sling my old billy-pot,
And while it is boiling the horses I seek,
And follow them down perhaps as far as the creek;
I take off the hobbles and let them go free,
And haste to tuck into my billy of tea.

And at night when I camp, if the day has been warm,
I give each of the horses their tucker of corn,
From the two in the pole to the one in the lead,
And the billy for each holds a comfortable feed;
Then the fire I start and the water I get,
And the corned beef and damper in order I set,
But I don't touch the grub, though hungry I be,
I will wait 'till it's ready — the billy of tea.

(Traditional bush song)

CAPE BARREN TEA

The remote islanders living on Cape Barren Island off Tasmania brew
the leaves of the *Corriea alba* as tea.

COFFEE

Although the coffee tree is native to Ethiopia and the Sudan it has
been widely cultivated for centuries. The creation of the drink itself
is surrounded in legend. Some have it discovered by a goatherd who
noticed his flock becoming agitated whenever they ate the red
berries that contained the coffee seeds. Another has a hermit
Dervish priest or mullah used the brew to stay awake so he could
pray. By the end of the nineteenth century, coffee drinking had
become an international fashion including Australia. Cappuccino,
so called because of its pale brown colour reminiscent of the robes
of the Capuchin monks, is one of the most popular coffee styles in
Australia.

There is a folk belief that drinking coffee will sober up an
intoxicated person. However, while it will keep them awake it
actually does little to remedy the affect of alcohol.

Bushies used to refer to coffee as 'slosh'.

A proper cup of coffee in a proper coffee cup.

Burn coffee and you'll have bad luck.

Never stir other people's coffee as you will surely stir up trouble.

CORDIAL

Cordial is a sweet syrup-based confectionery drink. Its name comes from the word 'cardio' as the drink was believed to add vigour and be good for the heart. In yesterday's Australia many people made homemade ginger beer up until the 1950s when commercially produced cordials became readily available. Most suburbs supported a cordial company that delivered the soft drinks or syrups door-to-door. Passiona, Sarsaparilla and GI were the most popular products, with the latter so named because of the American GIs who came to Australia during World War II.

DAD RUDD'S TEA

We couldn't very well go without tea, so Dad showed Mother how to make a new kind. He roasted a slice of bread on the fire till it was like a black coal. Then he poured the boiling water over it and let it draw well. Dad said it had a capital flavour — he liked it.'

(Steele Rudd's *On Our Selection*, 1899)

DANDELION

Dandelion is often considered a pest, however this has not stopped its popularity as a remedial tea used for liver, kidney disease and anaemia. It was often used as an alternative to coffee.

To find out how many children you will have find a dandelion that has gone to seed. Hold it up and blow the seeds into the wind. Count the number of seeds remaining and this will be the number of children.

The 'wet the bed' flower is a relative of the dandelion. These small flowers were widely believed to encourage children to wet their beds.

DEVONSHIRE TEA
The Australian version of England's 'cream tea' and usually comprised of scones, cream and strawberry jam. Devonshire teas were mostly served in roadway cafés in the country and at the swanky city hotels.

HARVEST TEA
Put 6 ounces (175 grams) sugar, $\frac{3}{4}$ pound (225 grams) fine oatmeal and half a lemon, sliced thinly, into a large jug or pan. Stir well, gradually adding just enough water to dissolve the sugar. Then add a gallon [4.5 litres] of boiling water, stir, and leave to get cold.

HOPS
Q: What are the equivalents for good beer, bad beer and ginger beer?
A: All slop, all sop and all pop.

To improve one's appetite drink a tea infused with hops and caraway seeds.

HOT BEEF TEA BRACER
Into a cup of hot beef tea put a wineglass of sherry, previously heated but not boiled.

HOT TODDY
A hot drink made with whisky, sugar or honey, hot water and lemon. Said to be good for whatever ails you!

JACK THE PAINTER
This was the term given to tea by old bushmen who carried a permanent brown tea stain around their mouths — 'He's been seeing Jack the Painter.'

KETTLES
Polly put the kettle on
Polly put the kettle on

Polly put the kettle on
And we'll all have tea

Sukey take it off again
Sukey take it off again
Sukey take it off again
They've all gone away

Blow the fire and make the toast
Put the muffins on to roast
Blow the fire and make the toast
We'll all have tea

A watched kettle never boils.

Let a kettle boil away and you will boil away your friends.

Place marbles in the bottom of your kettle to prevent lime building up.

There is an old custom called 'tin kettling' whereby various tin cans are tied to the rear of a wedding vehicle. As the bridal couple drives away the cans make a huge racket.

NEGUS
A bush drink made of hot port wine, spiced with sugar, nutmeg and lemon juice. The original meaning has slipped from time, however the concept of using China tea as a base for other flavourings — especially as a way of concealing alcohol — was popular in the nineteenth century.

PARSNIP COFFEE
When coffee was unavailable a version was made with parsnips. They were scraped, minced and spread on flat plates and baked in a slow oven. This was then added sparingly to hot milk and water then boiled again to produce the drink.

POST AND RAIL TEA

A tea so called because of the large leaves that float in the mug, resembling the distinctive outback post and rail wooden fencing.

SUNDOWNER'S CUP

A confused yet popular late-nineteenth century drink made from sauterne, soda water, lemon, white grapes, mint, caster sugar and Australian quince liquor brandy (Marnique).

TEA

One, two, three
mother caught a flea
put it in a teapot
and had a cup of tea
the flea jumped out
mother gave a shout
in came daddy with
his shirt hanging out

To stir a teapot is to stir up trouble.

If you add boiling water before the tea you can have trouble.

Strong tea means strong friendships.

If two women handle the teapot at the same time, one will give birth to ginger twins.

Love is crossed when milk before tea.

To pour tea back in the pot is trouble.

TEA COSIES

The cover on a teapot is known as a tea cosy. They come in all shapes, sizes and designs and folk art thrives with cosies made to look like cats, rabbits, mice and many other animals. They actually do keep the tea hot. Many tea cosies have embroidery on the side, sometimes with old sayings like this:

All those who love good tea
Must please remember me
Be sure allow the water to boil
Then the tea you will not spoil.

TEA LADY

The tea lady was a familiar fixture at most factories and offices up until the 1980s. They were employed to ensure the staff always had enough milk, tea, coffee and biscuits, and hot water in the urns. Most factories and offices had a designated morning and afternoon tea break as the tea lady pushed her trolley through the various departments. Biscuits, if not provided by the employer, were on an honour basis of around twenty cents a day. The tea lady was replaced by automatic 'time saving' café bars that disbursed hot water to go with tasteless tea bags, insipid coffee, packaged sugar, and wooden paddle pop sticks to stir the concoction. The old tea ladies would have been embarrassed.

TEA LEAVES

Reading tea leaves to tell fortunes has been in local circulation for well over 150 years. Once the skill of gypsies, it is now performed socially. Reading cups is called tasseography.

Always burn tea leaves for luck.

If a single tea leaf floats to the top of the cup expect a friend or a parcel.

Dinner is served
Home cooking

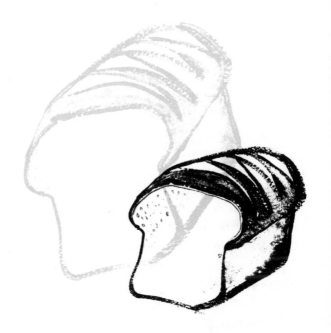

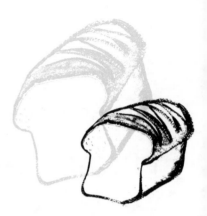

Meals of my youth were planned and appeared to be on some type of roster that you could set your watch by! I now accept this as traditional family custom. Monday was leftovers from the Sunday baked dinner, usually a bubble and squeak dish; Tuesday was sausages or mince with three vegetables; Wednesday was grilled lamb chops with three vegetables; Thursday was a stew or rabbit casserole; Friday was fish and chips; and Saturday was a savoury pie. Saturday was also baking day with two cakes, a tray of biscuits and two puddings — one of rice, the other milk or bread pudding. These were consumed over the week. We hardly ate rice, never had pasta and chicken was reserved for very special celebrations.

Both my parents were fond of old sayings and my father loved to sing little ditties like 'Polly Put the Kettle On' or 'The Keys of Canterbury'. Most of these were widely known; however, to a very young boy, they were mighty mysterious and I sometimes thought my parents were from another time — and of course they were. I now appreciate how they had both inherited their own family customs and folklore and brought them together under our roof. I never tired of hearing the same old lines whenever someone spilt the salt, burnt the toast or allowed the milk to boil over. Such is the familiarity and charm of folklore.

Cleaning and washing up was also part of the kitchen ritual. In the average household this was a job for the children — it certainly was in ours — and, for many, it was also a time for stories and a song. The folklore collector, the late John Meredith told of his recording sessions with Mrs Sally Sloane, in Lithgow, in the 1950s. He had to set up his tape machine in the kitchen for this was the place Mrs Sloane always sang and the best place for her to remember the words.

Home cooking should not be seen as being in competition to restaurant food. They are — and should be — miles apart, and many the home 'super cook' has been frustrated in an attempt to reproduce restaurant fare. That's not to say it isn't possible, but it should not be seen as a competition. In this day and age of 'celebrity chefs', and they do seem to be around every corner, we are being conditioned to be too fancy and encouraged to 'cook like your favourite restaurant chef— at home'. Not only is this killing the restaurant industry — 'I'm not going to pay those prices when I cook the bloody thing at home for half the price!' — but it is also turning families into guinea pigs. There is nothing wrong with good traditional home cooking and, in most cases, nothing tastes better!

Most lore associated with the kitchen or dining table was created for a reason, be it as a warning, education or simply as an entertainment. It is important to realise that the dining table, be it rich or poor, is singularly the most important place in the home. It is here the family gathers regularly, it is usually where group discussions are conducted, and it is here that most family values are cemented.

ASPIC

In the nineteenth and early half of the twentieth centuries meat in aspic was a popular dish. Aspic jellies were also made with vegetable, fruit and seafood, many of them in decorative shapes and moulds. Folklore has it that the name derived from the asp, a serpent whose icy coldness recalls that of the jelly.

BAKED DINNER

For many Australian families the Sunday lunchtime meal was known as 'having a baked dinner' and usually centred on a roasted lamb leg with baked pumpkin, potato and carrots. Gravy was a necessity along with freshly peeled peas or steamed cauliflower. The British referred to a similar dish as 'a roast'. For many of us, the best part of the baked lamb was the burnt ends and it was a struggle to gnaw at the bone before the family dog. The baked dinner was typically followed by a dessert of stewed fruit and homemade custard.

In the bush of yesterday's Australia the workers used to refer to stew as 'the complete baked dinner'.

BÉCHAMEL

Béchamel is considered the 'queen of sauces' because it harmonises with fish, meat, eggs, game and vegetables.

BRAWN

Brawn is traditionally made out of the meat from the pig's head (excluding the brain) and moulded in a brawn pot where it is pressed into shape. Sometimes it is set in aspic made from the reduced liquid. It is also known as 'head cheese' and was popular in the first half of the twentieth century when it was served with salad. Had I known what it was made of I doubt I would have eaten it as a child.

BUBBLE AND SQUEAK

A popular breakfast dish traditionally made with potatoes, onions, corned beef and 'anything else lurking at the rear of the refrigerator'. It is fried and served with eggs, and is said to 'put hairs on your chest'— which could be quite embarrassing if you are a girl.

Bubble and squeak is a popular hangover cure for the morning after. It is usually served with two fried eggs ('bull's eyes') on top.

BURNT FOOD

There's an old saying: 'If you burn anything edible you will have to pick it out of the fires of hell.'

Too many cooks may spoil the broth, but it only takes one to burn it.

(Madeleine Bingham, *The Bad Cook's Guide*)

CHEW YOUR FOOD

Eminent Victorian-era medics advised chewing food at least forty times before swallowing. Experts flourish in all ages but this advice was a difficult bite to swallow. Can you imagine sitting down to dinner and having to chew each mouthful forty to sixty times? Apart from the food being reduced to muck, the art of conversation would be dead in the water.

COOKS

Bad luck to the two people who cook the same thing in the same house on the same day.

Too many cooks spoil the broth.

She did not so much cook as assassinate food.
(Margaret Storm Jameson, British novelist, 1891–1986)

Never trust a skinny cook!

CRUMPETS

Crumpets are now a commercial product with aerated holes and a flat pancake texture. Although a campfire version existed they became commercially popular in the 1940s and many the crumpet was burnt to cinders as it cooked on the grill of the cosy kerosene heater.

He won't be worth a crumpet in action, not worth a bloody crumpet.
(Henry Lawson)

RECIPE FOR MOCK CRUMPETS

Mash some boiled potatoes until quite smooth, add a little salt, and press into round shapes. Brush with a little milk, and dredge with flour. Prick with a fork to prevent bursting and bake on a griddle. Eaten with butter or dripping they are equal to real crumpets and very nutritious.

(Koop family recipe)

CUTLERY

Lore has it that knives should never be crossed as they evoke both the cross on which St Anthony was crucified and the murderous gesture of crossing swords with an enemy.

If you drop a knife someone else should pick it up and you will receive a nice surprise.

Knife falls, gentleman calls
Fork falls, lady calls
Spoon falls, baby squalls

Stir with a knife, stir up strife
Stir with a fork, stir up talk

If a knife drops accidentally you can expect disappointment.

If a blade sticks in the ground then there will be good luck. Whoever picks it up will have very good luck however if the person who dropped it picks it up they will have bad luck.

If I knife falls and lands right side up expect misfortune and grief but if it lands upside-down you will get a pleasant surprise.

If a knife falls and lands standing up someone will soon leave the house.

The arm a baby uses to reach for its first spoon defines whether it will be left or right handed.

Don't play spin the knife as the blade could indicate a death.

Don't cross knife and fork on plate because this is an invitation to an argument.

Place a knife under the bed of a woman in labour and she will have less pain.

Never stir with the spoon in your left hand for you'll lose seven years of your life.

FEED A COLD AND STARVE A FEVER
There is no evidence to prove either piece of advice true; however, this is a saying common to many households.

GRAVY
There was a time when no respectable baked dinner could be served without being accompanied by this homemade sauce. Gravy is defined as a sauce made from meat juices, often combined with broth or milk and thickened with a starch in the pan juices. It can also be the reduced juices left from cooking proteins such as meat, fish or poultry. Although it is fairly simple to make, many home cooks have a difficult time making successful, smooth gravy. A survey of today's grocery shelves proves that the demand for gravy has not diminished one iota — gravy cubes, gravy granules, gravy powders and even 'fresh' gravy in cartons. Manufacturers have seen the 'gravy train'!

JAFFLES
Jaffles are made in a jaffle iron and appear to be an Australian invention. Essentially a jaffle is a pie made from two buttered (on both sides) slices of bread and filled with whatever takes your fancy. The jaffle iron is popular with bushwalkers, however many the jaffle has been made on the grill of a kerosene heater. One needs to be inventive and careful that the innards don't leak out. Jaffles cannot be made in waffle irons for this reason. Fillings include cheese, baked beans, eggs, curried meat — anything. You need to allow the jaffle to cool before munching, as a hasty bite can be extremely dangerous.

JOHN THE CHINAMAN
Before supermarkets and shopping centres, many Australians had their fruit and vegetables delivered to their door by street vendors who usually arrived around the same time and on the same day each week. Many Chinese became market gardeners and also operated first the delivery horse carts and then the motorised vans. Most of

these Chinese people were men and simply referred to as 'John the Chinaman'. One suspects it was not a racist slur but a result of the average Australian's inability to pronounce Chinese names.

KITCHEN

As farms improved in colonial Australia the station owners built themselves cookout huts or a 'lean-to' that later became known as 'the kitchen' and often became a structural part of the house. Other small huts were built, as needed — a slaughterhouse, meat-smoking room, bread-baking room, storeroom, etc. As the stations got larger, better kitchen facilities were installed, including bread tables, an array of cooking pots and implements, a meat safe, water filters, and kitchen safes to protect against the inevitable ants and flies.

At the turn of the twentieth century the Australian kitchen changed dramatically with the massive population shift from the bush to the coast and cities. This coincided with the growth of factories and the availability of more time-saving household inventions. In most urban areas the kitchen was incorporated into the main body of the house and was connected to what was known as the dining room, despite the reality that most families ate their meals around the kitchen table.

Everyday products like butter and bread became available commercially, which reduced the kitchen space but also freed up more time for the housewife. Newspapers and magazines, especially those aimed at women, featured advertisements for 'modern' gas and electric stoves, kerosene and then electric refrigerators, marble and steel sinks — and the parade has never stopped.

KITCHEN GADGETS

One of the most important kitchen inventions was the tin opener. Australia had been a pioneer for canning, sending Australian lamb and beef to Britain in the nineteenth century. The tin cans were very thick and required a hammer to open them. With the development of thinner cans it became a challenge to invent an efficient opener. In 1858, an American, Ezra Warner, patented the first can opener however it was William Lyman who went on to design the familiar opener with the wheel that rolled and cut around the rim. In 1925 the Star Can Company of California added a serrated edge to the wheel and this became universally popular.

New inventions and improvements on existing appliances rolled out including flour sifters, mincing grinders, vegetable peelers, jaffle irons, and a variety of lighter cooking pans and saucepans. It is truly fascinating to do a checklist of today's kitchen and all the inventions we take for granted. Imagine life without the blender (invented in 1922 by American, Stephen Poplawski) or those familiar green plastic garbage bags (invented by Canadian, Harry Wasylyk in 1950), not forgetting Tupperware (invented by Earl Silas Tupper who patented the air-tight sealed plastic container in 1947) to name but a few.

There are so many inventions that revolutionised our lives, from the toaster to the pressure cooker, but if one were to nominate only one example of an invention that has received international acceptance it might possibly be the microwave oven. Dr Percy Spencer, a self-taught engineer with the Raytheon Corporation, noticed something very unusual during a radar-related research project, around 1946. He was testing a new vacuum tube called a magnetron when he discovered that a chocolate bar in his pocket had melted. This interested Dr Spencer, leading to another experiment where he placed some popcorn kernels near the tube and watched as the kernels exploded. Microwave cooking had begun!

KITCHEN SAFE

Insects were always the scourge of the Australian bush cook and our pioneers invented all manner of things to protect their foodstuffs. The four legs of the kitchen safe would stand in old jam tins full of water to deter ants, or the meat safe would be suspended high from a nearby tree. The Coolgardie safe was the best-known brand.

MEATBALLS

This parody was circulated in the 1960s.

HOW THE MEATBALLS ROLL IN
(Air: 'My Bonnie Lies Over the Ocean')

My dad is a very fine fellow,
You can tell by the lift of his chin;
But whenever that man bends his elbow,
Oh, boy, how the meatballs roll in.
Roll in, roll in,
Oh, boy, how the meatballs roll in, roll in;
Roll in, roll in,
Oh, boy, how the meatballs roll in!

My dad dines on meatballs for breakfast,
He eats them at lunchtime, and then,
When he comes to the table for supper,
Oh, boy, how the meatballs roll in.
Roll in, roll in,
Oh, boy, how the meatballs roll in (again!);
Roll in, roll in,
Oh, boy, how the meatballs roll in!

MINCE

There was a time not so long ago in the mid-twentieth century when most butcher shops had a mincing machine in public view. To a bug-eyed kid it resembled a medieval torture machine as the butcher forced pieces of meat down its greedy gullet. It was fascinating to watch when the mince appeared at the other end, usually in long wavy strands.

Mince was a staple for most households and usually served with small triangles of white toast. If you were really posh the crusts were removed from the bread.

PAPERBAG COOKING

During the 1920s there was a craze for cooking food wrapped in greased paper. Bon vivant Leo Schofield alerted me to this peculiar phenomenon and the following song, which smacks of music hall repertoire. I eventually collected several versions.

You've heard about the latest kind of cooking,
In little paper bags, it's quite the craze,
My wife she's got the fever, and I'm sure I'll have to leave her,
If she doesn't change her paper-cooking ways.
It's not the paper bags that I object to,
It's her method, that's so very, very crude;
For the paper bags she uses are all made from 'Worldly News',
And the print comes off and boils out on the food.

Chorus
There's a breach of promise case upon the mutton,
And a murder right across the pickled pork;
You can read about the Navy on the surface of the gravy,
While the spinach bears the latest news from Cork.
The motto on the fish is 'Votes for Women',
While a scandal on the veal attention begs.
On the bacon we are getting all the latest London betting,
With the names of all the winners on the eggs.

My wife is very fond of reading novels,
The good old melodrama kind, I mean,
With a cottage ivy-laden,
And a youth and village maiden,
Who struggles with the villain on the green.
She uses all their pages up for cooking,
Which doesn't quite conduce to married bliss,
For although you're fond of reading,
You don't want it when you're feeding,
Served in chapters on your eatables like this —

Chorus
There's a breach of promise case upon the mutton,
And a murder right across the pickled pork;
You can read about the Navy on the surface of the gravy,
While the spinach bears the latest news from Cork.
The motto on the fish is 'Votes for Women',

While a scandal on the veal attention begs.
On the bacon we are getting all the latest London betting,
With the names of all the winners on the eggs.

First the hero meets the maiden on the cod-fish,
And murmurs, 'Just one kiss before we part',
Then the villain his 'Ha, ha!' snips
In the middle of the parsnips,
And he swears his love upon the apple tart,
He murmurs 'Fly with me!' upon the cabbage,
She spurns him — then the villain, getting vexed,
Cries 'Your jewels I will purloin!'
But she stabs him on the sirloin,
And the wedding is 'Continued in our next'.

Upon our food last week, instead of 'reading',
We'd pictures from the Sunday morning 'News'.
We'd photographs of actors,
And some famous benefactors,
And the very latest panoramic views,
I'd snapshots of the 'Cambridge' on my breakfast;
For lunch I'd aeroplanes and motor-cars;
And no wonder I get thinner,
For upon my Sunday dinner
I had photographs of all our leading stars!

Chorus
There's a breach of promise case upon the mutton,
And a murder right across the pickled pork;
You can read about the Navy on the surface of the gravy,
While the spinach bears the latest news from Cork.
The motto on the fish is 'Votes for Women',
While a scandal on the veal attention begs.
On the bacon we are getting all the latest London betting,
With the names of all the winners on the eggs.

There was Nellie Stewart reclining on the cutlets,
Upon the rabbit pie was Cyril Maud;
There was nothing on the mustard,
But all mixed up with the custard
Was a chorus girl just married to a lord!
We'd Lockhart's Elephants upon the jelly,
Upon the cheese an acrobatic group;
But what really took the biscuit
Was La Milo on the brisket,
With a picture of Salome in the soup.

POT

Beware! A watched pot never boils.

QUICHE

One of the most recognisable phrases of the 1990s, and the title of a highly successful book, was *Real Men Don't Eat Quiche*. No doubt this reference came from the fact that the quiche traditionally doesn't have any meat other than bacon pieces.

Although quiche is now a classic dish of French cuisine, it is said to have originated in Germany, in the medieval kingdom of Lothringen (later named Lorraine by the French), under German rule. The word 'quiche' is from the German *Kuchen*, meaning cake. However, *Larousse Gastronomique* gives its birthplace as Nancy in France around the sixteenth century.

The original 'quiche Lorraine' was an open pie with a filling consisting of an egg and cream custard with smoked bacon. It was only later that cheese was added. Wussy food indeed!

RISSOLES

Ground-meat rissoles were a regular dish on most counter lunch and boarding house menus. The standing joke was they were first rolled into balls and then finished off by placing in your armpits.

See ya' round like a rissole

SAUCE

There are some who would suggest that sauces and gravies were invented to hide spoiled meat. Not so. The noble sauce has a long and illustrious history. In Australia we find all types of sauces including Cumberland, bread sauce, onion sauce, white sauce, hollandaise, horseradish sauce, mint sauce, apple sauce and, of course, tomato sauce. In some ways it looks as if modern society has grown lazy in the sauce department and supermarket shelves now offer a huge range. A case of sauces for courses! I well remember making mint sauce every Sunday: fresh mint, vinegar, a touch of salt and sugar.

Sauce can be a touchy subject, especially with the French. There's a famous French quip that the English have sixty religions and only one sauce. They were referring to the English love of white sauce. Another Frenchman went even further, suggesting, 'The English have three taps in their kitchens. One for hot water, one for cold and one for white sauce.'

SAUCE ALBERT

A traditional British sauce named after Prince Albert, husband and consort of Queen Victoria. It is made from a white consommé seasoned with grated horseradish, thickened with breadcrumbs and enriched with egg yolks and cream. Lemon juice is added to give the final taste. It was popularly served with roast beef. The good Prince also lent his name to a fashionable Wellington boot and penile jewellery!

SHEPHERD'S PIE

Traditionally this British dish consists of minced meat sauce topped with mashed potato, baked until crisp on top. It uses lamb mince rather than beef, which is more closely associated with the cottage pie. How many kids have had nightmares picturing the poor old shepherd being ground down, boots and all, to make the stuffing for a shepherd's pie. Those apostrophes are cruel things!

SOUP

The word 'soup' comes from the Middle Ages English *sop*, which referred to a slice of bread over which stew gravy or dripping was poured.

The most popular folklore associated with soup is the old chestnut 'Waiter, there's a fly in my soup.'

Captain Cook was saved by soup. When the intrepid explorer set out on his second voyage of discovery in 1772, he sailed out on the *Resolution* to circumnavigate the South Pole in an attempt to lay claim to *Terra Australis Incognito*. Ice packs forced him back into the Pacific where he fell violently ill. His salvation was a soup made from a trusty ship's dog.

As ships go out to sea
I spoon the soup away from me.

Troubles are easier to take with soup than without.

(Yiddish saying)

Q: Which hand should you use to stir soup?
A: Neither — you should use a spoon

MULLIGATAWNY SOUP

A spicy soup of Indian origin adopted by the British and, for no apparent reason, particularly popular in Australia throughout the late nineteenth and early twentieth century. Its first recorded entry here was in 1809. (Other popular soups were made from turkey, duck and chicken giblets, potatoes, nettle, barley and peas.) Mulligatawny is essentially a chicken consommé to which are added vegetables such as onions, leeks and celery. It is then highly seasoned with curry and spices and garnished with chicken meat and rice. The Australian additions included bacon pieces and tomatoes.

Memories are like mulligatawny soup in a cheap restaurant. It is best not to stir them.

(P. G. Wodehouse, English novelist, 1881–1975)

PEA AND HAM SOUP

Pea and ham soup has been a staple of Australian winter fare. The best soup is heavy with a thick fog or torrential rain being referred to as a 'pea souper'. This soup dish is common to many cultures. The following recipe is for the typical Irish pea and ham soup served traditionally on St Patrick's Day.

500 grams (2 cups) dried peas or split peas
125 grams ($\frac{1}{2}$ cup) diced pieces of cooked ham or a ham bone
1 large onion and a little fat (optional)
$1\frac{1}{2}$ litres (6 cups) ham stock or water
cream (optional)
parsley (optional)
seasoning

Soak the peas as directed on the packet. Chop the onion, if used, and soften in a little fat over a low heat. Add the peas and water or stock, and the ham bone. Cook gently until the peas are soft — about an hour. Remove the bone and strip off any meat. This should be cut into small dice and reserved. Purée the peas in a blender or pass through a sieve. Adjust the seasoning. Add the diced ham and serve with a swirl of cream or a sprinkling of chopped parsley on top. Serves six.

SOUP LINE

During the Great Depression of the 1930s free soup was given out to the poor in soup kitchens. The queue was called the soup line.

It's a long way down the soup-line,
It's a long way to go.
It's a long way down the soup-line,
And the soup is thick I know.
Goodbye, dear old pork-chops,
Farewell, beefsteak rare;
It's a long way down the soup-line,
But my soup is there.

(Depression parody)

We're spending our nights in the doss-house
We're spending our days on the street
We're looking for work but we find none
We wish we had something to eat.

Soup, soup, soup, soup,
They gave us a big plate of loop-the-loop.
Soup, soup, soup, soup,
They gave us a big plate of soup.

(Depression song)

Beautiful soup, so rich and green,
Waiting in a hot tureen.

STEW

Hold the forks, the knives are coming
The plates are on the way
Shout the chorus to your neighbour
Send the stew this way

(Sydney boarding-house rhyme, 1877)

IRISH HOME STEW

Take 2 pounds [900 grams] of mutton and cut into fair pieces. Add 4 pounds [1.8 kilograms] of potatoes and cut them in half, as well as six onions peeled and sliced. Put a layer of the spuds on the bottom of the dish and then add some of the meat and onions, a small spoonful of pepper and some salt won't go astray. Pour over 2 cups of stock or water. The secret of the stew is that it must simmer and not boil for about two hours.

(Mrs Marsden, Cairns, Queensland)

TABLE

It is around the table that we gather to dine and, in many ways —
along with the kitchen sink — it is our high altar of food folklore.

Having thirteen people at one table is considered unlucky
because of the association with the Last Supper and Judas Iscariot.

It is particularly unlucky if the table is set for thirteen and the kitchen has only prepared for twelve!

Get off the table, Mabel, the money's for the beer.
(Classic Dad & Dave sexist humour and the inspiration for the title of one of my earlier books, *How Mabel Laid the Table*.)

It is extremely unlucky to place shoes on a kitchen or dining table.

TEST FOR LIARS
If you bite your tongue while eating it means you have been lying.

TV DINNER
2004 saw the fiftieth anniversary of the TV dinner. The brainchild of frozen food manufacturer Swanson and Sons overestimated its 1953 supply of Thanksgiving turkey and one Gerry Thomas had a bright idea to package up frozen trays with various compartments for the meat, vegetables and gravy. Thomas happened to be the right person at the right time and the TV dinner became a reality. Its success was astonishing and reflected the new craze for television and supermarkets — over 25 million TV dinners were sold in 1954 in the USA — with chicken, beef steak and meatloaf trays joining the turkey. My memory of TV dinners in Australia was that they tasted bloody awful but were fun to look at and play with.

VINEGAR
Vinegar is made from sour wine and comes to us from the French *vinaigre*. It has been used for centuries and legend has it that Cleopatra dissolved precious pearls in vinegar to win a wager that she could consume a fortune in a single meal.

It has many household folk uses ranging from an ant deterrent to removing bathtub film. When mixed with water and rubbed on plastic it will reduce static; the same mixture will also reduce discolouration in aluminium.

Vinegar will clean the toilet and disinfect it. It also cleans enamel stains.

Boiled beef will cook tender if you add vinegar and, oh yes, it is great mixed with oil in salad dressings!

WATER

Australians consume an enormous quantity of bottled water. Some may be attributed with almost miraculous powers, like the Unique Water brand in New South Wales that has been described in the media as inhibiting all sorts of chronic illness. The way stories spread about the amazing recuperative powers of such mineral spring water is the same as for most folklore — word gets around!

WINE

Drink wine and have the gout. Drink no wine and have it too.

Eat at pleasure, drink by measure.

WORCESTERSHIRE SAUCE

An English condiment, the recipe for which was discovered in the East Indies by Sir Marcus Sandys of Worcestershire. On returning home, he asked the English grocers Lea and Perrins to make up a sauce based on his favourite condiment. It was launched commercially in 1838 and soon exported to Australia where it was extremely popular with city and bush cooks alike. It is still sold in supermarkets.

Times were tough and the old cookie had to make do with what he could muster up as tucker. One of the saving graces of many meals was the ample supply of Worcestershire sauce that disguised the near-rotten meat. One day, the boss looked deep into the stew pot and took the cook aside.

'I notice that the stew is getting pretty black. How do you work out the right amount of sauce?'

'Oh, it's not too difficult, boss. I gets the old billygoat and I ties him upwind at the rear of the cookhouse, and then I set the stew pot downwind and then I steps in the dead centre line. If I smell the goat before the stew, then I know she needs more sauce.'

Feed the man meat

Beef, lamb, pork and others

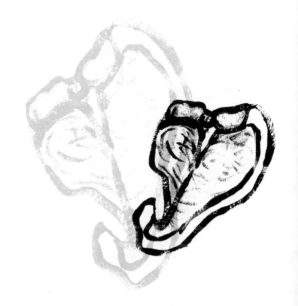

Red meat is one of our main food groups and has been since the dawn of humankind. For a small number of cultures, mainly on religious grounds, it is taboo; however, for the majority of the world's people it is a major element of their diet. Some nations eat more meat than others — this being dictated by availability, traditional custom, cost and, in some cases, religious doctrine. In all cases, animal produce is referred to as 'meat' rather than 'flesh'. Were this use of the generic name meat to include all flesh — be it bovine, pig or some best not spoken about — not centuries old we could be forgiven for thinking it was a giant marketing campaign. We simply would not be comfortable being encouraged to eat cow, sheep or pig, and it is more acceptable to order beef, lamb or pork.

Vegetarians oppose the eating of meat for various reasons including religious observance, humanitarian, dietary and sometimes a physical intolerance to meat products.

> My hearse will be followed not by mourning coaches but by herds of oxen, sheep, swine, flocks of poultry and a small travelling aquarium of live fish, all wearing white scarves in honour of the man who perished rather than eat his fellow creatures.
>
> (George Bernard Shaw, Irish playwright, 1856–1950)

Australians are big meat eaters, a legacy of our successful cattle and sheep industry, but also something that evolved as part and parcel of 'being true-blue Australian'. We used to be a 'meat and three vegies' nation, and there was a time when no respectful woman would allow her husband to venture off to a day's work without a mixed grill (lamb chop, piece of steak, lamb's fry and bacon) topped with a fried egg. We have become more sophisticated in our eating but we still consume more red meat than is good for us and, as if to reinforce the mixed grill custom, the livestock marketing campaigns continue to send out the 'Feed the man meat' message.

There are many traditions and customs surrounding the preparation and eating of meat. Like all food, fads come and go — and often return for a second helping! Some like their meat well cooked and others request theirs be served blue, implying rare. There was a time when butcher shop windows were full of staring pig's heads, huge beef tongues, ox tails, hanging meats, haunches of lamb, pork and beef, and trays of bloody offal and mince of several styles. Cartons of dripping stood in a row and strings of sausages hung across the window. Signs invited customers to 'Join the Xmas Ham Club' and pay off the ham and turkey on a weekly basis. Jokes were told about butchers backing into the sausage machine and 'getting a little behind in their orders'. The butchers were also known as flirts and many the pregnant lass was rumoured to 'have had it off with the butcher boy'. Nowadays the butcher displays neat trays of 'ready to cook' meat cuts — everything from pre-seasoned, rolled and tied roasts to fancy cuts like New York and Chateaubriand.

The media plays a part in spreading folklore about food and especially meat. Pork is never referred to as pig and is more likely to be promoted as 'the other white meat'. You don't eat cow, you eat beef and then there's the promise of 'iron' for healthy bodies. Our ancestors believed that mothers on a vegetarian diet were more likely to have a girl and meat-eaters would have a robust boy. Possibly this association with meat and manliness resulted in the custom of having the man of the house carve the roast at the table. Why on earth a man would have skills in this area is puzzling, especially nowadays when most seem completely dumbfounded by the very idea. Of course, there was a time — maybe seventy years ago — when men took pride in their carving skill but these same men also shaved with a cut-throat razor! These days most men wouldn't even know how to sharpen a knife.

Australian meat is clean meat and it is also usually tasty; however, we appear to be going down the American track and our animals are increasingly subjected to some rather strange additives, externally and internally. God forbid we end up with big, plump, juicy and near perfect looking steaks like those on the plates of our American chums, for they usually taste like wet newspaper.

There is an old saying that 'God sends meat and the devil sends cooks'. The blazing Australian barbecue, under the burning Australian sun, must make the devil feel right at home!

A little bit of sugar
And a little bit of tea
A little bit of flour you can hardly see,
And without any meat between you and me
It's a bugger of a life, by Jesus.

(Traditional swagman's toast)

Give them great meals of beef.
They will eat like wolves and fight like devils.

(Shakespeare, King Henry V)

Wine is the intellectual part of a meal while meat is the material.

(Alexandre Dumas, 1802–70)

BACON

Bacon is the flesh of the pig salted, dried and usually smoked. Green bacon is when the meat is salted, dried and not smoked.

The lightning crashed, the thunder roared,
Around the homestead station
The little pig curled up his tail
And ran to save his bacon.

(Children's rhyme)

You sexist pigs had better start shaking
For today's pigs are tomorrow's bacon.

(Feminist graffiti, Sydney, circa 1970)

To cure the worst sore throat, take a piece of bacon fat (raw) and tie
a length of cotton round it. Hold the cotton and swallow the fat. Pull up the
fat, and then swallow it again. Do this half a dozen times and the sore
throat will be cured.

(Old bush remedy)

BANGER

A popular name for any Australian beef, pork or lamb sausage;
however, sausages are also called 'snags' or 'mystery bags'.

BARBECUE

Australians make them out of anything handy, be it an old washing
copper, a barrel, wheelbarrow or whatever else is sitting in the back
shed.

We also love to abbreviate most names and the barbecue is
affectionately referred to as 'the barbie'. In print we often reduce it
even further to 'BBQ'.

Charcoal-burnt steaks, fried onions, flagon wine, lashings of
tomato sauce, slices of buttered white bread and lots of blowflies are
the mythical makings for the typical Australian BBQ.

Three sausages short of a barbecue.

(Popular Australian saying implying dim-wittedness)

BEEF

Here's to the bull that roams in the wood
That does the heifer a great deal of good.
If it wasn't for him, and his great red rod,
What would you do for beef, by God?

(Traditional drinking toast)

BONES

When we say 'I've got a bone to pick with you', we infer that the accused party has done something inappropriate and it must be discussed and resolved.

The closer the bone the sweeter the meat.

BULLY BEEF

This is the slang name given to tinned corned beef — a not-so-popular part of a soldier's diet. It was also known as 'canned dog'.

The term 'corned beef' comes from Anglo-Saxon times before refrigeration. In those days, the meat was dry-cured in coarse 'corns' of salt. Pellets of salt — some the size of kernels of corn — were rubbed into the beef to keep it from spoiling and to preserve it.

Corned beef and cabbage is synonymous with the Irish and was a popular Sunday lunch.

BUTCHER'S TALK

Australian butchers developed a special language whereby they talked backwards. Butcher's talk would become 'srehctub klat', or if something was no good it was 'on doog'. It was extremely popular thirty years ago when the butchery trade employed far larger numbers and the butchers worked in front of customers at the storefront. By using butcher's talk the men could openly discuss the customers — good or bad. (Maybe that should read 'doog ro dab'?)

CHOP

A piece of meat — usually lamb, veal or pork — on a single bone is usually referred to simply as 'a chop'. Food fashion often changes how we describe our food, including cuts of meat. The chop appears to have retained its dignity and has been so called for centuries.

We have also adopted the term into our slanguage: 'carry on like a pork chop', 'get the chop', 'not much chop'.

During the first half of the twentieth century, Australians ate lamb chops with eggs for breakfast and quite often lamb chops and three vegetables for dinner.

RECIPE FOR SAVOURY CHOPS

4 lamb shoulder chops

1 onion

1 tablespoon rice

1 tablespoon sugar

2 tablespoons flour

2 tablespoons vinegar

2 tablespoons tomato sauce

1 teaspoon salt

¼ teaspoon pepper

¼ teaspoon ground ginger

¼ teaspoon mustard

¼ teaspoon curry powder

¼ teaspoon mixed spice

Place lamb chops in a casserole dish and cover with chopped onion and rice. Mix remaining ingredients and place over chops. Add enough water to cover. Stand for an hour and then cook at 175°C (325°F) for about two hours.

(Mrs J Moore, Bexley, NSW)

FAT

Jack Sprat could eat no fat,
His wife could eat no lean,
And so between the two of them
They licked the platter clean.

GUARD OF HONOUR

The Guard of Honour is a particularly British style of serving a lamb cutlet roast. Like the Crown Roast, it is prepared from the ends of the lamb neck. Trim each cutlet bare to a depth of 2.5 centimetres (1 inch). Interlace the bones, fat side outwards, to form an arch as a 'guard of honour'.

HAM

The golden rule for ham preparation and eating is:

Forty days in salt
Forty days hanging
Forty days to be eaten.

HUMBLE PIE

No one likes 'to eat humble pie'. The expression, popular in our idiom, comes from the old British dish 'umble pie' — made from unwanted animal organs (offal) — that was served to poor, humble servants. Samuel Pepys was served this dish in the seventeenth century and reported (with a certain disdain), 'He did give us the meanest dinner of beef shoulders and umbles of venison.'

JERKY

Jerked meat was meat, usually kangaroo or beef, with the fat removed, cut into thin strips, sprinkled with salt and strung up on the nearest barbed-wire fence and left in the sun to dry. These strips provided nourishment for travellers and many the stranded and desperate outback traveller turned his dying horse or camel into jerked meat.

It is highly likely the custom of drying meat strips was brought here by Scottish settlers, but how the colonials adopted the American name is a mystery. The Scots developed a custom of compressing raw deer flesh between two batons of wood until it was hard, dry and extremely chewy. A similar dried meat is made in South Africa and known as biltong.

KIDNEYS

I have never been able to fathom the eating of kidneys. Sorry, but I studied biology at school and know what purpose they have in the body machine. I have tried and tried to eat these little devils but I gag every time. I used to make my mother cook steak and kidney pie without the kidneys!

> Most of all he liked grilled mutton kidneys which gave to his palate a fine tang of scented urine.
>
> (James Joyce, Irish writer, 1882–1941)

KIMBERLEY MUTTON

Old bushies refer to goat meat as Kimberley mutton. The Kimberley Range is in far north Western Australia near the Ord River where, at the time, there were a great many wild goats.

LAMB

Mary had a little lamb
It was a greedy glutton
She fed it on ice-cream all day
And now it's frozen mutton.

Mary had a little lamb,
The lamb was very tough.
And in the circumstances
A little was enough.

Mary had a little lamb,
Her brother had some chicken,
And so between the two of them
They had some finger lickin'.

Mary had a little lamb,
She kept in the closet
And every time she let it out
It left a small deposit.

LAMB'S FRY

Originally the testicles of castrated lambs were called lamb's fry (that's when they weren't swallowed raw). It was only in the twentieth century that we started to call the lamb's liver the same name. Early memoirs describe the men riding home with whollops of testicles dangling from their saddles. Must have been a pretty sight!

LARD

Up until the 1960s most butchers did a roaring trade in selling beef fat and pork fat lard. It was used in baking and was especially good for the Sunday roast. Today's health-conscious crowds would run a mile at the thought of it. It is useful to remember that fat-free foods, like people, tend to lack personality.

LIVER

The African Maasai chiefs eat nothing but milk, blood, honey and roasted liver, believing that the organ is the carrier of all courage.

In Australia, liver became a staple for the typical hotel counter lunch, where it was smothered in fried onions and served with a mountain of mashed potato.

MUTTON

Mutton is the meat from sheep over a year old. A favourite Australian dish is boiled mutton and it's quite simple to prepare. Boil one leg of mutton with salt and pepper, occasionally removing the scum. The secret is the dish should be cooked but not overcooked!

It is surprising to many people that our pioneering ancestors actually preferred mutton to lamb, which they believed tasted too insipid. So much mutton was consumed, in fact, that it was often referred to as a 'muttonous diet'.

A BUSHMAN'S FAREWELL TO QUEENSLAND

To stay in thee, O land of mutton
I would not give a single button,
But bid thee now a long farewell
Thou scorching sunburnt land of hell.

Mutton-bird — Tasmanian

Mutton chops — sideburns

Mutton dressed up as lamb — not all as it seems.

F. Lancelott Esq., colonial poet and mineralogical surveyor, composed the following poem, which says it all:

ON MONDAY WE'VE MUTTON

You may talk of your dishes of Paris renown,
Or for plenty through London may range,
If variety's pleasing, oh, leave either town,
And come to the bush for a change.

On Monday we've mutton, with damper and tea;
On Tuesday, tea, damper and mutton,
Such dishes I'm certain all men must agree
Are fit for peer, peasant, or glutton.

On Wednesday we've damper, with mutton and tea;
On Thursday, tea, mutton and damper,
On Friday we've mutton, tea, damper, while we
With our flocks over hill and dale scamper.

Our Saturday feast may seem rather strange,
'Tis of damper with tea and fine mutton;
Now surely I've shown you that plenty of change
In the bush, is the friendly board put on.

But no, rest assured that another fine treat
Is ready for all men on one day,
For every bushman is sure that he'll meet
With the whole of the dishes on Sunday.

PORK

It is sometimes said that the only part of the pig that is not eaten is its squeal.

Q: Why is the letter K like a pig's tail?
A: Because it is at the end of pork.

Salt, mustard, vinegar, pepper
Pig's head and trotter
Bread and butter for your supper

O–U–T spells out.

(Skipping rhyme)

RAM-STAG MUTTON
A bush expression used to describe any sort of tough meat.

SAUSAGE
In colonial Australia we ate French sausages (garlic and meat paste), Oxford (pork), mutton (lamb), and veal, and we still do. Most sausage-eating countries take pride in their particular style of sausage and, according to this rhyme, regional individuality was also praised.

The sausage made of beef
Is fit for London thief:
The sausage made of pork
Is eaten but at York.

Dictation, dictation, dictation
Three sausages went to the station
One got lost
One got squashed
and the other — I ate 'im.

Two little sausages frying in the pan
One went pop and the other went bang.

Don't tie your dog to a leash of sausages.

(French proverb)

SHEEP'S TROTTERS
Sheep's trotters were generally thrown away in Australia, although they make an excellent dish stewed and are delicate for jelly.

To prepare trotters, clean and boil them, then soak in salt and vinegar for a day before drying them ready for frying. Dip in egg and breadcrumbs. Fry until brown.

SLIPPERY BOB

There was a recipe for this tempting dish — a kind of kangaroo brains croquette — in Australia's first cookbook: *The English and Australian Cookery Book: Cookery for the Many, as well as for the 'Upper Ten Thousand'*, by Edward Abbott the Younger, published in 1864. Since the usual recipes call for four or six kangaroo brains, one imagines the early settlers had their work cut out for them hunting down the supplies.

STEAK

'Done to a T' is a well-known term used when tasting meat cooked according to the taster's preference—be it rare, medium or burnt. One assumes it originates from 'done to a turn'.

Cuts of meat have names and some are steeped in history. The popular sirloin is said to have originated with King Charles II, who, when dining upon a loin of beef, asked the name of the cut. When offered a blank look, he declared that the meat was so good it should be knighted, and henceforth called Sir Loin. It's a good story but, in fact, the word derives from the French *surlonge*, meaning 'above the joint'.

TRIPE

Tripe, the stomach lining of cows, is a peculiar yet popular dish. Excuse the dreadful pun but I have never had the stomach for it. My mother made it for my father, although she never ate it herself, preferring dates and cheddar cheese on Vita Wheat biscuits on those occasions when tripe was served. I still remember the smell of the tripe cooking with onions, parsley and milk — I used to leave the house.

So popular was tripe that there were restaurants solely devoted to serving precooked dishes made from it. It can be boiled, roasted or fried. Aficionados tend to be extremely loyal to tripe and the correct way to prepare it. Some will swear that to fry it is to spoil it, while others say that it should only be boiled.

The word tripe is an accepted part of our colloquial language: 'beat the tripe out of them', 'he talks tripe', 'a load of old tripe'.

Down by the seaside

Food from the seas, rivers and billabongs

We all accumulate folklore, usually unconsciously, from family and friends. Some of it is discarded and some stored away in the back of our noggins. We bring it in and out of our memory as needed, and in many ways use is as a comfort to reassure both ourselves and our companions. We also change folklore to suit our own needs and that is why you sometimes find little rhymes and beliefs that were popular in the Northern Hemisphere being changed to suit the southern. A good example would be the old belief that one should only eat oysters in a month where the letter 'r' occurs. This folklore first applied to the northern winter months of September, November, December, January, February, March and April. The hot months covered the mating season when oysters are skinnier and less attractive. In our temperate climate we quickly threw that bit of lore out the window!

Seafood eating also experiences fashion changes. While there is nothing quite as good as freshly cooked fish — steamed, baked, fried or grilled, served with lemon and pepper and salt — that hasn't stopped us experimenting with all manner of exotic sauces and spices. Some work and some definitely do not. Who could forgive the person who invented that brightly coloured sauce that accompanies the perennial prawn cocktail? The Victorians boiled all sorts of fish, mostly boiling the flavour out of them. They also fried their fish in, wait for it, lard or dripping — it must have tasted unbelievably greasy. Then there was the fad for preparing whiting and similar fish with their little tails tucked into their mouths. This fad was abandoned when everyone realised how difficult it was to cook the little devils.

We are blessed with such a variety of seafood in Australia and a trip to any coastal fish market will amaze. We have also become more adventurous with our eating, thanks to the various migrant streams that have entered Australia and brought their seafood traditions with them. There was a time when squid, octopus and many varieties of fish were ignored, but no longer. And above all foods, it is fish that must be eaten fresh. As some anonymous wit observed, 'Fish should smell like the ocean. If they smell like fish, it's too late.'

Fish, to taste right, must swim three times — in water, in butter, and in wine.

(Polish proverb)

A loaf of bread, the Walrus said,
Is what we chiefly need:
Pepper and vinegar besides
Are very good indeed —
Now if you're ready, Oysters, dear,
We can begin to feed!'

(Lewis Carroll, 1832–98, *Alice Through the Looking-Glass*)

BALMAIN BUG
The Sydney Balmain bug is a small shovel-nosed lobster or flapjack. It most probably got its name from local fishermen, many of whom lived in the working class Balmain area near the Sydney fish markets at Blackwattle Bay.

CARP
Vietnamese Australians eat carp at their New Year celebrations, believing that this fish, according to mythology, carried the god of good luck on its back and is therefore lucky.

EELS

There is a plentiful supply of eels in Australian rivers and creeks and there are several eel recipes, including eel pie, jellied eel, and smoked eel. Folklore also has stories or yarns about gigantic eels that snapped at fishermen and sometimes stole dogs. Nasty creatures!

FISH

Fish is regarded as a 'brain food' in folklore. This relates to the discovery by Jean Dumas (1822–95) who was the first to state that fish contained phosphorus. At the same time it was discovered that our brain contained phosphorus, so putting two and two together…

The British never really started to eat fish until the Romans departed their shores. It became a fashion in the fourteenth century by which time the church had decreed something like 200 meatless days a year — fish dishes took on a new meaning!

Fish bones should always be buried rather than thrown away if you want Lady Luck to stay with you.

Always eat fish from the head down to the tail if you want luck on your side.

If you dream of fish someone close to you is pregnant.

A raw egg, quickly swallowed, will usually dislodge a fishbone caught in the throat.

They tell me there's fish in the ocean
They tell me there's fish in the sea
But I buy my fish in the fish shop
So it all sounds fishy to me.

Q: One day two fathers and two sons went fishing. Each fisherman caught a fish, yet only three fish were caught. How is this possible?
A: A boy, his father, and his grandfather went fishing.

To remove the fishy smell from a pan, empty used tea leaves into it, fill with water and leave for fifteen minutes. The smell will disappear.

At high tide the fish eat ants; at low tide the ants eat fish.

(Thai proverb)

FISH AND CHIPS

These names were given to two rail trains that operated in New South Wales. 'The Fish' was originally the Blue Mountains Express. It was named after the 1860s engine driver Jock Heron who, through a corruption of his name to 'Herring', became known as 'The Big Fish'. 'The Chips' came later because you can't have fish without chips. Similarly, 'Tea' and 'Sugar' run between Kalgoorlie and Port Augusta.

FISH FRIDAY

Roman Catholics adopted the Christian custom of not eating meat on Fridays, so fish and chips became the standard meal and Friday was usually referred to as 'fish Friday'. The Church officially abandoned this custom in the 1970s.

FISH SPEAK

We use a variety of seafood references in our everyday language:

'That sounds fishy' implies something out of the ordinary or wrong.

A 'red herring' is something introduced to a conversation as a diversion.

If someone is out of sorts and irritated we say they are 'crabby'.

If we are looking for something we 'fish' for it.

If we miss out on something we are likely to say 'there's plenty more fish in the sea'.

If we are lost and confused we are 'floundering'.

If something is useless we say it is 'as useful as a fish on a bicycle'.

There's also 'not the only fish in the sea', 'bigger fish to fry', 'tight as a fish's arsehole', 'what's that got to do with the price of fish?' and 'fish out of water'.

LOBSTER

A truly destitute man is not one without riches, but the poor wretch who has never partaken of lobster.

(Anonymous)

A woman should never be seen eating or drinking, unless it be lobster, salad and champagne. The only true feminine and becoming viands.

(Lord Byron 1788–1824)

My temples throb, my pulses boil,
 I'm sick of song, and ode, and ballad —
So, Thyrsis, take the midnight oil,
And pour it on a lobster salad.

(Thomas Hood 1799–1845)

MERMAID BRAWN

This next recipe, tongue-in-cheek, serves up one of the largest marine species of the north of Australia. The dugong is also known as the sea cow because it grazes on sea grasses. The indigenous people of Australia have been eating them for centuries and still have licence to hunt in certain restricted areas.

RECIPE FOR MERMAID BRAWN

Ingredients: one dugong. As they weigh up to 90 kilograms (200 pounds), this is a recipe for a large dinner party. Boil a large chunk of dugong along with some buffalo shin or ox-tongue and add some salt, pepper, cloves and any other suitable spice. Boil and remove fat. When it is well cooked, chop it all up and press into a suitable dish for brawn, draining off the excess liquid to allow for settling. Serve sliced with salad and damper.

MURRAY COD

The Murray cod is legendary in Australia, with many yarns telling of its massive size and strength. The fish, if lucky, grows extremely large for a river fish. Some folk yarns tell of pioneer fishermen catching one that was so strong it changed the course of the river or pulled a riverboat onto the shore.

To prepare a Murray cod, forget about cleaning the fish. Dig a hole in the riverbank about 30 centimetres (1 foot) deep and build a fire in the hole. When the coals start to glow cover them with wet mud, adding eucalyptus leaves and the fish itself also coated in heavy mud. Cover with more leaves and more mud. The fish will slowly cook in the steam for about three-quarters of an hour. Another version of this dish was called 'bushranger fish', and involved coating the fish with mud and then wrapping it in wet newspaper.

MURRUMBIDGEE OYSTERS

A legendary concoction of a raw egg with a little brown vinegar, salt and pepper.

OYSTERS

I don't wish to spoil your fun but when you devour an oyster you are eating the intestine, gills, liver and rather remarkable stomach of a hermaphrodite.

Australian coastal dwellers have had a long history of oyster eating. Indigenous Australians collected them and ate them cooked on their open fires, our First Fleeters delighted in them and, right through the Colonial era, we ate them fresh, stewed, pickled and however else we could manage. Every major coastal city boasted oyster bars and Sydney's fashionable King Street had six around the time of Federation.

Irish Australians used to eat oyster stew on Christmas Day, continuing a food tradition from their original homeland. As oyster beds reduced in the early twentieth century the custom died out.

Oysters are considered an aphrodisiac. History tells us it was Casanova's prescription for stimulation and he started his evening meal with a round dozen before starting his lovemaking antics.

Eat fish and live longer,

Eat oysters and love longer.

He was a bold man who first ate an oyster.

(Jonathan Swift)

According to a companion, Thackeray, when presented with a half-dozen 6 to 8 inch oysters common at the time: 'He first selected the smallest one ... and then bowed his head as though he were saying grace. Opening his mouth very wide, he struggled for a moment, after which all was over. I shall never forget the comic look of despair he cast upon the other five over-occupied shells. I asked him how he felt. 'Profoundly grateful,' he said, 'as if I had swallowed a small baby.'

(William Makepeace Thackeray, 1811–63)

Any noise annoys an oyster,
But a noisy noise annoys an oyster more.

Q: Which is the laziest food in the world?
A: Oysters, because they spend all their time in their beds.

Before I was born my mother was in great agony of spirit and in a tragic situation. She could take no food except iced oysters and champagne. If people ask me when I began to dance, I reply, 'In my mother's womb, probably as a result of the oysters and champagne — the food of Aphrodite.'

(Isadora Duncan, American dancer, 1878–1927)

SMOKED OYSTERS

General D. MacArthur introduced smoked oysters when he headed the Japanese Provisional Government following World War II. He liked them so much that he arranged for them to be exported to America. Mind you, the Yanks have done some bloody awful things to the humble oyster, including covering it with ketchup, and the idea of covering them with grated cheese and grilling them does nothing for the tastebuds either. Not that we haven't tried similarly strange recipes — oysters marinaded in Japanese green tea or served with wasabi. What about New Orleans Rockefeller where oysters are served with chopped spinach, parsley, spring onion and crispy bacon and then rolled in breadcrumbs and deep-fried? Other options include sprinkled with paprika, cooked with cream and curry powder, French-style with a dribbling of Pernod, poached in champagne, and, those final insults, steak and kidney pie with oysters or the legendary and oddly strange carpetbag steak.

PRAWNS

Australians love their prawns. We eat them fried in batter, in stir-fries, with seafood sauce in what we call a 'prawn cocktail' and — to some, best of all — freshly peeled with buttered bread and pepper.

We refer to anyone trying to pull the wool over our eyes as 'coming the raw prawn'.

The stockman had never been to Sydney and was staying at the posh Australia Hotel. Not being able to read or write he asked the waiter to bring him something special for his lunch. The waiter, an obliging chap, returned with a large plate of fresh Sydney Harbour prawns on a bed of shredded lettuce leaves.

After a while the bushie signalled the waiter. 'Mate, how much do I owe you for the tucker?'

'That will be one pound ten shillings, sir.'

As the waiter handed the stockman his bill, he noticed that the prawns had all been pushed to the side of the plate, untouched. 'But sir, you didn't eat your meal, was there something wrong?'

'Well,' the stockman muttered, 'the grass was just okay, but be blowed if I'm going to eat the bloody grasshoppers!'

RED SNAPPER

Japanese Australians eat red snapper, a good luck symbol, on their New Year's Eve. (Red is a good luck omen in most Asian cultures.)

SHARK

If you buy fish and chips in Australia it is likely that the fish is actually shark. We call it flake and since Australians eat it so often it seems only fair that a shark gets to eat an Australian every so often.

SHELLFISH

Never eat shellfish with ice-cream — it was believed to be a deadly combination!

SLUMGULLION

Slumgullion was a word invented in the nineteenth century to describe a dish made from the innards of a gutted fish — a nasty dish one would have thought.

ST PETER'S FISH

Haddock is sometimes called this because of the two black spots near the gills. The two spots are said to replicate the thumb — and fingerprint of St Peter when he took the tribute money out of the fish's mouth.

SUSHI

Sushi began as a method of preserving fish. Traditionally fresh, raw fish was pressed between layers of salt and rice, with a stone placed on top for weight. The stone was eventually replaced with a cover. After storing for a few weeks, the fish was ready to eat. In the eighteenth century, a chef named Yohei eliminated the fermentation process and served something which resembled the sushi eaten today.

Sushi does not mean 'raw fish', but refers to the vinegar rice used in making sushi. It should not be confused with sashimi, which is raw fish.

YABBIES

The yabby is a small freshwater crayfish from New South Wales, the Australian Capital Territory, South Australia and Victoria. In Queensland they are called 'lobbies', and in Western Australia 'gilgies'. Whatever their name, they are traditionally caught by drag-fishing, using rotten meat in a sock or stocking.

Bush turkey, chooks and
underground mutton

Poultry and rabbit

There was a time when a large percentage of the Australian population, country and city, maintained a chicken coop. Although chickens have been with us since the First Fleet, poultry only became popular in the late 1950s. Before that, chicken was reserved for special occasions such as Christmas, birthdays and weddings. In colonial Australia we attempted to eat just about anything that could fly and some that couldn't even manage that. We ate scrub turkey, bush pigeon, parrot, quail and emu, and even had a go at lyre- and bowerbirds. In just about every case we prepared the birds like those of Old England. The classic bush yarn tells of the best recipe for cooking parrot: pluck four plump parrots and place them in a billy along with two medium-sized rocks. Salt to taste. When the rocks are soft the parrots are ready to eat.

Eggs have long been associated with magic. The Romans attached great importance to the egg as a symbol of all things whole and pure. It was thought to be bad luck and bad manners to break an eggshell after the egg had been eaten. On the other hand some believed that the shell must be crushed after the egg had been eaten — this prevented magicians using the eggshell to draw out mischievous spirits.

Australians do not eat a lot of rabbits these days although they were part of the bushman's staple diet in the late nineteenth century — often a lucky substitute for poultry — and up to the end of the 1950s. Our current distaste most probably has something to do with the eradication program and a scare that the poison bait, myxomatosis, had tainted the rabbit meat.

One of the most contentious topics debated in the poultry industry has been the community response to genetically engineered food for poultry. In 2005, a Greenpeace campaigner, John Hepburn, was quoted as saying that the import of 300,000 tonnes of soy by poultry companies was 'the biggest single source of GE contamination of the Australian food chain'. In February of the same year the country's three major poultry producers, representing over 80 per cent of chicken sold in Australia, announced their decision to stop using GE feed. Let us hope that other producers in the food market also stop the contamination of our food.

And how do the people fight back? Well, one way is through the circulation of urban myths. Whether consciously or unconsciously we spread food urban myths as a reaction to fear of the unknown. If we 'think' food might be contaminated, and this is certainly the case with take-away convenience foods, we will readily bounce on emails or relate stories that tell of ordinary people finding horrific things in their food. Photoshop, the relatively new technology of modifying photographs, has also emerged as a vehicle similar to urban myths. Photographs, some modified to suit a particular animal rights philosophy, are regularly circulated via the Internet. These include two-headed chickens, chickens without beaks, etc. It is obviously very difficult for the average person to establish fact from fiction and although the old saying of 'seeing is believing' does not necessarily stand up today, the average person tends to accept such images as fact.

> Poultry is for cookery what canvas is for painting, and the cap of Fortunatus
> for the charlatans. It is served to us boiled, roast, hot or cold, whole or in
> portions, with or without sauce, and always with equal success.
>
> (Jean-Anthelme Brillat-Savarin 1755–1826)

CHICKEN

Fifty years ago chickens were for special occasions. Most chickens were purchased from street vendors who also supplied livers, heart and gizzards, which were used to make giblet soup. They were relatively expensive and even if you had a coop in the garden, and many Australian families did, the drama associated with slaughtering a chook for the pot was simply too horrific for many of us. The fact that the headless chicken was likely to dance around the yard for two minutes didn't help matters. One thing is for sure, chickens that scratched the earth for a living tasted fantastic compared to the frozen zombies we are now offered at the local supermarket.

Oddly enough, chicken meat was always readily available in Chinese restaurants, and its general scarcity elsewhere prior to the 1950s might have contributed to the myth of Chinese serving cat meat.

> If you cook a greasy chicken put a red apple (or an eggshell) in pot and it will absorb the grease.

> Stick two nails in a tough chicken and they will make the bird tender during the cooking process.

CHICKEN SOUP

Chicken soup has long been attributed with magical properties for cleansing the blood and reducing chest phlegm. There's little scientific proof of this — although the clean broth is certainly easy to digest and might possibly reduce nasal congestion because of its heat— but chicken soup sure tastes good when you have a cold. It is often known as 'Jewish penicillin'.

CHICKEN ON A RAFT

This is how children popularly describe a poached or fried egg on a slice of toast.

CHOOK

Australians affectionately refer to chicken as 'chook'. Unfortunately this term is also applied to some females: 'she's an old chook' (as in 'old boiler').

Captain Cook chased a chook

All around Australia

He lost his pants in the middle of France

And found them in Tasmania

EGGS

Australians eat chicken, quail and duck eggs. Emu eggs were also consumed in the colonial era as were some native bird eggs.

Finding two yolks in an egg is considered lucky. Such an egg is known as a double-yolker.

Greeks and Russian Orthodox Christians give painted or dyed eggs as gifts at Easter. Red eggs are the most lucky as the colour is said to resemble the blood of Christ. The Chinese also believe the red egg is a symbol of good fortune.

At the Jewish Seder Passover feast the egg plays a significant role in the traditional dinner.

Brown eggs are considered healthier, however there is no evidence to support this belief.

Egg and spoon races and egg throwing competitions are part of traditional Australian sport's day activities.

Eggshells attract other eggshells. I am not sure why this is so but it's a fact. If you drop a piece of shell in a pan you can chase it all around with a spoon but touch it with another eggshell and whammo! It sticks to it with glee.

When Australians have eaten or drunk too much they will often say they are 'full as a googy egg'. There is no doubt the egg is a remarkable creation and a perfect container, allowing no waste of space, but the origins of the word 'goog' have been lost in time.

What's that got to do with the price of eggs?

Don't put all your eggs in one basket.

She had breasts like two fried eggs (implying they were flat).

He was a bad egg.

She had egg on her face (implying embarrassment).

He taught her to suck eggs (taught her the obvious).

It was like treading on eggshells (a fragile conversation with a temperamental person).

Crushed shells in a crystal decanter or glasses with a little water will restore sparkle.

To test an egg's freshness put your tongue on the larger end. If it's warm it is fresh, if it's cold it is stale. Also, when about to boil, if an egg floats to the top of a saucepan of water it is going off.

Break an egg
Break your leg,
Break three
Woe to thee;
Break two,
Your love's true.
   (Old rhyme recited when collecting eggs on a farm or chookhouse run)

Throwing the shell of an egg into the fire prevents the hen from laying again.

Bringing chicken eggs into the house after sunset is unlucky.

Finding a chicken egg without a yolk is extremely unlucky.

Eggshells thrown into a coffee pot will settle the grounds.

The outback hotel offered a very limited menu — stewed galah or stewed mountain goat. The young bush worker knew enough about the tough old galah not to go that way, so he pointed to the goat.

   'Nar, can't have the goat, mate,' rasped the waitress, 'that's reserved for the weekly boarders.'

Not wanting to chew on the nigh impossible bird, he asked the waitress for 'some boiled eggs, please, Miss'. When the waitress returned, she plonked down a dozen newly boiled eggs.

'Struth! I can't eat that many eggs, I only wanted a couple!' protested the young man.

'Look, love, if yer can't find a couple of good ones in that lot let me know and I'll boil yer up another dozen.'

A hen laying two eggs on the same day is unlucky.

Always burn eggshells to prevent bad luck.

Cracking an egg at the small end is unlucky.

Dreaming of broken eggs will lead to a lawsuit.

Dream of a lap full of eggs and you'll be rich.

Rubbing a birthmark with an egg then burying it under the doorstep causes the blemish to vanish.

Playing with eggshells causes warts to grow.

Feeding children ground eggshells cures bed-wetting.

Hinka, pinka, I smell a stinka.
By egg or by bacon
I think you're mistaken.

EGGNOG

There is a tradition of making eggnog, a warm egg and brandy (or rum) drink, at Christmas time. Neighbours are often invited to share this drink to toast Christmas. While it's not really the thing for a hot Australian December morning, many believe the combination of milk, egg yolks, vanilla and sugar provides the ideal stomach lining for the diverse indulgences to follow.

EGGS BENEDICT

It is not uncommon for popular dishes to have several origins. *The American Century Cookbook* by Jean Anderson provides two contenders for this internationally renowned breakfast dish. The original Eggs Benedict dates back to 1894 when, it's said, a Wall Streeter named Lemuel Benedict, suffering from a hangover, made his way along the buffet table at the newly opened Waldorf-Astoria, slapping bacon and poached eggs on dry toast, then topping the lot with hollandaise sauce. Later, the Waldorf's formidable maître d'hôtel, Oscar Tschirky, fine-tuned the recipe, substituting English muffins for toast and Canadian bacon for ham. A second legend attributes Eggs Benedict to Delmonico's and Mrs LeGrand Benedict, a regular there. Finding nothing to her liking one day, Mrs Benedict huddled with the maître d'hôtel, who concocted the combo now known as Eggs Benedict.

EMU

The large flightless bird of the outback can be as tall as 1.8 metres (6 foot) and it has been a staple part of Aboriginal diet for centuries.

> The American tourist had been driving the coach driver crazy with his comments that everything was bigger back in Texas. When they passed a flock of emus the American gasped, 'What on earth are they?' The driver looked over and said, 'Oh, those are baby chickens, they get really big when they're older.'

NED KELLY'S EYE

A popular breakfast dish consisting of a slice of bread with a hole in the centre for an egg to fry in. It is cooked and gently turned over. A colonial *croque madame*!

PARSON'S NOSE

The knobby, fleshy, fatty stump that sticks out at the rump of a chicken (or turkey). On a fried chicken it's that super crunchy, extra greasy part that almost everybody loves although they may not know what it is or that it has a nickname.

In Australia it is known as the parson's nose or the pope's nose; in the Middle East, as the sultan's nose. For the curious, the proper name for this part is the pygostyle.

Some say that the monikers originated as a derogatory term meant to demean Catholics in England during the late seventeenth century.

RABBIT

Often referred to as 'underground mutton', 'bush chicken' or 'bush turkey', rabbits were introduced to Australia as early as the First Fleet. Environmentalist and sometimes food writer, Eric Rolls, has commented that, 'It was after Thomas Austin brought twenty-four wild rabbits from England in 1859 and released them on his property in southern Victoria that the rabbit became established on the mainland.

The establishment of the rabbit was initially regarded as a great success for the sporting gentleman. In 1866, only seven years after its introduction, 14,253 rabbits were shot for sport alone on Austin's property.'

As a kid growing up in Ramsgate, a Sydney suburb, I remember the rabbit-o coming around every week. He had a horse and small cart where the bunnies were kept cool with dry ice. He would call out, 'Rabbit-o! Rabbit-o! — two for three and sixpence!' We ate stewed rabbit every fortnight.

There is a wonderful story within the 'Crooked Mick of the Speewah' legend where Crooked Mick finds himself surrounded by millions of crazed rabbits and is saved by a snap freeze, as one can only find in the mysterious outback. Crooked Mick ended up a millionaire after flogging the frozen rabbits to some Yank bloke called Birdseye. Apparently the underground rabbit was extremely popular with the American market.

RECIPE FOR RABBIT PIE

Cut all the meat from the rabbit and mince it, then add one chopped onion, one cup of green peas, one tablespoon of flour, a pinch of salt and pepper, plus a little water or stock. Mix all together and place in a pie dish. Cover with pastry and bake for one and a half hours at 200°C (400°F). Reduce heat after about half an hour to 150°C (300°F). Serve with roast pumpkin.

(Fahey family recipe)

RECIPE FOR MOCK CHICKEN CASSEROLE

1 plump rabbit
flour
1 medium onion, chopped
chopped parsley
a pinch of thyme
salt and pepper
2 tablespoons chicken stock powder
milk
bacon rashers

Joint the rabbit and dip pieces in flour then place in a camp baking dish or casserole, adding chopped onion and parsley and thyme. Add salt and pepper to taste. Mix the stock powder in a cup of hot water and pour over the rabbit, then pour in enough milk to just cover the meat. Put the lid on and cook for about two hours in an oven of 150 to 160°C (300 to 315°F) or until tender (which depends on the age of the rabbit). Before serving, remove lid and cover contents of dish with rashers of bacon and allow to cook for a further 15 minutes.

(Mrs E T Roberts, Canterbury, NSW)

Tuppence a half, fourpence a whole,
Everyone eats rabbit on the Dole.
(1930s Depression ditty)

Rabbits hot, rabbits cold;
Rabbits young, rabbits old;
Rabbits fat, rabbits lean;
Rabbits dirty, rabbits clean;
Rabbits short, rabbits tall;
Rabbits big, rabbits small;
Rabbits black, rabbits white;
Rabbits for breakfast, rabbits at night;

Rabbits stewed, rabbits roast;

Rabbits on gravy, rabbits on toast;

Rabbits by the dozen, rabbits by the score;

Rabbits by the hundreds, rabbits by the door;

Rabbits tender, rabbits tough —

Lord, spare me from rabbits,

I've bloody well had enough!

TURKEY

The modern desire to serve turkey at Christmas appears to owe much to Charles Dickens and his evocative *A Christmas Carol*, where Ebenezer Scrooge attempts to right his wrongful ways by serving the largest turkey available.

The 'turkey trot' was a popular dance in Australia in the early 1900s.

He laid her on the table

So white, clean and bare

His forehead wet with beads of sweat

He rubbed her here and there

He touched her neck and then he felt her breast

And then drooling felt her thigh

The slit was wet and all was set

He gave a joyous cry

The hole was wide — he looked inside

All was dark and murky

He rubbed his hands and stretched his arms

And then he stuffed the turkey.

(From James McFarland, via mobile SMS text message, Christmas 2004)

Turkey boiled

Is turkey spoiled.

And turkey roast

Is turkey lost;

But turkey braised,

The Lord be praised!

WHITE MEAT

We talk about chicken and turkey having 'white' and 'dark' meat, and there is a reason for this difference in colour. Oxygen-storing myoglobin, proteins located in the muscle cells, retain oxygen brought by the blood until the cells need it. The myoglobin act as a holding station. The muscles that require a lot of oxygen have a greater storage capacity than those that only need a little, so they are consequently darker red in colour. Good old chickens and turkeys do a lot of strutting, clucking and scratching but they hardly ever fly — so their breast meat is white and their legs dark. Wild duck, bush turkey and game birds, by contrast, spend more time flying, so their breast meat is dark.

WISHBONE

The chicken or turkey wishbone is so called because of the custom of two people 'snapping' the bone, with the person retaining the bigger piece getting to make a wish. It is also called 'the lucky bone'.

Salad days

Salad and raw vegetables

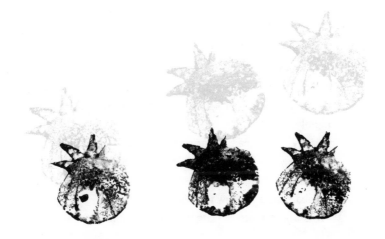

I can now trace social and gastronomic change from a family perspective: I was there to see the transformation of the salad. When I was a kid in the 1950s, salad was reserved for a hot summer's night meal or a Saturday lunch. It was never viewed as a 'real' meal — how could anything served cold be so? I can see it now: three slices of sliced beetroot, some grated Kraft Coon cheddar cheese, shredded iceberg lettuce leaves, sliced tomato (sometimes soaked in brown vinegar and sprinkled with sugar), grated carrot, three slices of cucumber, sliced egg and either cold corned beef, Devon or mortadella sausage, ham or lamb slices. We usually accompanied salads with mayonnaise and chutney but never dressing. Sometime during the 1960s the European migrants started to set an example of what a salad should be, and showed us that all salads should have a good oil and vinegar dressing. We were suspicious as usual as we whispered, 'Just look at what they eat!' and 'How can they stand all that oil?' However, we were soon dousing our salads along with the best of them. Thankfully, we generally rejected the lure of fancy American salad dressings, especially the creamy varieties like Thousand Island. Fifty-something years later a salad is considered a respectable meal and tinned beetroot, watery corn kernels and grated soapy cheese are all too embarrassed to show their faces.

It is appropriate here that I add another word about genetic engineering and food. The jury is still out on the potential and nutritional worth of such experimentation. Australian cookery pioneer Margaret Fulton is emphatically against genetic tampering of food and, I must admit, that the history of food additives scares me and has also taught me that such 'progress' rarely results in flavoursome or nutritional results, especially with fruit and vegetables. What is the use of developing a new vegetable, even if bigger and brighter, if it tastes of nothing? I'm sure readers, especially older ones, are nodding their heads in agreement, yet we all still accept tasteless and tampered-with fruit and vegetables when we shop. We learn in our youth that carrots are good for eyesight, beets are good for the blood, etc; however, our present-day vegetables might look better and bigger but are they as nutritious?

We can thank our twentieth-century migrants for widening our vegetable appetite to the extent where our greengrocers — I shall avoid that ridiculous word fruitologists — offer an abundance of salad vegetables that would do any table proud. In 2004, I interviewed Tony Terakes, a pioneer of the Sydney Markets. He told me how in the 1940s the range was unbelievably limited and anything exotic was usually brought in by market gardeners, especially the Chinese or Indian. It was only in the early 1970s that the range exploded and, in the 1980s, exploded again. Today the range is mind-boggling and every second vegetable has a 'baby' version.

BEETROOT

The beetroot in yesterday's Australia was usually boiled and pickled in vinegar then served cold and sliced in salad. It had a nasty habit of staining everything it sat next to, especially the pineapple rings!

The old Romans and Greeks used to eat the leaves and throw the root away. They also used the leaves for medical reasons. Pliny spurned the beet's root as 'those scarlet nether parts'.

Russian homeopaths used the beet to treat scurvy, toothache and tuberculosis, and the peasants used it as an insecticide.

Lore has it that beetroot will help clean your liver and cool the blood. Sorry, there is absolutely no evidence to support this belief. Of course, it is good for you but it is not high in iron and will not help with anaemia. One suspects the belief has more to do with the rich red colour of the vegetable. For many years the beet was used in Europe to treat cancer, as it is high in anti-carcinogens.

There was a time when beetroot was used as a natural dye and even as rouge and lipstick!

You can beat an egg but you can't beat a root!

You can't beat a root and you can't beat beetroot.

BULLOCK'S HEART
A large, seasonal, heart-shaped tomato. Oddly enough these beautiful-tasting tomatoes are not very popular and are considered ugly. Go figure!

CAPSICUMS
Capsicums have symbolic associations:
Black — purification
Green — growth and prosperity
Red — energy and strength
Yellow — creativity

CELERY
Celery was considered holy by the Ancient Greeks, with its leaves being used as a laurel in the Nemean Games from AD 573.

For many centuries both gastronomic writers and popular opinion considered celery to be a powerful aphrodisiac.

Celery water was thought to cure rheumatism's aches and pains.

The thought of 2000 people crunching celery at the same time horrified me.
(Noted vegetarian George Bernard Shaw on why he
refused to address a vegetarian society annual gala dinner.)

CHIVES
He who bears chives on his breath is safe from being kissed to death.
(Martial's Epigrams, AD 9)

COLESLAW

Many Australians still incorrectly call this dish 'cold slaw' because it is generally served cold.

CUCUMBER

A cucumber should be well sliced, and dressed with pepper and vinegar, and then thrown out, as good for nothing.

(Samuel Johnson, 1709–84, quoted in James Boswell's
Tour to the Hebrides)

Cool as a cucumber? Scientific research shows that the inside of a cucumber is usually cooler than the surrounding air.

Once thought to have a poisonous skin, the cucumber's poison had to be drawn out by slicing off both ends and rubbing the stubs against the cut ends until froth developed.

Cucumbers are believed to have soothing properties when slices are placed over the eyes.

Old-timers use slices of cucumber, strewn on the floor for several nights, to ward off cockroaches.

Cucumber sandwiches were often served in Australian afternoon teas and were thought to be terribly posh. In truth they didn't seem to travel well and the combination of white bread, butter, limp cucumber and water rendered them more like Wettex sandwiches.

And one final note about cucumbers — in the 1980s there was a book published bearing the title *One Hundred Reasons Why Cucumbers are Better than Men*.

KALE

Kale is a plant with mystical powers. The Irish say fairies ride on the stalks in the dark of the moon. When the Irish farmer finds his kale plants in disarray it means his crops will be good and tall since the little people have been playing in it.

Good kale is half a meal.

(Old saying)

LETTUCE

Early ocean travellers suggested eating a head of lettuce to avoid seasickness.

Eating lettuce was also believed to counteract an over indulgence of wine.

MAYONNAISE

Old-timers used to rub mayonnaise on their exposed skin as a way of preventing sun- and windburn.

Pregnant women should never stir mayonnaise, as it will inevitably curdle.

NASTURTIUMS

Most people have never considered eating flowers. However, if you have ever eaten artichokes or broccoli you have eaten immature flowers and herbal teas often contain flowers such as rose or hibiscus. Nasturtiums can be added to salads providing a delicious bite and an intriguing splash of colour. They are also popular pickled.

To pickle nasturtiums pick the green seeds after the flowers have fallen off. Stems should be about 4 centimetres (1½ inches) long. Lay stems in salted water for 48 hours then in fresh water for 24 hours. Drain and bottle, adding boiling water. They are best eaten after about a month in storage.

ROCKET

Eating rocket was considered to bring luck; however, this might possibly have been a way of encouraging people to eat something that looks very similar to common garden weeds.

A popular use was to mix rocket with honey to remove freckles. No, it didn't work!

SALAD DRESSING

It takes four men to dress a salad: a wise man for the salt, a madman for the pepper, a miser for the vinegar, and a spendthrift for the oil.

(Anonymous)

SWISS CHARD

A beetroot top gone wild — apparently the leaf shriveled in the cold Swiss winter and the name spread. In Australia it is commonly confused with spinach.

TOMATOES

Tomatoes, originally called 'love apples', have been grown in Australia since the early 1800s and became popular in the 1840s, especially as a soup ingredient. It took the English a bit longer to catch on to their flavour and appeal. The round, red tomato, flourished in our hot climate, became a backyard staple, and ended up in jams, relishes, chutney and stews.

Christians snubbed the tomato for over 150 years, and it wasn't until the early 1700s that they started to look at it as a possible decorative and garnish item. Most people believed the evil blood-red fruit would cause your teeth to fall out or that one whiff would send you crazy.

During the Victorian era a great deal of emphasis was placed on the parlour room and it became the perfect place in which to display the novelty pincushions of the era. Pincushions were made in the shape of shoes, fans, umbrellas, dolls, teacups, animals, fruits and vegetables. They were hung on the walls or placed on occasional tables. The tomato was a popular design.

My sister Mary went to market with Jim.

Someone threw a tomato at him.

Tomatoes are soft and don't bruise the skin,

But this one killed Jim 'cause it was wrapped in a tin.

Place a tomato on the windowsill for luck as it guards against evil.

RECIPE FOR TOMATO RELISH

Tomato relish was so called after the French word *relaissier,* meaning to leave something behind.

6 pounds (2.7 kilograms) ripe tomatoes

a small handful of salt

2 pounds onions

2 pounds sugar

2 tablespoons plain flour

2 tablespoons curry powder

½ teaspoon cayenne pepper

3 tablespoons mustard

vinegar

Cut up the tomatoes, sprinkle with salt and let stand overnight. Slice onions into a separate dish, sprinkle them with salt and let them also stand overnight. When ready strain the tomatoes and onions through a colander before placing in a pan with the sugar and barely cover with vinegar. Boil for five minutes. Mix flour, curry powder, cayenne pepper and mustard with a little brown vinegar and then add to the tomatoes and onions and boil for one hour.

(Mrs Betty Griffith, Adelaide, SA)

TOMATO SAUCE

Tomato sauce, ever popular on pies, chips, and as an integral part of any barbecue, is also known in rhyming slang as 'dead horse'.

Thump and shake the tomato sauce bottle
None'll come and then a lot'll

A new bag of fruit

Fruits and berries

The history of fruit, like that of the vegetable, is a study that takes many evolutionary roads as ancient varieties disappear and new ones take pride of place. We are certainly blessed in Australia to have so many fruits on our doorstep. Some have been nurtured here for over 200 years and others have come with the various waves of migration and from our bountiful Asia–Pacific neighbourhood. There are also numerous indigenous fruits and berries, although it took us over 150 years to recognise them as edible. Fruit also attracts a wide field of folklore in the form of superstitions, customs, charms, songs and lore.

We are introduced to fruit through nursery rhymes where Little Jack Horner has a pie made of plums; in alphabet rhymes where 'A' inevitably stood for apple; and in games such as Here We Go Round the Mulberry Bush. Fruit, being easily digestible, is also some of our earliest food. Traditional folk tales of all countries use fruit as important motifs and this was reinforced in the twentieth century when children's producers like Walt Disney brought fruit motifs into contemporary times. The apple in *Snow White* is the perfect example, with its bright, shiny red surface and wicked poison under the skin.

In adulthood fruit remains an important and somewhat symbolic part of our life, especially apparent in our use of language, with expressions such as 'talks rather fruity', implying a 'plum in his mouth'. We also refer to women losing their virginity as 'losing (or popping) their cherry', while their complexion can be described as 'all peaches and cream' or 'a raspberry blush'. Fair hair may be that particular shade known as 'strawberry blonde'. Shifty people can be described as being 'bent like a banana' and mean-spirited people are 'as sour as a lemon'. These are just a few examples of how we use fruit to colour our language.

Today's fruit and vegetable shop, usually known as the 'fruit shop' or 'greengrocer', carries a staggering variety of produce ranging from specialty fruits to dried fruits. It is not unusual to find exotic Asian fruits like durian or jackfruit alongside specialty berries and juices. Fruit-based teas, sometimes mixed with herbs, have also become popular, especially those derived from citrus fruit.

APPLE

Apples, a member of the rose family, have been grown in Australia since colonial times and this noble fruit continues to be surrounded by folklore. No doubt much of this lore is connected to the Christian belief in the story of Adam and Eve—the apple being the supposed fruit of temptation. In reality, 'the forbidden fruit' was probably a pomegranate or apricot, since agricultural history tells us that apples were unknown in biblical times.

A man's Adam's apple takes its name from the morsel of the forbidden apple that stuck in Adam's throat.

Ancient Greek men tossed an apple at the one they wanted to marry, and if the girl wanted to accept the proposal she caught the apple.

There was a time when 'an apple for the teacher' was given as a sign of respect from a student.

It is through old sayings such as 'one rotten apple ruins the barrel' that we learn 'traditional wisdom', for indeed a bad apple will spread to its neighbours. However, like many old sayings, it also has another unrelated meaning. In this case it has come to mean one bad personality can encourage others in a group to lower their morals or behaviour to that same level.

Apples and apple by-products like pectin and cider vinegar have a place in alternative medicine, however green apples were often thought to cause stomach-ache. Such green apples were often called 'cooking apples'.

Having a snap-cold climate the island of Tasmania is ideally suited for apple growing. Tasmania's reputation as the 'Apple Isle' dates back to when the island shipped apples to Britain during the European off-season. By 1950 there were 1400 apple orchards in Tasmania, however with the introduction of cool storage the export demand for Tasmanian apples reduced considerably.

'Apple speak' has entered the Australian slanguage:

'Everything's apples' means everything is in good order. 'Apples and spice' is rhyming slang for nice. Useless people are sometimes described as not able 'to eat an apple through a picket fence'. She was the 'apple of his eye', but he 'upset the apple cart' or was 'a bad apple'.

> You cannot sell a blemished apple in the supermarket, but you can sell
> a tasteless one provided it is shiny, smooth, even, uniform and bright.
>
> (Elspeth Huxley)

Q: How many apples did our parents eat in the Garden of Eden?
A: Ten. Eve ate and Adam too.

'An apple a day keeps the doctor away.' This old saying is probably one of the best-known folk beliefs in the Western world. It is true that apples are high in potassium and also offer Vitamin C and fibre. The folk belief contributed to the circulation of the original poem:

An apple a day
Send the doctor away
An apple in the morning
Doctor's warning

Roast apple at night
Starve the doctor outright
Eat an apple going to bed
Knock the doctor in the head

Three each day
Seven days a week
Ruddy apples
Ruddy cheeks

There is some truth in the belief 'eating an apple will keep your teeth clean' as they contain malic acid. The following ditty is also ages old and another slice from the same folklore.

Eat an apple going to bed
Make the doctor beg his bread.

My boyfriend gave me an apple
My boyfriend gave me a pear,
My boyfriend gave me a kiss on the lips,
And threw me down the stairs
I gave him back the apple
I gave him back the pear
I gave him back the kiss on the lips
And I threw him down the stairs

(Children's clapping rhyme)

A was an apple pie. B bit it. C cut it. D dealt it and E eat it.

A cure for indigestion: three spoonfuls of apple cider vinegar a day.

Apple crumble makes you rumble
Apple tart makes you — hiccup

(Children's rhyme)

Rub an apple slice on a baby's tongue to produce a good singer.

You should never take all apples from the tree — leave one or two for the birds (for luck) and an offering for a better crop next year.
It is a sign of bad luck if an apple breaks while you are eating it.

To find out your lucky number, count the pips in an apple.

To discover if your dream lover feels the same about you, count the pips in an apple saying 'I love you, I love you not' until you run out of pips and end up with the answer.

To discover your true love's name think of the names of six people you love. Twist the apple stem as you recite the names. The name at which the stem breaks is the name of your true love.

To find the name of the person you will marry, peel an apple in one continuous peel until it breaks. Throw the peel on the ground and the letter it forms will be the first letter of your intended's Christian name.

APPLE MAN

Tanny Lanny was a cattle duffer in the southern highlands of New South Wales in the 1840s. He would hide in the limestone caves near the Burragorang Valley. Tanny was also known as the 'Apple Man' because of his habit of distributing apple seeds as he crisscrossed the country. This possibly explains the number of wild apple trees that appear in the most unusual places in rural New South Wales.

APRICOTS

The apricot tree grew wild in China several thousand years ago and was said to have been brought to Greece by Alexander the Great.

The Persians called the fruit 'egg of the sun' because of its round shape and golden colour.

The phrase 'nectar of the gods' comes from the belief that the juice was the favoured refreshment of the Roman and Greek gods.

AVOCADO

Avocados are also known as 'crocodile-skin pears' because of their variegated, rough skin and the pear shape that resembles the reptile's head. Avocados were also known as 'poor man's butter'.

Avocado comes from the Aztec *ahuacatl*, which translates as 'green testicles'.

The fruit is also known as a 'lawyer's pear' in France and Germany because in the Spanish language *abogado* means 'lawyer'.

'Avocado seafood cocktail' was a prime mover and shaker in the eating stakes of the 1950s and 60s and had a brief revival in the late 1990s. The combination of fresh seafood, especially prawns, and avocado is very palatable; however, the cream-based, orange-coloured mayonnaise dressing somewhat killed the more subtle flavours and colour scheme.

To ripen avocados put them in a paper bag along with a banana. The banana emits a gas that encourages the avocado to ripen.

> What is round like a pear but isn't a fruit
> Rich like cream but isn't from a dairy
> Savoury as a vegetable but isn't one
> Perfectly contained like an egg but needs no cooking?
> (Answer: avocado)

BAG OF FRUIT
Popular rhyming slang for a suit of clothing.

BANANA
The banana originally came from India where it was known as 'the fruit of the wise'.

According to an Indian legend, Paradise was situated on the island of Sri Lanka and it was here that Adam and Eve were banished from the Garden of Eden because they ate a banana! When they left the garden they covered their private parts with banana leaves which might explain why Europeans first referred to the banana as 'Adam's fig' and by the even earlier name, 'Paradise banana'.

> Bananas should always be broken and never cut.

> Banana wish: cut a slice from the stalk end of the banana while making
> a wish. If there is a Y-shaped mark (for 'yes') your wish will come true.
> Rub banana skins on chilblains to remove the growth.

BANANABENDERS

Queenslanders are called 'bananabenders'. This gained popularity after Henry Lawson wrote the immortal line: 'The Post Office is in New South Wales, and the Police Barracks in Bananaland.'

BLACKBERRY

The blackberry bush has a long history associated with folklore, including several ballads. It has even been said the human race sprang from the blackberry bush.

The blackberry was considered a valuable remedy for dysentery and diarrhoea and was generally taken as an infusion made from the root and leaves with water.

The berries were thought to cure the cold and stomach-ache, and infusions made from the leaves and fruit were used as a diuretic and also to treat hoarseness and general infections of the throat.

> What is white as snow, but snow it's not;
> Green as grass, but grass it's not;
> Red as fire, but fire it's not;
> Black as ink, but ink it's not?
> (Answer: blackberries)

CHERRY

'You only get one bite at the cherry.' This old saying makes sense when you realise how small a cherry is, but referring to losing one's virginity as 'losing one's cherry', gives it added meaning!

> To find out when you will marry count out cherry stones saying: 'this time, next year, sometime, never'. When you run out of stones that is the decision.

DATES

Dates, the fruit of the date palm, are thought to have originated in the Persian Gulf. The Chaldeans called the date 'the tree of life' and ate both the fruit and the buds, drank the sap, used its fibres for weaving cloth and burned its nuts for fuel.

Dates were thought to increase fertility. In Arabian tradition there is said to be over 800 uses for dates, including a popular alcoholic drink.

In Australia the rectum is often referred to as 'the date' ('all he does is sit on his date') and toilet paper as 'a date roll'.

DURIAN

This Asian fruit is now making its way smelt in Australia. Considered both an aphrodisiac and a delicacy, the durian has an extremely strong smell — a cross between strong onions and rotten fruit — and is so offensive it is best eaten by the entire household or not at all.

FIG

The fig is the oldest cultivated fruit in the world, grown for well over 6000 years, and the oldest symbol of a woman's sexuality (in texture, shape and seeds). It is also dated by the reference to fig leaves in the Garden of Eden.

Because Mohammed swore by it, like the date, it is sacred. It is considered 'intelligent' by Muslims, and simply a step removed from the animal kingdom. The fig is regarded as the fruit of Heaven.

FRUITOLOGIST

This term appeared some time in the 1960s and was taken up across Australia with enthusiasm. In reality it is a rather silly name for a retail outlet that predominantly sells vegetables. I suppose a 'vegologist' doesn't have the same ring about it! Anyway, although one can still see the occasional fruitologist sign, it has all but disappeared from sight with 'greengrocer' being reinstated on the awning.

FRUIT SPEAK

We delight in referring to people as 'fruit loops' (implying craziness) or being 'fruity' (straight-laced) or 'a fruit' (homosexual).

FRUIT SYMBOLISM

Fruit has long been associated with symbolism born of folklore. Here are some of the more popular associations:

Apple — temptation

Currants — you try to please all
Fig — longevity
Pear — affection
Pineapple — perfection
Raspberry — remorse
Strawberry — excellence

GOOSEBERRY
Baby boys are said to come from the gooseberry bush — especially the naughty boys!

GRANNY SMITH
Maria Ann Smith (1801–70) had an orchard in what is now the Sydney suburb of Eastwood. It is said that in the 1860s she bought Tasmanian cooking apples, probably French crab apples, and planted the seeds on her property. Her apples thrived and grew far bigger than the Tasmanian variety and much greener. She took them to market and they became extremely popular so she started selling cuttings to other growers. The 'Granny Smith' became highly regarded for apple pies and conserves. It became a successful export in 1930.

GRAPEFRUIT
A grapefruit is a lemon who had a chance and took advantage of it.

(Anonymous)

There is a lot more juice in a grapefruit than meets the eye.

(Anonymous)

JUNIPER BERRIES
Australia had numerous juniper groves, as the berry is a principal ingredient in gin. Paddington, an inner-city Sydney suburb, was built on juniper groves. One of its most significant buildings is the National Trust property Juniper Hall that was built by the original landholders, the Cooper family, who also made gin for the colony.

The potent juice of the berry was believed to prevent pestilence and even ward off snakebite.

There was a time when men carried juniper berries in their pockets to improve sexual prowess.

Tibetans burn juniper sprigs every day to purify temples.

Grow junipers near the front door to discourage thieves.

LEMON

Lemon juice has a long history as a natural bleach.

Oranges and Lemons
Say the bells of St Clements.

Rub lemon juice on cut apple quarters and they will remain white.

LIME

In the eighteenth century scurvy had devastated the ranks of the British navy far worse than any enemy. Good old Captain Cook and a Scottish doctor named Lind recognised that scurvy could be avoided by increasing vitamin C intake. Between 1795 and 1815, some 1.6 million gallons of lime juice drastically reduced the mortality rate of seamen. Along with their daily ration of rum, British sailors were required to consume a daily ration of lime juice mixed with vinegar; hence British seamen became known as 'limeys'. Limes imported cheaply from the English colony of Jamaica were substituted as the citrus of choice.

Lime leaves were boiled into a tea for a blood purifier.

Lime was also used to supposedly cure epilepsy and palpitations of the heart.

One old song, 'According To The Act', had a chorus:

Now when you've signed your articles, of course you've heard them read,
They'll tell you of the beef and pork, the butter and the bread,
The sugar and the marmalade, and with quantity exact
Of limejuice and vinegar, according to the Act.

The British ships running the Australian and New Zealand lines, mainly with new chum migrants, were known as 'Limejuice Tubs'.

MANGO

There is a folk saying that 'the only way to eat a mango is in the bath'. The mango, oddly enough, is a member of the cashew family and nobody eats cashews in the bath!

MULBERRY

This is a delicious berry similar in colour to the blackberry, but, as any child who has sat under a tree eating the fruit knows, mulberries stain the hands.

Australian children often keep silkworms that feed exclusively on the leaves of this tree.

All around the mulberry bush
The monkey chased the weasel.
The monkey thought 'twas all in fun.
Pop! goes the weasel.

A penny for a spool of thread,
A penny for a needle.
That's the way the money goes.
Pop! goes the weasel.

Up and down the City Road,
In and out of the Eagle,
That's the way the money goes.
Pop! goes the weasel.

Half a pound of tuppenny rice,
Half a pound of treacle,
Mix it up and make it nice,
Pop! goes the weasel.

OLIVES

Olives have been grown in Australia for well over 100 years. Originally from Asia Minor, olives have a noble place in folklore, signifying peace and tranquillity. When Noah looked out of his Ark after the great biblical deluge the first sign of hope was a dove carrying an olive branch. We still see the olive branch as an international symbol of peace, witness its adoption by the United Nations.

The term 'pouring oil over troubled waters' relates to olive oil's original use as a calming balm.

Olive oil is still used as holy oil in most Christian ceremonies such as baptism and last rites.

Some cultures believe the olive tree to be the 'tree of life'.

Drinking olive oil for nine consecutive mornings will cure drunkenness.

Take a tablespoon of olive oil before you drink alcohol to prevent a hangover.

ORANGES

What came first — the fruit or the colour? Whatever the case, oranges and other citrus fruits were grown in *orangeries* in seventeenth-century Europe.

A chaplain on one of the early convict transportation ships brought the first orange seeds to Australia.

Italian Australians eat slices of orange for good luck on Christmas Eve. In Italian folklore the colour orange (and gold) implies strength, courage, luck, power and justice. The orange fruit is also believed to be strong in luck by Indians and most Asian cultures.

Orange blossoms are considered good luck for weddings, ensuring a happy marriage and lots of children

Champagne and orange juice is a great drink. The orange improves the champagne. The champagne definitely improves the orange.

(Philip, Duke of Edinburgh)

PARSON'S LEMON

Back in the mid-nineteenth century the Reverend Selwyn was a well-known character in Victoria. A travelling bush parson, the reverend gentleman took it into his head to distribute citrus seeds, particularly lemons, as he rode through the bush. Wild lemons, especially those found off the beaten track, are now known as 'parson's lemons'.

PASSIONFRUIT

Parts of the passionfruit are said to represent the crucifixion. Its leaf shows the Roman soldiers, the tendrils the sword and the scourge, the ovary columns the pillar of the cross, the anthers the hammer, and the styles the nails. The blue and white flowers indicate the blue of heaven and the white of purity.

The name 'passion fruit' came from the diaries of early Spanish missionaries who recorded accounts of seeing the flowers during church holiday seasons, especially during the Lent and Easter holidays, reminding them of the Passion of Christ.

PAWPAW

Pawpaw, or papaya, is highly regarded for its healing properties. The fruit will aid digestion and some folk believe eating the pips will also relieve indigestion.

The paste made from the fruit is also widely used to treat open wounds and as a rub for lumbago.

Tenderise meat by adding pawpaw.

PEACH

The peach tree originated in China, where it had grown since the tenth century BC. It was introduced to Japan and then Persia, before being introduced to the Greeks by Alexander the Great.

Chinese legends attribute the peach with the power to confer immortality. One legend tells of the Peach Tree of the Gods which bloomed only once every 3000 years, yielding the fruits of eternal life and granting health, virility and immortality to those who partook of the fruit. It is considered the most sacred plant of the Chinese Taoist religion. Even today, the peach is customarily served at birthday celebrations in China as a symbol and hope of longevity.

Japanese folklore tells of a beloved child born of a large peach and who grew up surrounded by the love and devotion of his foster parents. When the child matured to manhood, he contested the demons on the Island of the Devils, winning their treasure for his destitute, beloved foster parents.

Peach leaves were sometimes used instead of bay leaves as a flavouring substitute.

Peaches will ripen quicker if a breeze flows over them.

An apple is an excellent thing — until you have tried a peach.
(George du Maurier 1834–96)

PEAR

Everybody knows the old Christmas song in which the true love gives his lady a partridge in a pear tree, two turtle-doves, three French hens, four calling birds, as well as swans-a-swimming and geese-a-laying. What you may not know is that these were traditional Christmas gifts intended to end up on the table for dinner! All of them!

The Greek poet Homer (eighth century BC) referred to pears as a 'gift of the gods'. Evidently, the Romans agreed and proceeded to use grafting techniques to develop more than fifty varieties. Today there are over 2500 pear varieties, many of which are cultivated in Australia.

Pears grow well here and were one of the first introduced fruits. For many years, along with apples, pears were the most readily available tinned fruit and fruit used in bulk jams.

Pears will ripen quicker if a banana is placed in with them.

A popular hot drink, similar to apple cider, was made with pear juice and called Hot Perry.

PINEAPPLE

Pineapples are a sign of welcome and this is why many buildings incorporate the fruit in their exterior ornamental design.

The explorer Columbus was given some pineapples when he visited the island of Guadeloupe in 1493. One imagines he never thought the sweet fruit would end up on pizzas or faux Chinese sweet and sour dishes.

The Big Pineapple in Nambour, Queensland, attracts huge crowds every year where they stare at the plaster fruit and buy pineapple paraphernalia.

RECIPE FOR QUEENSLAND PINEAPPLE CAKE

225 grams (8 ounces) raisins

125 grams (4½ ounces) glacé cherries

225 grams (8 ounces) sultanas

1 cup pineapple juice

225 grams (8 ounces) butter

225 grams (8 ounces) sugar

4 eggs

4 cups plain flour

4 teaspoons baking powder

2 teaspoons cinnamon

1 teaspoon salt

125 grams (4½ ounces) preserved ginger

125 grams (4½ ounces) almonds

125 grams (4½ ounces) mixed peel

1 cup chopped pineapple

Soak the raisins and sultanas overnight in the pineapple juice. Cream the butter and sugar, adding the eggs one by one, and beat well. Add the sifted flour and then alternate adding the other dry ingredients and the rest of the fruit. Bake the batter for 4 hours at 145°C (275°F).

(Mrs Coffey, Hawthorne, Queensland)

PINEAPPLE BOAT

In the 1960s, party-givers favoured so-called 'pineapple boats'. These were pineapple halves with the fruit scooped out and then filled with prawns and mayonnaise and other fillings.

PLUMS

This fruit dates back to the Hanging Gardens of Babylon and it was the Crusaders who introduced the plum to Western Europe.

For most of the nineteenth century plum jam was the most available jam in Australia. It was sold in large tins that were placed directly on the table. If you were really posh you would surround the tin with some crêpe paper.

The fruit found its most popular home in the nursery rhyme where Little Jack Horner eats his plum pie.

Little Jack Horner
Sat in the corner
Eating his Christmas pie.
He put in his thumb
And pulled out a plum
Saying, what a good boy am I.

POMEGRANATE

Known as the 'apple of many seeds', the pomegranate was regarded as a symbol of love and fertility. It has also been suggested that the 'apple' in the Garden of Eden was actually a pomegranate, especially since apples were a relatively late arrival on the fruit scene. The pomegranate, however, is mentioned in Greek mythology as well as being depicted in Christian symbolism.

PRICKLY PEAR

This scrub fruit is known to lower cholesterol levels and alleviate diabetes.

According to old bush lore, the fruit of the prickly pear can be eaten 'after it has been soaked in cold water, the prickles removed by using hard gloves or a rag, and then stewed'. (Not sure if that means you throw the pear away and eat the prickles, gloves or rag. Hmm!) It can also be eaten raw with a squeeze of lemon. They are not as bad as they seem.

PRUNES

Prunes have a reputation as a cure for constipation.

Elizabethan men considered the humble prune to be an enormous help in sustaining an erection and brothels kept a jar handy on the sideboard.

There is even a song, 'The Prune Song' by Frank Crumit, which was popular here in the 1940s:

Nowadays we often gaze
On women over fifty
Without the slightest trace
Of wrinkles on their face
Doctors go and take their dough
To make them young and nifty
But Doctors I defy
To tell me just why
No matter how young a prune may be
It's always full of wrinkles
We may get them on our face
Prunes get 'em every place
Prohibition worries us
But prunes don't sit and brood
For no matter how young a prune may be
It's always getting stewed

In the kingdom of the fruits
The prune is snubbed by others
And they are not allowed
To mingle with the crowd
Though they're never on display
With all their highbrow brothers
They never seem to mind
To this fact they're resigned
That no matter how young a prune may be
It's always full of wrinkles
Beauty treatments always fail

They've tried all to no avail
Other fruits are envious
Because they know real well
That no matter how young a prune may be
Hot water makes 'em swell

Baby prunes look like their dad
But not wrinkled quite as bad

Every day in every way
The world is getting better
We've even learned to fly
As days go passing by
But how about the poor old prune
His life is only wetter
No wonder he can't win
In the awful stew he's in
No matter how young a prune may be
He's always full of wrinkles
We may get them on our face
Prunes get 'em every place
Nothing ever worries them
Their life's an open book
But no matter how young a prune may be
It has a worried look

Prunes act very kind they say
When sickly people moan
But no matter how young a prune may be
It has a heart of stone

QUINCE

The quince, originally from Persia, was used for eye care. An astringent lotion was made from the seeds (often with the herb goldenseal) and used in the treatment of diseases of the eye, including weakness of vision.

In Iran, and some other parts of western Asia, it was known as 'the pear of Cydonia', a reference to its age as Cydonia was an ancient city of northwest Crete.

The quince was also extremely popular with the Ancient Greeks who hollowed it out, filled it with honey and cooked it in a pastry case.

The quince grew well in Australia and was chiefly used to make quince jam and chutney.

RASPBERRY

Vinegar made from raspberries is believed to help clear phlegm in chest conditions. It should be taken in very small doses with crushed berries to improve the gawd-awful taste.

RHUBARB

It was the English who first brought rhubarb to the kitchen table— up until the eighteenth century, it was only considered for its ornamental and medicinal value.

The plant originated in Asia but, oddly enough, was not eaten there.

It's difficult to map when rhubarb first appeared in Australia; however, it almost became mandatory in the twentieth century to have a patch in the back garden. The stalky rhubarb appeared to enjoy life in the Australian yard and could never get enough chook manure.

STRAWBERRIES

The strawberry is recognised as the best of all berries.

It is closely associated with love because of its sweetness and the belief that it was the favoured food of Venus, the god of love.

If you break a double strawberry in half and give it to someone you fancy they will fall in love with you.

Pregnant women should never eat strawberries as they could give the baby a birthmark in the shape of the berry.

WATERMELON

This fruit is originally from the African continent, possibly a fruit of the Kalahari Desert. Hieroglyphics show that the watermelon was harvested nearly 5000 years ago in Egypt and the melons were often placed in burial tombs to nourish the dead as they travelled to the afterlife. Somewhere along the line, merchant sailors carried the melon along the Mediterranean and, eventually, to China where it is still a major crop. Around the thirteenth century the Moors carried the watermelon to Europe.

Q: What is red and white and green all over?
A: A watermelon.

Don't eat pips because they will grow out your ears.

Do not swallow seeds, as they will grow in your stomach.

If you eat the pulp of the watermelon you will have a fever.

Nuts to you

Grains, lentils and nuts

Nuts have a long association with fertility and that is why they are often included in traditional fruit cakes, especially at occasions such as weddings. They also appear as good luck charms and are often seen on key rings, bracelets and necklaces.

Grains and lentils also offer a noble history surrounded by superstition and other lore. In many ways nuts, grains and lentils represent the ever-lasting circle of regeneration and completeness.

Australians, because of the various migration streams, are now eating a lot more of these vital foods.

Avoid fruits and nuts. You are what you eat.

(Jim Davis, 'Garfield')

ALMONDS

Almonds are the fruit of the almond tree. They originated in Asia and were quickly adopted by the Romans who called them 'Greek nuts'.

In the Middle Ages the milk of the almond was used to prepare a soup made from crushed kernels, onions, wine and spices. It was usually consumed between courses.

Almonds, especially sugared almonds, are enjoyed at Australian, Middle Eastern and Greek weddings signifying the sweetness of marriage They are also a popular gift at Orthodox Easter and Christmas in a combination of white, pink and blue.

An early European tradition of wrapping sugar-coated almonds in sheer netting and presenting them to wedding guests symbolised fertility, happiness, romance, good health and fortune. Today we still carry on this tradition with white sugar-coated almonds for weddings as part of the cake decoration.

Medieval Europeans used the milk of the almond nut to get around restrictions on holy day fasting, particularly the requirement to avoid dairy products.

Jews regard the almond as a symbol of haste because the tree blossoms suddenly before leafing. Muslims see it as a symbol of hope and renewal. Czechs, Greeks and Italians see the nut as a symbol of good luck and long life.

Swedish tradition has the almond as symbol of good fortune at Christmas time, serving rice pudding with an almond hidden in one of the servings. The one who finds it is promised an especially good year.

One superstition holds that eating almonds before drinking reduces the chances of getting drunk and having a hangover.

Dreaming of almonds points to temporary sorrow ahead.

Eating a bitter almond usually means that there is serious trouble ahead.

BARLEY

Many Australians were brought up on barley water and tea. Barley water contains considerable nutritional value and was widely used in the treatment of those in convalescence.

Barley's main use was as an ingredient for beer and there are several folk songs praising 'John Barleycorn'.

There were three men came out of the West
Their fortunes for to try,
They made a vow, a solemn vow,
John Barleycorn must die.
They ploughed him in the furrows deep
Threw clods upon his head

And these three men rejoiced
That John Barleycorn was dead.

The old song goes on to tell that it then rained and 'John Barleycorn sprouted up again'. The men then came and cut him down, beat him, then put him in a vat to drown him but he ended up proving to be the best man.

So come put your wine into glasses
Your cider in old tin cans
Put young Barleycorn in the old brown jug
For he proved the stronger man.

BEANS

Folklore has it that eating beans results in flatulence. Beans create gas for a reason. When we eat lentils they travel down into the digestion system; however, since they are so high in sugar content, the little devils are not totally digested until they reach the lower intestine. The bacteria greedily digest the beans and create wind. It's these bacteria that are actually farting! A note for the cautious — the fewer beans you eat the more wind you create. Go figure!

A parody of a commercial brand advertisement runs 'Beanz Meanz Fartz'

Beans, beans, they make you glow,
The more you eat the more you go.
The more you go, the better you feel —
So let's have more beans with every meal.
Baked beans are good for your heart,
The more you eat the more you fart.
The more you eat the more you'll say
Eat baked beans every single day.

(A children's rhyme that looks suspiciously like
the work of an advertising copywriter)

214

COCONUT

This is an old food — globetrotter Marco Polo recognised it as 'Pharaoh's nut'.

Before the trade winds started sending the coconut to Europe it was considered a rare prize and the shells would be polished and mounted on gold or silver bases. They were often used for scrimshaw carvings in a similar way to emu and ostrich eggs. By the end of the nineteenth century, the nut had become extremely popular and who could forget the song 'I've Got a Lovely Bunch of Coconuts (Have a Banana)'?

The coconut got its name from the Portuguese who declared *coco* ('grinning face') when they saw the husk with its distinctive three spots looking like a mouth and two eyes. Well, that's their story and they're sticking to it.

Balinese women are forbidden to touch the coconut tree because of the belief that doing so will transfer the tree's fertility to the woman.

In Papua New Guinea there is a belief that the tree grew from the head of the first man to die.

CASHEWS

These nuts are a relative of the poison ivy, so it's no wonder rumours circulate that the nut is associated with death. The shells do contain a poison; however, they also taste fairly disgusting so it's unlikely anyone would eat them.

CHICKPEAS

Sometimes called garbanzo beans, the chickpea is also universally known as the 'ram's head' bean because it resembles a ram's head complete with curly horns.

Chickpeas are reputed to increase sexual potency in both women and men.

CORN

Corncobs are a marvellous work of mathematical design with every ear having an even number of rows.

Recipe for perfect corn: Place corn ears in a large saucepan of cold water. Sugar lightly (never salt because it toughens the corn), bring to the boil then cover with a lid and say the 'Lord's Prayer' quickly — the corn is now perfect.

The ancients referred to corn 'reaching to heaven as it grows'.

Corn was grown in Australia from early times and was mainly used for its flour rather than eaten on the cob.

One for the blackbird,
Another for the crow,
Three for the ground worm,
And four to grow.

The sooner it's cooked the better it tastes.

You can stroll out to pick it but you surely should run back to the kitchen with it.

(This old adage is, in fact, true as corn commences to turn starchy as soon as it is picked.)

CORN DOUGHBOY

This was an early settler favourite of boiled cornflour dumplings. It was simple food like the doughboy — essentially a rough ball mixture of flour and water — that kept hunger at bay.

CORN ON THE CORN

A term used to describe prison porridge. Also called 'hominy mush'.

FROG'S EYES

Sago pudding and other sago desserts were extremely popular in Australia and children delighted in referring to the cooked grains as 'frog's eyes'.

HAZELNUTS

For quite some time the Europeans called the hazelnut 'filbert' because the nuts were considered ready to harvest on 22 August, St Philbert's Day.

MACADAMIA

Macadamia nuts are native to Queensland and are sometimes referred to as 'the Queensland nut'. They are named after the Scottish chemist John Macadam who discovered that the round nut was edible in 1858.

Australian cooks experimented with the macadamia and, because of its extremely high fat content, it became a rather posh additive to dishes — such as barramundi cooked in butter and macadamia nut flakes. Similarly coated king prawns were served on Qantas first class.

NUTS

We say: 'he's nuts', 'nutty as a fruit cake', 'a nutter', 'she's a nut case'— all implying craziness. One imagines this has something to do with the variety found in packets of mixed nuts with all shapes and sizes and flavours.

A good nut harvest year also means a good baby year.

If you discover two kernels in a shell, eat one and throw the other over your left shoulder. Never eat both, as this is extremely bad luck. (However, some people believe if you discover two kernels in one shell it is a sign of luck!)

To discover if your love is true take two hazelnuts and place them on a fire griddle. If they move apart or refuse to burn the love is false; however, if they burn together then love is true.

Make a wish and throw a nut in the fire; if it flares the wish will come true.

PEAS

Peas were cultivated in the East for centuries before being introduced to Britain in the Middle Ages.

In Australia we followed the British custom of adding bicarbonate of soda to the water to retain the green colour of the peas after boiling. It was also popular to add crushed mint leaves. Like most kids, shelling the peas was a normal part of life — I was delighted when they introduced snap frozen peas to the market and doubly delighted when they were followed by minted peas.

Peas were thought to be a cure for warts. Rub the wart with a different pea every day saying 'wart, wart, dry away'. Keep all the peas until the warts dry up.

We refer to people who behave in a like-minded and close manner as being like 'two peas in a pod'.

> I eat my peas with honey
> I've done it all my life:
> It makes the peas taste funny
> But it keeps them on my knife.

> Opening a pea pod containing a single pea is a sign of good luck.

> Finding nine peas in a pod is considered very lucky for a woman, and the next single man she meets will marry her.

PEANUTS

These originated from the Mayans and Incans of South America and were taken to Europe by the Conquistadors, from where the peanut spread to the world.

The peanut is actually a bean although it tastes like a nut, smells like a nut, behaves like a nut and is called a nut. It's still a bean!

Free peanuts in hotels are to be avoided since research in the 1990s revealed up to 80 per cent had been tainted by guests carrying urine on their hands!

PISTACHIO

Along with almonds, pistachios enjoy a rare mention in the Old Testament, giving them the distinction of being the only two nuts found in the Bible.

> So their father, Jacob, finally said to them, 'If it must be, then do this: put some of the best products of the land in your bags and take them down to the man as gifts — a little balm, a little honey, some spices and myrrh, some pistachio nuts and almonds.'

(Genesis 43:11)

Muslim legend has Adam bringing the pistachio nut with him and Eve.

The Queen of Sheba was convinced that pistachios were a powerful aphrodisiac and ordered the pistachio harvest from the best trees grown in Assyria to be used for her and her royal guests only.

PORRIDGE

Porridge was usually known as 'Scot's Porridge' in early Australia and manners were often judged by how it was eaten. It was considered bad manners to add sugar to porridge and most recipes called for a good pinch of salt during the cooking process. Good manners dictated that one stood while eating porridge, or walked around the room with the bowl in one hand and spoon in the other. It was acceptable to add a dollop of butter.

PULSES

Italians believe pulses, particularly fava beans, are lucky. It is not uncommon to carry a few dried beans around in your purse or pocket.

RICE

If you're planning to boil rice then remember the golden rule: 'rice is shy and doesn't like to be looked at'. A watched pot of rice never boils!

On leaving a wedding ceremony — much to the chagrin of the clergy — it was customary to throw rice at the bride and groom as a symbol of plenty ('may your pantry always be full'). Nowadays paper confetti appears to have replaced the grain; however, it is just as annoying. This tradition most probably originated in China or India where rice has a long association with fertility. Hindus also believed that by feeding the evil spirits with rice they would ignore the bride, of whom they were very jealous.

Ancient Romans also threw nuts and sweets at the bride as a sign of fertility.

RICE PUDDING

So mean he wouldn't give you the skin off a rice pudding.

SAGO

This edible starch is extracted from the centre of cycads and some east-Asian palms. It is eaten in many ways and also used as a stiffening glue for traditional textiles. It is the staple diet for many Australian neighbours including some Papua New Guinean territories. In Australia we eat the granules which we make into puddings and other dishes.

RECIPE FOR LEMON SAGO PUDDING

2 ounces (55 grams) sago
1 pint (550 millilitres) cold water
1 tablespoon golden syrup
sugar
juice and grated rind of 1 lemon

Mix together all ingredients and then simmer until sago is clear. Serve hot or cold with custard or cream.

(Mrs Howe, Brisbane)

WALNUTS

The Greeks called the walnut *caryon*, meaning 'head'. They saw the shell as a skull and the fleshy nut as a brain. Not surprisingly they took this association and decided the nut was a cure for headache.

The Greeks also believed the gods lived on walnuts and referred to them as 'Jupiter's nuts'.

Later, the Romans believed the walnut helped to prevent rotting teeth and, mixed with figs, was a cure for indigestion.

WHEAT

The king of all grains! Wheat, as the main ingredient of bread, has always been credited with supernatural power. It is probably the oldest cereal cultivated, with records showing it was grown in Mesopotamia more than 10,000 years ago.

Eat your greens

Cooked vegetables

Our attitude to fresh fruit and vegetables, and how to cook them, has changed with the years. Sadly, for a long time, the main influence on our vegetable consumption was the British. It was boil, boil, boil, and any green vegetables — especially peas and beans — were given extra torment with the addition of bicarbonate of soda. We also inherited our love of cabbage from the Brits, reminding me of the old French joke: 'The English have three vegetables and two of them are cabbage.'

Change occurred for a number of reasons, not least of which was the availability of certain produce. Our colonial selection was understandably limited until the 1850s when Chinese gold seekers discovered there was more reliable money to be made by feeding the diggers. Chinese market gardens became a fixture of outer suburbia and many country towns. Every ethnic group since has either introduced new produce and new methods of cooking it or increased the market demand. It stands to reason that they would also introduce the folklore associated with these foods.

ARTICHOKE

Known as the 'tooth of the dog' or 'the strangler', the artichoke is a member of the perennial thistle group of the sunflower family. It is one of the earliest documented foods of modern man.

The Jerusalem artichoke is a very distant relative and is a member of the sunflower family although it grows underground as a tuber. It is believed to be a native of North America where it was known as the sunroot. A French explorer named Champlain took it back to France and called it a 'sunchoke' because it tasted similar to the artichoke. It then travelled to Italy sometime before 1633 when the locals called it *girasole*, which means 'turning the sun'. This, according to fable, was corrupted to the word 'Jerusalem'.

It has been said that the artichoke was created by a jealous Greek god who turned a beautiful woman into a thistle because she was considered more attractive than him.

Ancient Greeks boiled their artichokes in water and wine and sometimes drank the residue as a restorative. This could very likely be the original 'hair of the dog' when one considers the artichoke's nickname of 'tooth of the dog'.

In France the word *artichaut* ('artichoke') is a derogatory description of a loose woman — perhaps because of its supposed power as an aphrodisiac?

Italian women often rub two artichokes together in the markets. If the vegetables squeak they are considered good for eating.

Artichokes are associated with protection because of their tough skin and sharp leaves. For this reason they are sometimes incorporated in furniture, carpet and room decorative patterns.

And if you really appreciate trivia you will be delighted to know that Marilyn Monroe was the first official Californian Artichoke Queen, in 1949.

> These things are just plain annoying. After all the trouble you go to, you get about as much actual 'food' out of eating an artichoke as you would from licking 30 or 40 postage stamps. Have the shrimp cocktail instead.
>
> (Miss Piggy)

ASPARAGUS
A member of the lily-of-the-valley family, asparagus is unique among vegetables in having no leaves. Before it was eaten history tells us that it was used for heart trouble, toothache and dropsy when taken as an infusion.

The slender sticks of the asparagus were thought to be an aphrodisiac. French country folk used to insist that three courses of the vegetable were to be served at the traditional bride and groom's nuptial dinner.

Its most vulgar attribute is, of course, the strong effect it has on urine and there's nothing aphrodisiac about that! One can only imagine what the above-mentioned French post-dinner loo must have smelt like! Popular myth has it that 'asparagus urine' is linked to higher intelligence. In fact, it's the result of a simple chemical reaction. Asparagus contains a sulphur compound called mercaptan. (This is also found in rotten eggs, onions and garlic.) When your digestive tract breaks down this substance, by-products are released that cause the distinctive smell. It is true that some people do not emit the smell but there is no truth to the intelligence myth.

The English referred to asparagus as 'sparrow's grass', which in turn, became 'sperage' and eventually 'grass'.

Australians have had an ongoing love affair with tinned asparagus and used to place it alongside the pineapple ring and tinned beetroot in salads. Today we find beautiful fresh varieties including the seasonal white asparagus; however, we still need to remind ourselves that the taste lies in the cooking and less is more. Emperor Augustus was known to order executions 'quicker than you can cook asparagus'.

BICARBONATE OF SODA

Bicarbonate of soda was once a necessary addition to any green vegetable. It made the peas or beans turn bright green even when Australian housewives insisted on boiling them forever and a day.

There was a belief that if taken when pregnant bicarbonate of soda would ensure a boy child.

Bushmen often took twenty grains of bicarbonate of soda last thing at night to ensure a good night's sleep.

Mixed with cream of tartar, it is the rising agent in the Australian scone and no bush cook would have ever been without it.

BROCCOLI

Broccoli originated in Italy where its name translates to 'cabbage sprout'. It is a member of the Brassica family and was introduced to Australia in the twentieth century by Italian migrants.

Long before the modern European cooks were serving broccoli with rich sauces, the Romans were presenting it with all sorts of creamy sauces, some cooked with wine, others flavoured with herbs.

Emperor Tiberius had a son named Drusius who took his love of broccoli to excess. Excluding all other foods, he gorged on broccoli prepared in the Apician manner for an entire month. When his urine turned bright green and his father scolded him severely for 'living precariously', Drusius finally abandoned his broccoli addiction.

Broccoli is sometimes known as 'the poor man's asparagus' or 'five fingers of Jupiter'.

BRUSSELS SPROUT

Eat your sprouts! This is the tiny cabbage-like sprout that has received very bad press. Children are not supposed to like them. Personally I always loved them with pepper and butter.

People have long known that sprouts are good for you. More than 5000 years ago, sprouts were prescribed by Ancient Chinese physicians for a range of ills. In the 1700s, Captain Cook had his crew eat sprouts as well as limes and lemons to combat scurvy.

Originally found in Iran, Pakistan and Afghanistan, their existence in Europe was first recorded in 1587. They became known as the 'Brussels' sprout due to their popularity in Belgium.

Waste not, want not,
For you may live to say
Oh how I wish I had the sprout
That I once threw away.

BUBBLE AND SQUEAK

The most remarkable thing about my mother is that for over forty years she served the family nothing but leftovers. The original meal has never been found but it was always suggested it was hiding in bubble and squeak.

Lightly fry some cold shredded leftover meat. Corned beef is particularly good. Add cold shredded cabbage and small pieces of any other available vegetable like pumpkin, choko, marrow, cauliflower or bell pepper. Salt and pepper to taste as you continue to fry the mixture. Some folks like to add tomato sauce or Tabasco sauce. Place two fried eggs on top and you have a meal fit for any table.

(Ernie Goodrich, Rockhampton, 1975)

CABBAGE

'Cabbage' is a corruption of the Old French word *caboche*, which means 'head'.

The explorer Captain James Cook reportedly used a compress made from aged cabbage and vinegar to treat the wounds his soldiers suffered in a fierce storm in 1769.

Romans believed that the cabbage sprang from the tears of Lycurgus, King of the Edonians.

The Emperor Claudius called a Senate vote to see whether any dish could surpass corned beef and cabbage — the nays had it!

Ancient Greeks used to eat a whole cabbage head to treat insanity. (They must have been mad!)

Russians eat seven times more cabbage than Australians. The Germans hold that sauerkraut is good for everything and anything that ails you.

One indication of its supposed healing power lies in the belief that the cabbage is 'the medicine of the poor'.

Scots send their daughters out blindfolded into the cabbage patch on All Hallows Eve and, as lore has it, they can tell the physique of their future spouse by handling the cabbage heads.

The Irish sometimes wrap cabbage leaves around a minced meat and vegetable mixture to be served on St Patrick's Day, ensuring good fortune.

The Man in the Moon was banished to the sky after being caught stealing cabbages from his neighbour on Christmas Eve.

Cabbage was not supposed to be eaten on St Stephen's Day, because the saint, according to legend, hid in a cabbage patch to escape from his persecutors.

Australian bush cooks referred to cabbage as 'chow' or 'leprosy' because they were equally despised.

A grub in the cabbage is better than no meat at all.

(Bushman's saying)

CABBAGE PATCH
Babies were said to be 'delivered by storks' or 'found under cabbage leaves'. This quaint story goes as far back as the third century BC and is survived by those peculiar Cabbage Patch dolls.

CARROTS
The earliest carrot eaters appear to be the Afghan people who were sun worshippers. They believed that eating orange or yellow-coloured foods would make them more righteous.

Ancient Greeks called carrots *philtron* and used them as love tokens. This no doubt has something to do with the vegetable's penis shape.

Emperor Caligula is supposed to have fed the entire Roman Senate a banquet composed solely of carrot dishes to see if they would turn to 'fornicating like beasts in the fields' — the vegetable had a reputation as an aphrodisiac. One suspects it was more of an ordeal than an orgy.

It was the Flemish settlers who introduced the carrot to Elizabethan Britain. One assumes this is where the term Dutch carrot originated, although today this designates the smaller carrots.

Carrots are said to be good for one's eyesight and children were told they would see in the dark if they ate their carrots. (Mind you, they were also told that's why rabbits eat them and who has ever seen a rabbit wearing glasses?) This traditional wisdom was substantiated by the discovery of vitamin A in carrots, which is beneficial in cases of night blindness.

Write the word 'carrot' on a piece of paper and hide it. Then ask someone to quickly answer your questioning. Ask what is $1 + 1$, $2 + 2$, etc, until you reach 128 — then ask them to name a vegetable. More often than not it will be a carrot.

If a carrot is allowed to go to seed someone in the family will die.

(Old saying)

Do you carrot all for me?
My heart beets for you,
With your turnip nose
And your radish face.
You are a peach.
If we cantaloupe,
Lettuce marry;
Weed make a swell pear.

(Vegetable and fruit poetic puns from the schoolyard)

Go hop, carrot top!
Drop dead, potato head!
Get real, banana peel!

(Schoolyard taunts)

I never worry about diets. The only carrots that interest me are the number you get in a diamond.

(Mae West)

CAULIFLOWER

Cauliflowers were originally brought to Europe when the Moors invaded Spain. It was given the name *cavoli a fiore* ('the cabbage that flowers') and folk therefore considered it ornamental rather than culinary.

Mark Twain, never one lost for words, offered: 'The cauliflower is a cabbage with a college education.'

CHICORY

This popular plant was once grown commercially to take advantage of the fashionable demand for it as an additive to coffee. It has a diuretic, laxative effect and is considered an excellent tonic for the liver.

CHOKO

The choko is a cross between a pear and climbing ivy. It looks inedible but is delicious peeled, steamed and eaten with pepper, salt and butter. The vine delights in growing over fences and its favourite challenge is the old outdoor lavatory building, garden shed or back fence. Neighbours joke that no one has ever actually planted a choko vine.

EGGPLANTS

The aubergine, or eggplant, was thought to be poisonous because it belonged to the deadly nightshade family. It is so called because of its egg shape.

FENNEL

The fennel is, beyond every other vegetable, delicious. It greatly resembles in appearance the largest size celery, perfectly white, and there is no vegetable equals its flavour. It is eaten at dessert, crude, and with, or without dry salt, indeed I preferred it to every other vegetable, or to any fruit.

(Thomas Jefferson, quoted in *Consuming Passions*, Jonathan Green ed., 1985)

There's fennel for you, and columbines; there's rue for you; and here's some for me; we may call it herb of grace o'Sundays.

(*Hamlet*, William Shakespeare, 1564–1616)

GREENS

Australians now call a range of green herbs, vegetables, and mixed green salad by the generic name 'greens'. Eat your greens!

LEEKS

Leeks are associated with Wales. It began in AD 640 when Welsh soldiers wore pieces of leek in their helmets to distinguish themselves from their Saxon foes in battle. Even today the leek is worn as the national flower of Wales on St David's Day.

Leeks date back to the early Bronze Age, around 4000 BC. It is said they were part of the diet of those who built the Egyptian pyramids.

Hippocrates, the father of medicine, prescribed the leek as a cure for nosebleeds.

OKRA

Arabs called this member of the mallow family 'sun vessels', because it was believed their ripening seeds contained therapeutic properties that, once consumed, remained in a man's body forever. The okra was only consumed on special occasions and the Arab name for okra, *uehka*, translates to 'gift'.

It was also an old belief that no mallow should be torn from the ground without leaving a stigma of retribution on the hands of the thief. This most probably has something to do with the fact that the green leaves will cause a scarlet rash if touched.

Australians often refer to okra as 'little boy's dicks', however the more refined side of society calls them 'lady fingers'.

ONIONS

Ancient Egyptians used onions when making an oath or promise, believing the onion, with its many layers of skin, was magical.

A seventeenth-century herbalist said: 'The juice of an onion anointed upon a bald head in the sun brineth the haire again very speedily.' However, the same writer also added, '…though it be boyled, the onion causeth head ache, hurteth the eyes and make a man dim-sighted and dull.'

Raw onions were thought to attract germs so that's why you often see half a raw onion on a kitchen windowsill.

Onion's skin very thin
Mild winter coming in;
Onion's skin thick and tough
Coming weather cold and rough.

Onions hanging in a room prevent disease.

To prevent tears, peel from the root upwards.

To avoid crying, place a slice of potato in your mouth and the fumes will go into the potato.

To keep from crying while peeling onions, place a piece of onion skin on your head or place a piece of bread in your mouth or drink milk.

Having a cut onion in the house leads to arguments.

Onions rubbed on the back of the neck will stop a nosebleed.

To cure coughs, cut an onion in half, scoop out the middle, fill with brown sugar, leave till liquid and drink.

Include onions in soup to prevent colds.

Hold an onion in your hand to scare off snakes, as they dislike the smell.

And, most dear actors, eat no onions nor garlic, for we are to utter sweet breath.

(A Midsummer Night's Dream, William Shakespeare, 1564–1616)

PICKLED ONIONS

Pickled onions will give birthmarks if eaten by pregnant women.

PIGWEED

A widely available Australian native weed. The small leaves and stems are quite succulent when boiled, but can also be eaten raw. The early settlers used it in salads and as a replacement for spinach, and later bushmen took to using its dried seeds in their damper as a spice.

POTATOES

Considering our Irish heritage it is not surprising that Australians love their potatoes, or, as we affectionately call them, 'spuds'.

Over the last few years many new varieties have been introduced to join the classic potato. They come in all shapes and sizes and hardly any main meat or fish course is served without them. Pink Eye Purple, Congo, Desirée, Craig, Bintje, Pontiac, Dargo Goldfield, Manhattan, Winlock, Kipfler, Toolangi Delight … it's strange to think back to the days when Australia had two types of potato — washed and unwashed!

Potatoes were said to be 'the devil's food' because they're not mentioned in the Bible.

Scottish Presbyterian clergy in 1770 declared the potato unsafe to eat (because it was not mentioned in the Bible). One hundred years later, an American clergyman pointed to the potato as the cause of moral decay: Reverend Richard Sewell declared that potato cookery led to wantonness in housewives because it required far too little preparation and left hands idle!

Pregnant women were advised not to eat potato because it would result in their newborn having a small head.

Although the Irish are credited with being Europe's leading potato lovers, the Germans were there first. In 1581, Gutenberg's Press offered a cookbook containing the first annotated potato recipes.

Irish Australians used potato water as a rubbing for sore feet, joints, etc.

Chipping potatoes was considered one of the hardest rural jobs of all. One bushman, keen for work, tramped into a Victorian spud farm and on discovering the job was digging potatoes he suggested to the cocky 'that you hire the bloke who planted them — he'll probably know where they are!'

If you don't wash your ears, potatoes will grow out of them.

One potato, two potatoes
Three potatoes, four
Five potatoes, six potatoes,
Seven potatoes, more.
O-U-T spells out

A potato fast boiled is a potato spoiled.

Carrying an old blackened spud cures rheumatism.

Not the cleanest potato.
> (An 1870s colloquial saying implying a bad reputation)

A pan of potatoes burning dry means rain.

Rub a dub dub
Three men in a tub
And who do you think they were?
The butcher, the baker,
The candlestick maker
And they all ran after
The rotten potater.

POTATO CHIPS

These were invented in 1853 by an American chef, George Crum, in response to a complaint that his French fries were too thick. They appeared in Australia in the 1940s.

PUMPKIN

Pumpkins grow in most parts of Australia. The wild variety kept many a starving bushman alive during the hard times. This probably explains why many post-Depression Australians viewed the marrow with suspicion as 'pig food'. Explorer Ludwig Leichhardt, in a letter to his brother-in-law, 1844, described pumpkins as 'the potato of the Colony'.

It was believed that pointing at a growing pumpkin would stop it growing.

The word 'pumpkin' was voted the fortieth most beautiful word in the English language, according to a 2002 survey conducted by the British Council. The word also takes out the winning stakes as the only vegetable name that is also used as a term of endearment — 'you sweet little pumpkin'.

Peter, Peter, pumpkin eater
Had a wife but he couldn't keep her
He put her in a pumpkin skin
And there he kept her, very well

RADISH

There are many varieties of radish, a cruciferous (or 'cross-bearing') plant, cultivated for its edible root.

It has been grown in China for over 3000 years and was prized by the Greeks and Romans before it travelled around the rest of the world.

> There are some oligarchs that make me want to bite them just as one crunches into a carrot or a radish.
>
> (Evita Perón)

SPINACH

Spinach has a long and inaccurate history of being good for you. Popeye, King Nebuchadnezzar and Richard the Lionheart have all been champions of the green beet. It is said to be 'iron man' food but is actually relatively low in iron.

The ancient inhabitants of Medea prescribed twelve washings for every leaf of spinach that went into a pot — eleven of which were meant to wash away the earthly associations, while the twelfth, washed in human tears, was supposed to season the leaf with God's wisdom.

An old belief instructed one to 'eat spinach and be calm'.

TURNIP

There was a time when women drank boiled turnip water to make themselves more beautiful. This might possibly have something to do with the popular belief that turnips act as a blood purifier, leading to clearer skin.

VEGETABLE SYMBOLISM

Edwardians and Victorians loved to attribute special powers to vegetables:

Cabbage — gain/profit
Cucumber — criticism
Lettuce — coldness
Olive — peace
Potato — benevolence
Rhubarb — advice
Turnip — charity

ZUCCHINI

The zucchini is a member of the cucumber and melon family. The locals down in Central and South America have been eating zucchini for several thousand years, but the zucchini we know today is a relatively new variety of summer squash developed in Italy. The word 'zucchini' comes from the Italian *zucchino,* meaning 'a small squash'. The term 'squash' comes from the Indian *skutasquash* meaning 'green thing eaten green'.

Good old Christopher Columbus originally brought seeds to the Mediterranean region and Africa.

The French snubbed zucchini for a long time until chefs learned to choose the small zucchinis that have more flavour and less water. The French word for zucchini is *courgette* and the vegetable sometimes appears in our markets under that name.

Happy birthday!

Festive and ritual foods

Of all social events, weddings attract the most folklore — especially surrounding the food served. Wedding cakes are rarely made by the bride for that is extremely bad luck, and the cake is usually made of fruits and nuts signifying fertility and coated with white icing signifying purity. There is also lore associated with the actual cutting of the cake and the distribution of the slices. Refusing a slice is an invitation to bad luck.

Other events and festivals, particularly those with a religious observance, are celebrated with particular foods, but many of these traditions have been adapted to suit Australian conditions — as anyone who has slaved in a steaming kitchen cooking a traditional hot Christmas lunch knows, it isn't much fun. Far better to go with the seafood option!

My own memories of Christmas are haunted by the inevitable, everlasting ham, as it sat in the refrigerator, wrapped in a tea-towel, waiting to be dragged out for yet another meal. It was fried, mashed, bubble and squeaked, covered in breadcrumbs, curried and, finally, when it started to think about going green, it was ceremoniously dumped in the garbage. My other childhood memory is of collecting the rare-as-hen's-teeth sixpenny pieces that miraculously appeared in the Christmas pudding. I kept them in a box in my room along with the two-shilling pieces that also mysteriously appeared under my pillow whenever the Tooth Fairy visited. The pudding sixpences were easily recognisable because they always retained some grimy pudding around Queen Elizabeth's face.

APRIL FOOL'S DAY

Australians have adopted the French April Fool Day of 1 April when a trick or joke is played on an unsuspecting victim. In Europe, especially France, it is traditional to offer chocolate in the shape of a fish. There is a good story behind this festivity. Apparently, the origin goes back to the sixteenth century, at which time the new year started on 1 April in France. In 1564 it was decreed to change this to 1 January; however, this move was not popular, so as a protest and a joke, people started to send each other worthless gifts on 1 April as mock new year presents. As the sun was in the constellation of Pisces, at that time, the custom of giving chocolate fish came into circulation. Today we traditionally give a 'pinch and a punch for the first of the month' (unless your victim has yelled 'Bar!') and also play practical jokes.

BIRTHDAY CAKE

At birthday celebrations it is usual to have a cake with one candle for each year of the recipient's age. The celebrant who, according to tradition, is also entitled to make a wish, blows out the candles. To come true the wish should not be told to anyone.

Some historians suggest that the concept of a birthday or anniversary cake started with the Ancient Greeks, who would have presented a nut and honey cake. The Romans certainly celebrated birthdays, including those of temples, buildings and members of the Imperial family. In Medieval Britain it was a custom to celebrate with a small gift inside the cake, usually a coin or token.

The candles on a birthday cake were initially thought to take the smoke to God and this developed into the custom of wishing.

The 'Happy Birthday' song appears to be American in composition however it is now universally popular.

Happy birthday to you
Happy birthday to you
Happy birthday dear [name]
Happy birthday to you.

(Which is usually followed by:)

Why was he [or she] born so beautiful
Why was he [or she] born at all
You're no bloody good to any of us
You're no bloody good at all

(and yet another one)

Hooray for [name]
Hooray at last
Hooray for [name]
He's [or she's] a horses' arse

BISCOTI NATALE
A traditional Christmas biscuit from southern Italy made from almonds, fruit and honey.

CHRISTMAS CAKE
The Christmas cake is considered the epitome of all the Christmas food customs. Rich in fruit, nuts, and sherry or brandy, the cake is usually made some weeks prior to Christmas Day. There is also a tradition of giving Xmas cakes as gifts. Many Australians start or finish their Christmas Day by visiting friends and neighbours for a drink (egg nog) and a slice of cake. It is said that every slice of Christmas cake eaten in a friend's home will add an extra month to your life. The combination of fruit and nuts is of course rich in traditional symbolism of long life, fertility and joy. The cake is traditionally decorated with frosting, glacé cherries and sprigs of holly.

RECIPE FOR CHRISTMAS CAKE

1 cup water

1 teaspoon baking soda

1 cup sugar

1 teaspoon salt

1 cup brown sugar

lemon juice

4 large eggs

nuts

1 bottle vodka

2 cups dried fruit

1. Sample the vodka to check quality.

2. Take a large bowl; check the vodka again.

3. To be sure it is of the highest quality; pour one level cup and drink.

4. Repeat.

5. Turn on the electric mixer.

6. Beat one cup of butter in a large fluffy bowl.

7. Add one teaspoon of sugar.

8. Beat again.

9. At this point it's best to make sure the vodka is still OK.

10. Try another cup … just in case

11. Turn off the mixerer.

12. Break 2 leggs and add to the bowl and chuck in the cup of dried fruit.

13. Pick fruit off flooooor.

14. Mix on the turner.

15. If the fried druit gets stuck in the beaterers pry it loose with a drewscriver.

16. Sample the vodka to check for tonsisticity.

17. Next, sift two cups of salt. Or something. Who giveshz a shit.

18. Check the vodka.

19. Now shift the lemon juice and strain your nuts.

20. Add one table.

21. Add a spoon of sugar, or somefink. Whatever you can find.

22. Greash the oven.

23. Turn the cake tin 360 degrees and try not to fall over.

24. Don't forget to beat off the turner.

25. *Finally, throw the bowl through the window, finish the vodka and kick the cat.*

CHERRY MISTMAS!

(Collected from the Internet, 2003)

CHRISTMAS HAM

In yesterday's Australia the Christmas ham was usually cooked in the laundry copper kettle, resting on a large enamel plate. The method was to cover the ham with cold water adding cloves, mixed spice and a cup of brown sugar. When the ham had simmered for an hour the fire was usually put out and the ham covered to allow it to sweat and slow cook. After about twelve hours or more, when the water was finally cool, the ham was taken out, skinned and then glazed.

CHRISTMAS IN JULY

The relatively new custom of hosting a traditional Christmas dinner in winter has become known as 'Christmas in July'. Since the traditional hot dinner of turkey, gravy, baked vegetables, etc, followed by plum pudding is far too heavy for our summer Christmas, this is obviously an opportunity too good to miss.

CHRISTMAS MINCE

Christmas mince is full of the symbolism associated with long life and good fortune. The word 'mince' comes from the fine chopping, or use of a meat-mincing device, required to make the fruit paste.

RECIPE FOR CHRISTMAS MINCE

2 apples

60 grams (2¼ ounces) currants

60 grams (2¼ ounces) raisins

60 grams (2¼ ounces) sultanas

30 grams (1 ounce) lemon peel

125 grams (4½ ounces) brown sugar

½ teaspoon mixed spice

rind and juice of 1 lemon

1 tablespoon sherry

Peel and core the apples and mince the currants, raisins, sultanas and lemon peel. Add the brown sugar, mixed spice, lemon rind and juice, and sherry. Let all of this stand for at least an hour before eating but, better still, make it a few days before Christmas as this mince improves with age.

(Mrs Callbeck, Cairns, Qld)

CHRISTMAS PUDDING

The Christmas pudding had its origin as an offering to fertility and the harvest. The more fruits it contained the more pleasing to the gods it was. Currants were traditionally very important as the grapevine is a sign of peace and plenty.

In Australia, we also add small silver coins to the mix and to discover one in your slice is an added good luck bonus for the year. To accidentally bite on it is not so lucky unless you are a dentist! As silver threepences and sixpences are no longer in currency some people recycle them each year but this takes away some of the fun.

The Christmas pudding has been around for centuries and has changed from a savoury medieval dish to the sweet, boiled, cannonball-shaped pudding we now recognise.

CHRISTMAS STOCKING

Christmas stockings were often filled with fruit, especially oranges. Later candied fruits, orange slices in chocolate, etc, replaced the fresh fruit. Nowadays simple chocolates and toffees are popular.

DORLATI

Fritti dorlati or 'golden fries' are the traditional breaded and fried vegetables eaten by Italians with fried fish from 23 December to Christmas Eve. Italian custom decrees a meatless diet at this time.

EASTER EGGS

Australians celebrate Easter by giving chocolate gifts, mainly in the shape of a rabbit or egg. The egg is universally symbolic of rebirth and is closely linked to the Christian observance of Christ's rebirth after the crucifixion. The Easter bunny appears to be a surprisingly old tradition originating in Germany and a pagan symbol for fertility.

243

There has been a recent move to replace the bunny with a bilby, a small Australian marsupial.

HOT CROSS BUNS

Hot cross buns are made with a cross cut into the dough, or, more recently, have a cross marked on them in icing. The cross signifies Christ's death on the cross. Eating them brings good fortune and the bun was originally eaten on the first day of Lent.

This is the ideal example of food folklore being taken over by commercialism, as most large bakers mass-produce these buns with them appearing on the shelves earlier and earlier each year.

Hot cross buns

Hot cross buns

One a penny

Two a penny

Hot cross buns

If you have no daughters

Give them to your sons

One a penny

Two a penny

Hot cross buns.

KITCHEN TEA

This is a social gathering, usually of women, where friends gather to celebrate the bride-to-be and offer gifts, usually kitchen related. The food is usually 'ladies bring a plate' — chicken sandwiches, cakes and lamingtons.

PANCAKE DAY

Pancake Day is traditionally Shrove Tuesday, the day before Lent commences. The tradition started because households had to use all their butter and eggs before the Lent fasting period. It was a popular celebration in my youth; however, it appears to be almost gone now.

PANETTONE

Traditionally, panettone originated in the Italian industrial city of Milan. There are several legends concerning its origins, but by far the most romantic of all is that of a Milanese baker named Toni di Borgo alle Grazie. Toni, so the story goes, ran his shop with an iron hand, as he did the life of his young and beautiful daughter, Adalgisa. Because of this, his faithful employee, Ughetto della Tela, knew that he would never receive Toni's consent to marry Adalgisa unless he could somehow raise his status from that of a simple kitchen hand.

Ughetto was a masterful baker but, rather than taking the glory for himself, he gave all the credit for the bakery's wonderful bread to Toni. And soon all of Milan was asking for 'Toni's bread' or *pan ad Toni*. And yes, he did win the fair lady's hand.

Another, less romantic, legend tells how Antonio, a lazy Milanese baker, happened to spill a jar of sugar, candied fruits and raisins into his daily bread dough and, as they say, the rest is history.

Panettone is now available in Australia as part of our Christmas celebrations. It is an accepted gift of friendship prior to Christmas; however, the rate they are flying around these days you'll very likely get your own back.

Panettone is usually toasted or, more often than not, used to make rich bread and butter puddings. It is also good sliced and filled with ice-cream and frozen as a *torta gelata*.

RAMADAN

The ninth month of the Muslim lunar year, during which the faithful must fast from dawn until dusk. During this time a Muslim must not drink (other to rinse the mouth out), eat, smoke or have sexual intercourse during the daytime. A meal is eaten at sundown (*iftar*) and another just before dawn (*suhur*). Halfway through the month a traditional meal is served. The end of Ramadan is celebrated with a feast, usually centred on lamb.

ROUND FOODS

Round foods have long been seen as lucky, especially round cakes and cheeses. This has a lot to do with circles being symbols of completion and closure. Many Asian cultures prepare decorated round cakes for particular celebrations. The Chinese mooncake is the best example.

SHOWER TEA

The 'shower tea' is a party, usually for women only, for a mother-to-be. Friends bring 'a plate' of cold finger food such as chicken sandwiches, cakes and lamingtons to accompany tea, coffee or light alcohol. The focus of the afternoon is the opening of the presents. The custom is also known as 'a baby shower'.

ST NICHOLAS'S MEAL

Many Australians leave a small glass of milk or sherry and a slice of fruit cake out for St Nicholas (alias Santa Claus) on Christmas Eve. Children are led to believe that the old gent scoffs these down as he zips from chimney to chimney. He should look out for RBT units!

TWELFTH NIGHT CAKE

A light fruit cake, covered with almond paste and eaten on 6 January to celebrate the visit of the Magi to the Christ Child twelve days after the birth.

TWENTY-FIRST BIRTHDAY CAKE

When celebrating a twenty-first birthday, the cake is sometimes made in the shape of a giant key and sometimes covered in silver-coloured icing. When the cake is cut the partygoers sing:

> She's [or he's] twenty-one today
> Twenty-one today
> She's [or he's] got the key of the door
> Never been twenty-one before
> We'll shout hip hip hooray
> For she's [or he's] a jolly good fellow
> She's [or he's] twenty-one today

VASILOPITA
A Greek cake made at New Year and named after St Basil who, according to legend, helped return the wealth stolen by the Ottoman Turks. It is baked with a coin inside to commemorate the event.

WEDDING BREAKFAST
Despite the fact that very few wedding feasts are staged in the early morning, the main meal at a wedding celebration is traditionally still referred to as 'breakfast'. There is a strict code of etiquette as to speeches, toasts, cake cutting, bridal waltz, throwing of the bouquet, etc.

WEDDING CAKE
The most important food at the wedding is the cake. Like the Christmas cake, it is traditionally made of fruit and nuts, symbolising fertility. On no account must the bride make the wedding cake herself or assist in its making.

Some Australian weddings also have a 'groom's cake', which is usually a dark chocolate cake. Perhaps this has something to do with pure white marzipan for the bride and devilish dark chocolate for the groom?

All the guests should partake of the wedding cake as a sign of good luck for the newlyweds. It is also important that the bride and groom be the first to cut the cake. The usual custom is for the groom to place his hand over the bride's as she cuts it, symbolising that they intend to share life's good fortune.

Remember me over the water
Remember me over the lake
Remember me at your wedding —
And send me a piece of the cake!

(A common Australian autograph book entry)

If the groom cuts the cake alone the marriage will be childless.

It is considered a sign of bad luck if the icing cracks.

If a girl places a small piece of the wedding cake through a ring, then places it in her left stocking and finally puts it under her pillow and sleeps on it, her future husband will appear in a dream that very night.

ZAMPONE

Italian Australians eat a traditional Christmas Eve sausage called a *zampone*. Made predominantly from the meat of the pig's trotter, the sausage is served with lentils. Tradition has it that the more lentils you consume the more money you will make in the coming year.

Some like it hot
Spice

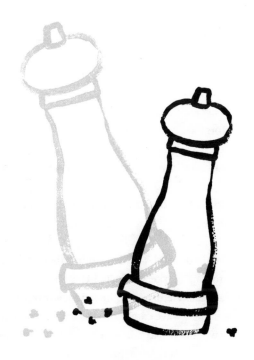

Australian cuisine has developed a surprisingly high tolerance for and love of hot spices, particularly chilli. Many visitors, especially British and American, are somewhat taken aback when they are confronted with restaurant menus where hot spices are used so freely, and that isn't necessarily the Asian or Indian restaurants! The popularity of Indian, Thai and other Asian cuisines has a lot to do with recent immigration and the generally adventurous Australian palate.

The thousands of Chinese who ventured here during the gold-rush era certainly spiced up many the dubious piece of old mutton, as did early Afghan hawkers who supplied country kitchens and rural stores with everything from top hats to curry powders. As gold petered out, the Chinese opened restaurants in both rural and urban Australia; however, for many years, the cuisine was bland and boring as the Chinese designed sweet and colourful dishes for the locals. Slowly they became more adventurous and introduced traditional dishes from the northern, colder regions of China. With the post-World War II arrival of refugees and immigrants from Vietnam, Cambodia and Thailand, our palate really got spiced up and our produce markets reflected these new directions with lemongrass, gangalal, Vietnamese mint, and many other Asian specialty products. A similar wave came with the Indian and Pakistani migrants, many of whom opened café-style eateries in busy suburban shopping strips.

No one could accuse present day Australians of being unadventurous eaters as we dish out the cumin, coriander, fennel and chilli to spice up all types of dishes.

CHILLI
There is some truth in the folk belief that eating scorching hot chillies can make you feel good. Capsaicin, the main fiery ingredient, is a gutsy hot weapon to combat all kinds of pain, especially headaches, muscle aches and hangovers.

Eat a small whole chilli to cure a cold.

A pepper plant in the garden will bring good luck to the household.

CINNAMON
Cinnamon was first mentioned in the writings of the Chinese in 2700 BC, and has been long used as a flavouring, perfume and traditional medicine. It is regarded as a 'warming' spice against 'cold' aliments like chills, rheumatic pain and digestive complaints.

CLOVE
The clove has been used as a means of alleviating toothache for centuries. Ancient Chinese, when dining with the Emperor, would chew a clove to ensure sweet breath.

PEPPER
Pepper was the most commonplace and widely used spice up until the end of the fifteenth century.

Pepper, particularly black pepper, is said to increase sexual urge and is also a great help as a gastrointestinal stimulant in the case of flatulence, congestive chills and indigestion.

The term 'peppercorn rent' implies a nominal rent; however, this is not its original meaning. Pepper was once a very expensive commodity, and during the Siege of Rome in AD 408 the spice was so highly thought of it was used as currency. It was not uncommon for bills, including large ones, to be paid in pepper.

Spill pepper and you will have an argument with a best friend.

Peter Piper picked a peck of pickled pepper.
If Peter Piper picked a peck of pickled pepper
Where's the peck of pickled pepper that Peter Piper picked?

Kids in the kitchen

School meals and other kids' food

Surely the manufacturers of processed baby food have either never tasted their squishy concoctions, or they despise babies. The stuff is horrible and that includes the organic, vitamin-enriched varieties. It is small wonder kids grow up thinking they are entitled to commercially packaged food rather than the offerings of the home kitchen. It's a natural progression from those tiny little jars to the frozen pizza slices in the supermarket freezer. When one considers the number of modern-day allergies and diseases, and the fact that so many of our children are mightily overweight, surely the connection between food and wellbeing must be considered. We are what we eat and it is imperative we appreciate this from a young age.

When I was a kid, we weren't allowed to eat many store-bought sweets. 'They'll rot your teeth' was the usual reply to 'Can I have …?' Our sweet tooth fantasies were given over to biscuits, cakes, cordials and fruit pies. Festive occasions usually meant trifles, jellies and ice-cream. The one exception to the 'no lollies' rule tended to be our weekly visit to the pictures, or 'flicks at the flea pit', as we fondly referred to our Saturday afternoons at the Kogarah Mecca or Rockdale Odeon. At one stage a green or pink musk stick was given out with the ticket. We sucked rainbow balls that changed colour as you sucked them furiously, chewed sticky Hopalong Cassidy Bars and Choo Choo Bars that somehow or other ended up all over your face, and bubble gum that went splat and also ended up sticking to your moosh or, worse still, your hair. Other favourites included Slate Pencils that tasted of aniseed when sucked, Chocolate Frogs, Liquorice Straps that we shredded strand by strand, Traffic Lights, Bullets, Nut Kisses, Kurls, White Knights, Fruit Tingles, Tarzan Jubes, Polly Waffles, Violet Crumble Bars, Jelly Beans, Wagon Wheels and Jaffas. Courting couples up the back of the theatre, in the 'passion pits', preferred Conversation Hearts, Columbines and Fantales.

One of the most memorable advertising slogans in Australia must be: 'It's moments like these you need Minties', followed closely by 'lollygobbleblissbombs'. Cadbury's would also get a gong for its long-running 'glass and a half of full cream milk' campaign. Whilst advertising plays an important role in popularising sweets, the folk are also inventive — as witnessed in the movement to freeze Mars Bars or, worse still, the recent custom of deep-frying them in batter.

Recent surveys have revealed that many Australian children are seriously overweight and organisations are now starting to act upon these frightening statistics. The fact is that many children are given far too much lunch money and what we call 'pocket money'. When I was a kid we had to scrounge around for empty soft drink bottles to earn the five pence refund and our pocket money was a few shillings a week, if we were lucky. School tuck shops these days seem to be a thriving business and it's nothing to see children with wads of money. Kids usually know what is good and bad to eat and I can't help but wonder what role folklore plays in their overall attitude to food. Most of the classic fairy tales use sweet foods in an alluring way, including houses made of gingerbread, giant lollypops, and sweet pies, etc. In recent years, television and film has taken up the sweet is good theme so kids are continually being presented with the concept that sweets are naughty but nice. Given the opportunity, most kids will go for the nice even if it is naughty. Of course, all attitudes to what is good and bad to eat are learned experiences and ultimately the responsibility of the parents and guardians.

CUT LUNCH

A 'cut lunch' is usually two sandwiches made in the morning and taken to school or work. The term has also entered the vocabulary in the phrase 'mad as a cut lunch', which is obviously a strange derivation of 'mad as a cut snake'.

FAIRY BREAD

A regular at children's parties and especially birthday parties, these are usually white-bread triangles buttered and sprinkled with hundreds and thousands.

FAIRY FLOSS

Spun coloured sugar has been a popular confectionery at fun fairs, the circus and agricultural shows for many years. It is usually coloured bright pink or yellow and eaten on a wand stick.

FÊTE FOOD

Fêtes are particular fund-raising events, usually mounted by schools, churches and other community groups, and consisting of various stalls selling bric-a-brac, potted plants and, of course, foods such as confectionery, cakes, biscuits and preserved pickles and fruits. Some of the mainstays of the fête are toffee apples, coconut ice, stickjaw toffees and lamingtons.

HEDGEHOGS

We don't have hedgehogs in Australia but we do have the echidna. Both marsupials have needle-like spines on their backs but, for some reason or other, our cooks decided long ago that this recipe was called 'hedgehogs'. One assumes the corn flakes create the hedgehog look.

RECIPE FOR HEDGEHOGS

250 grams (9 ounces) butter

25 grams (1 ounce) sugar

1 egg

1 teaspoon baking powder

1 ½ cups flour
1 tablespoon chopped walnuts
1 tablespoon chopped candied cherries
Kellogg's Corn Flakes

Beat the butter and sugar to a cream and add the egg. Sift together the baking powder and flour and add to the creamed mixture together with the chopped walnuts and candied cherries. Roll teaspoons of the mixture in Kellogg's Corn Flakes and bake in a moderate oven for 30 minutes.

(Mrs Fotheringham, Sans Souci, NSW)

HUNDREDS AND THOUSANDS
A brightly coloured confectionery devised as a cake and biscuit decoration. They're particularly popular on fairy bread.

ICE BLOCKS
Australian kids and some adults eat ice blocks — frozen drinks on a stick. There is now a zillion varieties to tempt the hot and bothered. When I was a kid there were three flavours — lime, raspberry and pineapple — and they were called 'icy poles' because they were cylindrical. Thankfully we have avoided the American word 'popsicle'.

OSLO LUNCH
The Oslo lunch, developed by Dr Carl Schiotz in 1932, was introduced to Australia in 1940 after a short test period at the Collingwood Primary School, Melbourne. Fifty children were randomly selected to lunch on a daily menu of three slices of wholemeal bread and butter with cheese, half a pint of milk, half an ounce of wheat hearts and an orange. The diet was deemed successful, especially in nourishing bone growth, and was subsequently introduced to all schools throughout Australia.

PLAY LUNCH
School children refer to their mid-morning snack, usually accompanied by a small bottle of milk, as 'play lunch'.

SOLDIERS

Pieces of toast cut into strips and usually eaten with boiled eggs were called 'soldiers'.

TUCK SHOP

It's tempting to think that the tuck shop earned its name from the fat friar in the Robin Hood stories; and considering the muck that some of these school outlets have offered in the past, the image of the big-bellied Friar Tuck might not be too far from the truth. Mountains of pies, sausage rolls, hot dogs and white bread rolls and sandwiches are still dished out every day. In my school days, in the 1950s, fruit was unheard of and wholemeal bread unwelcome. Times (thankfully) are changing but the average tuck shop still needs a healthy food injection.

I wouldn't eat that!

Migrant influence

It has often been said that Australia is a melting pot for the many cultures settled here. Be they European, Latin American, Asian or Callithumpian they all bring with them their traditions and into the pot they go. Some traditions are hardy, suit the new land and stick around while others quietly disappear. Folklore assimilates easily and, as the Celtic and British lore became 'Australianised' during the nineteenth century, so has the folklore of more recent Asian and European settlers of the twentieth century. One only has to look at how Middle Eastern pita bread, and especially so-called 'Turkish bread', has become part of the everyday eating habits of so many Australians.

'Tell me what you eat and I'll tell you where you live' is a well-known truism. We tend to live in communities and new settlers obviously find comfort in living in close proximity to their religious and social centres. This leads to specialist food suppliers also opening in those areas. Every capital city now boasts a Chinatown but they also have other Asian community shopping areas where you will find exotic Asian vegetables, spices and meat cuts. The same can be said of Arabic suburbs where Middle Eastern breads, goat meat and halal foods are available. There will also be a Greek suburb and a so-called 'Little Italy'; in some cities, there will be several such areas. Sydney and Melbourne have large Jewish communities and here you will find kosher butcheries and specialist groceries and takeaway food outlets.

Sydney even has a Japanese shopping centre. Sushi, yeeros, kebabs, couscous, pho, chow mein, falafel, and gelato all vie for the easy dollar along with takeaway chicken and whopper burgers of every description.

For my part the discovery of garlic, strong cheese and preserved sausage came with the arrival of the Italian and Maltese students to the Catholic school I attended in the 1950s. Here I was with baked bean or peanut butter sandwiches and these new kids were hoeing into what looked like huge sandwiches with fillings I had never seen before, let alone tasted. They had never eaten peanut butter or baked beans so we did what kids do — we swapped. We also swapped the folklore created around those foods, be it superstitions, customs or even the introduction of their names into skipping and clapping rhymes (even if mostly in a derisive form).

Cultural difference also creates folklore associated with racism. In many ways it is an innocent form of racism based on ignorance. When the post-World War II European migration of Italians and Greeks arrived we called their food 'dago or wop food' and 'wog food' as we sneered at the garlic, strange cheeses and oddities like pesto and feta. Gradually suburban corner stores started selling pasta and strange sausages. In Sydney's Paddington this prompted the local Australian-operated store to paste a message on its window: 'Shop Here Before the Day Goes'.

The Australian delicatessen, usually referred to simply as 'the deli', has come a long way but, sadly, a trip to France will send the average gourmand crazy with desire. The French charcuterie is a wonderland with beautiful prepared and masterfully decorated dishes in aspic, tureens of casseroled meats, smoked game and everything shouting 'Eat me!' Most of our deli counters have as much appeal as a cinema snack bar. I usually take one look at the coleslaw to see if it has come out of a giant factory-made vat — and most have — and run in the opposite direction. I also shy away from those shaved processed meats that dominate most supermarket deli counters and wonder why anyone in their right mind would buy slices that are curling up their toes.

Not surprisingly, Asian food was seen as suspicious as we sneered at the noodles and dumplings and avoided the chilli and coriander. That too is changing and every major city in Australia boasts a thriving Asian sector with fishmongers, butchers, greengrocers and general Asian food supplies. Middle Eastern cuisine is currently taking the heat; however, this too will easily assimilate and a journey into their shopping centres can be a real eye-opening treat.

Australia has one of the world's most vibrant cuisines and one of the most adventurous. None of us could imagine life without garlic, oils, noodles, chilli and all those other wonderful ingredients that have become part of our life. The following examples are but a tasting of why migrant-influenced food, and the lore surrounding it, is now so much part of our life.

BABA GHANOUSH

This *mezze* or vegetable side dish is eaten throughout the Middle East and is now available in most Australian supermarkets. Made from the smoked flesh of the aubergine it is puréed with garlic, lemon juice and olive oil. It is traditionally known as 'poor man's caviar'. In Lebanese it translates as a delightful 'spoiled old daddy'.

BALI BELLY

A familiar condition for Australians touring the island of Bali. Any form of stomach upset experienced in Asia is referred to as having a dose of 'Bali belly'.

BEAN CURD

In Chinese folk belief there are three gods invoked by the bean curd makers and sellers. The chief of these is Huai nan Tzu because he invented the dish. The other two are Chiao Kuan and Kuan Yu.

Australians now consume a healthy amount of soy bean curd in its various manifestations, including tofu.

BORSCH

This soup originated in Europe where it was made from just about any root vegetable available. In Australia it is made from beetroot. It has the same mythical recuperative power as Jewish chicken soup.

CHALLAH

A Jewish bread loaf made from white flour dough and eggs and sometimes flavoured with saffron. It is plaited and glazed with an egg and then sprinkled with poppy or sesame seeds. It is traditionally eaten on the Sabbath and at festival meals.

Originally 'a Challah' was a biblical tithe paid to the priests. Nowadays, to remember this biblical mitzvah, Jewish bakers follow the rabbinic commandment to burn a token amount of dough. A benediction is recited before removing a pinch of the dough and tossing it to the back of the oven.

CHINESE COOKERY

The two dominant philosophies of the Chinese culture are Confucianism and Taoism. Each influenced the course of Chinese history and the development of the culinary arts. Confucianism concerned itself with the art of cooking and placed great emphasis on the enjoyment of life and the Toaist approach sanctified preparation and consumption. To the Chinese, food and friends are inseparable. A gathering without food is considered incomplete and improper. The standard Australian joke about Chinese meals is that you can eat one and can eat another an hour later. I'm not sure where this belief originated other than for the fact that much Chinese food is bite-sized and fresh. It is one of the very few cuisines where food is cut up into portions before being served.

CHOPSTICKS

The term originates from the pidgin word *chop,* meaning 'speedy'. For all those chopstick klutzes out there, I've found the best way to handle them is by holding the bottom stick stationary between my thumb and third finger, while using that same thumb and my first two fingers to capture a bite-sized morsel and steer it toward my mouth. Yes, being left-handed only complicates the whole process but where there's a Wu there's a Wei.

It is considered unlucky to break chopsticks. It is also considered bad mannered to eat Chinese food with a knife and fork.

> The honorable and upright man keeps well away from both the slaughterhouse and the kitchen. And he allows no knives on his table.
>
> (Confucius)

CHOP SUEY

No one seems to know the true origins of this Chinese dish, but it was most likely created by Chinese immigrant cooks in America who wanted something easy to pronounce for their American customers. Along with chow mein, it is a staple of Australian Chinese restaurant menus.

According to a favoured bit of folklore, an angered Chinese cook mixed together the day's garbage in a bit of broth and presented it to San Francisco restaurant patrons who'd earned his ire. Not knowing any better, those being insulted loved the dish and, much to the amused bewilderment of their tormentor, returned time and again to order it. Chop suey, therefore, is a mispronunciation of 'chopped sewage'.

CHOWS

There was a time when Chinese food was considered exotic in Australia and ignorance always breeds folklore. Australians, always ready for a convenient abbreviated descriptive, adopted the old goldfields slur of 'chows' to describe the Chinese. The most widely distributed folklore, racist in intent, was that most Chinese restaurants served cat instead of chicken. It must be remembered that up until the 1960s chickens were not consumed on a regular basis — they were a special occasion dish — and this played a part in our view that the Chinese were using the next best available meat: cat meat! Of course this belief was spread the same way today's urban myths circulate, despite the fact they are falsehoods.

CORNISH PASTY

This is a pastry turnover traditionally made with short pastry but often made with puff pastry. Originally from the county of Cornwall, England, it was brought to Australia by Cornish miners who ended up in South Australia and the Hunter Valley, New South Wales. The pasties were designed as a snack for the miners; the pastry twists acted as 'handles' that the men, whose hands were usually black with coal soot, could discard after the middle had been eaten. A larger version was often made with a savoury filling on one side, sweet on the other.

CURRY

Australians tend to call any Indian or Pakistani dish a curry. It is a Tamil word, *kari*, meaning sauce. For many years you could only buy one or two brands of colonial curry powder and both were a bright yellow colour and rather insipid.

The first commercial curry powder appeared in 1780, and in 1846 its fame was assured when William Makepeace Thackeray wrote a 'Poem to Curry' in his *Kitchen Melodies*.

> Three pounds of veal my darling girl prepares,
> And chops it nicely into little squares;
> Five onions next prures the little minx,
> (The biggest are the best, her Samiwel thinks),
> And Epping butter nearly half a pound,
> And stews them in a pan until they're brown'd.
> What's next my dexterous little girl will do?
> She pops the meat into the savoury stew,
> With curry-powder table-spoonfuls three,
> And milk a pint (the richest that may be),
> And, when the dish has stewed for half an hour,
> A lemon's ready juice she'll o'er it pour.
> Then, bless her! Then she gives the luscious pot
> A very gentle boil — and serves quite hot.
> PS — Beef, mutton, rabbit, if you wish,
> Lobsters, or prawns, or any kind fish,
> Are fit to make a CURRY. 'Tis, when done,
> A dish for Emperors to feed upon.

To 'give someone curry' is to make it 'hot' or difficult for them. To 'curry favour' is to solicit favour.

In yesterday's Australia women made chutney and never made curry. These days many people make curry but hardly ever make chutney.

RECIPE FOR FRUITY CURRY

Grind and mix dry curry ingredients of curry leaves, coriander, cumin, fennel seeds and mustard seeds until you have a curry powder. Fry two sliced onions and then add the dry mix until the onions sweat and take in the curry. Now add your chopped meat (chicken, lamb or beef) and cook until it browns. Add whatever vegetables and dried fruits you have available. Sliced pumpkin, squash and carrots are good and so are raisins, sultanas and dried pineapple. Add whatever fruit is available — sliced banana, apple or pear are excellent. Add 4 cups of chicken stock and bring to the boil, then turn down to low and allow to simmer for one and a half hours. Serve with boiled rice and cold yoghurt. (Fahey family recipe)

FISH CAKES

As a child, I watched my mother make fish cakes with a mixture of mashed potato, tinned tuna or salmon, a raw egg, breadcrumbs and dill. They were served with horseradish. Today, showing the influence of Thailand and Indonesia on our cuisine, fish cakes have come to mean those flat, fried Asian cakes usually served with a sweet chilli sauce.

FOCACCIA

The Italian olive-oil flatbread known as focaccia has become extremely popular in Australia. A cross between a pizza and traditional bread it has been eaten in Italy for over 2000 years. It now sits with the Turkish pide flat bread in the sandwich shops of Australia.

FOOD FESTIVALS

Australia stages a large number of regional and metropolitan food festivals that celebrate a particular food or wine producing area, regional food or other related product. There are blessings of fishing fleets; festivals celebrating the chilli, the olive and the banana; and major wine shows and harvest festivals in regions like the Barossa in South Australia or the Hunter Valley in New South Wales. Many of these festivals also incorporate the traditions of the earliest settlers to that particular region: the Germans in the Barossa, the Yugoslavs in the Margaret River, the Maltese in the Queensland banana and sugar industries, etc.

PASTA

There are many types of pasta and most can be found in Australia. We eat mountains of it thanks to our various migration streams from Europe and Asia. The Italian-style pasta is primarily wheat and the Oriental pasta, usually referred to as noodles, is from a variety of flours and starches, including rice.

It is popularly believed that the fourteenth-century explorer Marco Polo introduced pasta to Italy from China, but the first-known reference can actually be traced back to Sicily in the Middle Ages. Catherine de Medici, generous soul that she was, introduced it to France where it spread to most of Europe. Both the Italian-style and Oriental come in all shapes and sizes and have just as many uses. In the first half of the twentieth century Australians ate mostly macaroni and vermicelli (the name means 'small worms'), usually cooked within an inch of its life. In the second half, after several waves of European immigration, other varieties appeared.

Everything you see I owe to spaghetti.

(Sophia Loren, Italian actress, 1934–)

The trouble with eating Italian food is that five or six days later you're hungry again.

(George Miller, British writer)

RISOTTO

This Italian rice-based dish is a regular on our restaurant menus, more often than not as the 'vegetarian option'. In 2004, Australia went for the world record for the Biggest Rissoto Ever. Cooked at First Fleet Park, Circular Quay, in Sydney on 26 November, the monster weighed in at 4,650,000 kilojoules and using 1600 kilograms of rice,

800 kilograms of peas, 4400 litres of stock and 320 kilograms of Parmesan cheese. It won the world title.

SPAGHETTI BOLOGNESE

Nearly everyone has a favourite spaghetti bolognese recipe and all other attempts, including restaurants', pail into insignificance by comparison. It's a good bet that the average Aussie recipe is nothing like the original from Bologna that used chicken livers, ground veal and pork, and cream or milk to make a rich ragù with tomato, onion, garlic, herbs and a little red wine. It should also be stated that the average Australian version is usually sitting under a mountain of inferior shredded cheese.

A woman who had never been to the bush before was finding things very different from what she was used to in the city. On her first visit to a country hotel dining room, she came out of the ladies toilet with a look of horror on her face.

As she was leaving the hotel, she said to the waitress, 'Please tell the owner of this establishment that I found your graffiti in very bad taste.'

'I will,' said the waitress, 'but next time, I suggest you try the spaghetti.'

This parody of a popular old song went into circulation in the 1960s.

ON TOP OF SPAGHETTI
(Air: 'On Top Of Old Smokey')

On top of spaghetti, all covered with cheese,
I lost my poor meatball when somebody sneezed.
It rolled off the table, and onto the floor,
And then my poor meatball rolled out of the door.
It rolled down the garden, and under a bush,
And then my poor meatball was nothing but mush!

The mush was as tasty, as tasty could be,
And then the next summer it grew into a tree.
The tree was all covered, all covered with moss,

And on it grew meatballs, all covered with sauce.

So if you have spaghetti, all covered with cheese,

Hold onto your meatball, 'cause someone might sneeze.

STROGANOV

A dish of thinly sliced beef, coated with a creamy sauce and garnished with mushrooms and onions, stroganov is usually served with pilaf rice. It is a traditional recipe from Russia and has been popular throughout Europe since the eighteenth century. (The Stroganovs were a Russian family of wealthy merchants, financiers and patrons of the arts.)

The dish appeared in Australia in the mid-1950s and was an extremely popular dinner party dish along with chicken cacciatore.

TARAMASALATA

Australians now eat a wide range of Greek, Asian and Middle Eastern dips. Taramasalata is a Greek dip made from fish roe and was historically consumed on the eve of the Assumption when it was prohibited to eat eggs, cheese and olive oil. This is only one of the many dips that you will find on today's supermarket shelf. Unfortunately, a lot of commercially prepared versions of taramasalata have the consistency of face cream and, sadly, some taste like it too.

TSOUREKI

This Greek Easter bread is traditionally round, plaited and features an egg painted bright red. The egg symbolises the resurrection of Christ. On Easter Sunday most Greek families have a traditional meal of taramasalata, soup and lamb, served with the tsoureki.

A little crêpe paper around
the jam tin

Entertaining and
etiquette

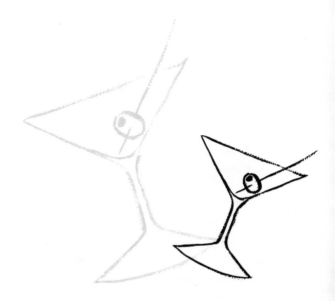

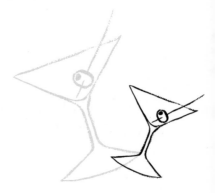

For many years, sex, politics and religion were the three conversational subjects traditionally avoided at the table. No one laid down this rule, it emerged as a suggested behavioural code for polite society and was adopted by the population at large. Nowadays dinner parties would be deemed dull if none of these subjects were vigorously discussed and some would require all three, including the religious and sexual behaviour of politicians! Likewise the use of vulgar or swear words was deemed inappropriate; however, this too has changed and, in some circles, the use of such language is accepted as everyday vocabulary. As with spices, and locally in the words of the old Peck's Paste commercial, 'a little bit goes a long way'.

Manners are customs accepted over a period of time as normal behaviour. Things were not always so: men did not always stand up when a lady entered the dining room, dishes were not always served from one particular side, and so on.

Larousse Gastronomique comments that:

Table manners have developed through the ages and attitudes towards them vary in every country. The Gauls used to eat sitting down, and the Romans lying down, while the Japanese traditionally squat on their heels at the table. The French are taught to keep their hands over the table throughout the meal, whereas the English etiquette requires that they should be placed in the lap when not actually eating. Belching, regarded as the grossest indelicacy in western countries, was a sign of politeness in ancient Rome and still is in the Middle East.

Colonial Australia, being a predominantly male society, developed 'rough and tumble' manners. For many years we followed the British pattern where women served and cleared the table and then retired to the kitchen so as to allow the menfolk the opportunity of hard talk along with hard liquor and cigarettes. Women were not allowed to drink in the public bar of hotels and were restricted to the saloon bar or made to drink their 'shandy' mix of beer and lemonade in the car in the parking lot.

Sadly, some things never change, and the embarrassing stereotyped image of the bush dancehall with men circling the keg at one end and women making sandwiches at the other still survives.

One of the biggest shifts in eating customs came in the aftermath of World War I. During the nineteenth century, both city and country families 'of means' would have domestic servants and especially a 'cookie'. Family cooks were highly regarded and usually underpaid which prompted the saying, 'She was a good cook, as cooks go and as good cooks go, she went.' After the war, women were accepting employment in the factories and commercial offices, so domestic labour became scarce. Having domestic staff was also seen as snobbish and, for the newly independent woman, unnecessary. This resulted in a flood of books encouraging women to 'do it themselves' — the modern cookbook was born.

The dinner party is a good example for comparative study on how dining customs have changed with time. Fashionable society created the dinner party as evidence of success. It was an opportunity to show manners, introduce eligible daughters and sons and, in many ways, act as an index of a family's taste. Giving a dinner party was a visible expression of a family's middle class position. Once a month was the norm, with the rich hosting once a week. In the first one hundred years of white Australian settlement, dinner parties emulated those of Britain, including the type of dishes presented, the musical entertainment offered and the social positioning it implied. The twentieth century presented different challenges, including two world wars and an international depression. Early film, radio and television also had a major affect on how we saw ourselves at the table. Did we eat the same food as Lucille Ball, Cary Grant and Gloria Swanson? Did we have the same manners as the stars of the *Carry On* films or were we more like Audrey Hepburn in *Breakfast At Tiffany's*?

As eating loses its traditional spiritual and social base — mainly because we are too darned busy to relax around the dining table — we also lose our tradition of table manners. These are real losses.

ANGELS ON HORSEBACK

A popular appetiser that dates back to the nineteenth century. Fresh oysters were sprinkled with a little cayenne pepper then rolled in a piece of bacon, skewered and lightly fried. Compare with 'devils on horseback'.

ASPARAGUS FINGERS

A party food made with brown bread, with the crusts cut off, encircling a finger of tinned asparagus and staked with a toothpick. (What were they thinking!)

BRING A PLATE

The popular custom of contributing to a common table by bringing a plate of food to a formal or casual gathering was widely referred to as 'bring a plate' or, in an earlier era, 'ladies bring a plate'.

BYOG

Equally widespread is the invitation (or order) to 'bring your own grog' — this usually refers to alcohol. Some restaurants also use BYOG as an incentive, allowing customers to bring their own wine.

CHEERIOS

Peculiar to Queensland, cheerios are small cocktail frankfurters skewered with a toothpick. In New South Wales, vulgar capital of the nation, they are referred to as 'little boys'.

COCKTAIL PARTY

Australians use the name 'cocktail party' to describe any social gathering where drinks are served, usually with what is described as 'cocktail food'. The latter can be anything from party pies or baby frankfurters to caviar and smoked salmon — sometimes all four and more!

A toast to the Cocktail Party
Where olives are speared
And friends are stabbed.

(Anonymous)

DEVILLED EGGS

A truly nasty cocktail food: boiled eggs halved with the yolk taken out and mixed with curry and then replaced in the egg white hollow. The very posh used a piping bag to create a wavy effect. They look rather scary after sitting on a plate for an hour or more.

DEVILS ON HORSEBACK

A suspicious 1950s Australian cocktail finger-food comprised of a grilled prune wrapped in bacon strips and skewered with a toothpick. The combined flavour does work; however, be warned: a hint of burnt prune leads to a nasty aftertaste and many the eager eater has been stabbed with a wayward toothpick.

DINNER

The times at which we eat have been developed as custom and have changed dramatically over the centuries. In eighteenth-century England, breakfast was eaten between 10 and 11am as a light meal, presumably after several hours of work. By the 1830s and '40s in Australia, it had become earlier, and by the gold-rush days of the 1860s it had settled around the 7.30 to 8.30am mark, being consumed before any work was undertaken.

It was also around this time that the concept of a light midday meal gained popularity. Initially this was known as 'luncheon', later becoming abbreviated to 'lunch'. In the country, it tended to be a cold meal; however, in the fashionable cities, the idea of a luncheon party appealed to the womenfolk, sometimes becoming an elegant affair where women steadfastly kept their hats firmly on their heads and men carried their hats into the drawing room.

Dinner has also experienced time shifts and in the late eighteenth-century it was usually consumed between 3 and 5pm, with a light supper following around 9 or 10pm. Around the 1850s we adopted 9am to 5.30pm as a working day and, at the same time, changed our evening dinner meal to between 7 and 8pm. Along with all these changes, we also adopted the English concept of 'tea', which was typically served around 5pm. However, this didn't suit our pioneering workday, so we simply started to refer to the main evening meal of the day as tea. Some still refer to the evening meal as tea.

Q: What is it you eat every day and no one else eats
A: Your dinner

After dinner, rest a while,
After supper, walk a mile

DINNER PARTY

By the 1860s the fashionable of our capital cities, especially in Melbourne and Sydney, discovered the dinner party. This was often a grand affair and an opportunity to show class solidarity — and to show off. Essentially, one could not provide a better opportunity for acceptance than to allow a stranger to join the family table. The emergence of the canning, refrigeration and processing industries also meant that typical British meals could be served. The interesting aspect of all this is, of course, the survival of the dinner party into the twenty-first century, including many of its trappings and customs.

FINGER BOWL

The rinsing of one's fingers when eating seafood, asparagus, corn on the cob, artichokes, etc, is done in a finger bowl. There are, however, recent moves to adopt the Asian preference for a heated towel. The custom dates back to the ritualistic washing of hands performed by the Ancient Greeks and Romans and was adopted by Europeans until the invention of the fork when such washing was deemed unnecessary.

FINGER FOOD

Finger foods come in all shapes and sizes and are very fashion conscious, swinging in and out of social favour. Perennial favourites include cucumber sandwiches, chopped egg sandwiches, salmon spread on Jatz biscuits, stuffed avocados, cheese bites, Middle Eastern dips, tomato salsa, vegetable crudités, toasted bread circles topped with reduced cream, wafer-thin ham, cocktail sticks and, of course, good old sausage rolls and pies. The last few decades have seen the emergence of fat-free, gluten-free, lactose-free and often taste-free alternatives.

Some of the most doubtful recipes include French onion soup packet mix combined with sour cream to make a dip — ouch! Then there's deep-fried Camembert cheese wedges and that other dip made from Philadelphia cream cheese mixed with chopped walnuts and prunes. One of the nastiest must be the smoked oyster served on an egg slice on a water biscuit.

Recently finger food has seen 'man-sized' portions (mini hamburgers, individual noodles, Peking duck, etc), but now the golden rule — for this month at least — is 'nothing larger than a twenty cent piece' (scallops, tiny chicken sandwiches, prawns, etc).

RECIPE FOR PARTY CHEESE STRAWS

125 grams (4 $^{1}/_{2}$ ounces) flour
150 grams (5 $^{1}/_{2}$ ounces) butter
175 grams (6 ounces) grated cheddar cheese
$^{1}/_{2}$ teaspoon cayenne pepper
$^{1}/_{2}$ teaspoon salt
$^{1}/_{2}$ teaspoon baking powder

Mix all the ingredients into a dough. Roll out three times, then cut into pieces about 1 centimetre ($^{1}/_{2}$ inch) wide and 10 centimetres (4 inches) long. Brush with a beaten egg and place in a hot oven for about 5 minutes.

DIP

1 packet of onion soup

1 cup reduced cream

2 tablespoons tomato sauce

1 tablespoon vinegar

chives, chopped (optional)

Mix all the ingredients and chill before serving with the cheese straws.

(Mrs O'Malley, Five Dock, NSW)

HORSES' DUVERS

Colloquial name for *hors d'oeuvres*. Duvers can also refer to genitals so this is an interesting description in any slanguage.

NOUVELLE CUISINE

Many food fashions have entered Australia, done the circuit and, thankfully, disappeared. It is doubtful that any hearty eater would have been sorry to see *nouvelle cuisine* (often referred to as 'mean cuisine') disappear. *Nouvelle cuisine,* roughly translated, means: 'I can't believe I paid ninety-six dollars and I'm still hungry.'

It's so beautifully arranged on the plate — you know someone's fingers have been all over it.

(Julia Child, food writer)

The so-called nouvelle cuisine usually means not enough on your plate and too much on your bill.

(Paul Bocuse, chef)

PORCUPINE

The posh made their porcupines out of watermelons and the poor used the humble orange. Either way the porcupine was seen with its toothpicks through the hide gallantly brandishing cheese cubes and brightly coloured miniature pickled onions.

SMORGASBORD

Originally this was a spread of hot and cold dishes served in Sweden as *hors d'oeuvres* or a full buffet meal, usually where guests served themselves. Its literal translation is 'a table of buttered bread'. It became popular in Australia in the 1970s when hotels started advertising 'all you can eat' smorgasbord lunches — caterers viewed it as a labour and timesaving opportunity.

TABLE DECORATION

There's an old saying that 'you can't eat the tablecloth', but that doesn't stop us sometimes pulling out all the stops to make our tables look like they jumped out of a gourmet magazine. Some families have a traditional centrepiece that dominates the table all year round, some crochet elaborately designed spreads, and others like to make displays out of Australian bush flowers. However, tables are meeting places where the true centrepiece should be those seated around it — although a little embellishment never hurt anyone!

Take it away!
Fast food and eating out

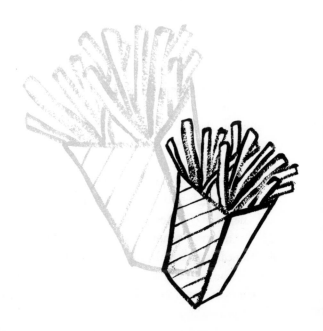

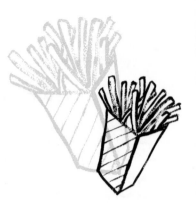

Australians eat in and out — at restaurants, bistros, cafés, pubs, dining rooms, mess halls, cafeterias, snack bars, delis, pizzerias, steakhouses, and roadhouses. We eat, dine, pork out, pig out, hog in, sup, feast, snack, graze, chow down or gobble.

Colonial Australia, and the first half of the twentieth century, saw the restaurants emulating those of Paris, New York and London. French food, particularly if prepared by a French chef, was the preferred dining style. *Cordon bleu* chefs, those of the distinctive blue ribbon, were prized and promoted in newspaper advertising, while their favourite recipes were published in leading magazines. There were many fine dining establishments, particularly but not exclusively, in Sydney and Melbourne where the classic dishes of the French style were served. Around the mid-1900s another international fad reached our shores: *à la Russe* ('in the Russian style') had first been introduced to France and Britain in 1814, after the Peace Agreement, and 'out of compliment to the Emperor of Russia'. Essentially the concept of bringing dishes to the table as hot as humanly possible dates back far earlier than the Russian Court but it was a new thing for most of Europe and definitely new for Australia. Our fine restaurants enthusiastically embraced *à la Russe* serving food from a nearby side table, or 'serving table', direct to the table and guest. Meat was carved at the same side table and waiters would present each part of the dish, including the gravy, in a progression.

A grand dinner in Victorian times could run to as many as fifteen or more individual courses and just as many diverse drinks. No wonder gout was such a common complaint!

In 1888 the *Boomerang* magazine suggested the following menu as suitable for an Antipodean repast:

Soups: macaroni or oxtail

Fish: fried mullet or boiled bream and parsley sauce

Poultry: roast turkey and bread sauce or boiled fowl and ham

Meat: roast beef or veal

Vegetables: French beans, potatoes and marrow

Puddings: plum pudding and custard, blancmange and apricots

Desserts: almonds and raisins, oranges, bananas, muscatels and watermelons, apples and grapes

Beverages: tea, coffee, lemon squash

Queen Victoria's son, Prince Alfred, the Duke of Edinburgh, visited Australia in 1867, and was scheduled to attend a Christmas banquet in Melbourne. This dinner was attended by thousands of freeloading Melburnians and appears to have been the subject of much satire including this parody set to the tune of 'Four & Twenty Blackbirds':

THE FREE BANQUET OF MELBOURNE

Sixty thousand loafers, all jammed together,

At the monster banquet, in very hot weather

Sixty thousand hungry brutes, gnashing their teeth

Eager to drink and gorge the roast beef.

Sixty thousand sausages, dirty and greasy

Dr Louis Lawrence Smith, clean and uneasy.

Sixty thousand drunken louts, roaring out 'Wine!'

A squadron of troopers drawn up in line.

Hundreds of pretty girls, amidst these wretches huddled,

Sixty thousand Christians stupid and fuddled.

Wasn't this a picture to make the doctor wince,

Wasn't this a dainty dish to set before the Prince?

New South Wales also decided to celebrate the Prince's visit with a picnic, at the northern beaches resort of Clontarf. By all reports it was 'straight out of Mrs Beeton's illustrious book' with a grand menu of oysters and stout, chicken, lobster and champagne. Unfortunately this meal also became a fiasco when a local Irishman decided to take a potshot at the Prince. The Duke was whisked away with a superficial wound in the shoulder and the remaining guests decided to toast his recovery with 1100 magnums of French champagne and nearly 800 bottles of beer. Those were the days!

I should explain the confusion over course names. Visitors to America are often amused to see the main course described as 'the entrée' and what we know as the entrée described as 'a starter'. With our use of the English language 'entrée' appears to be directly linked to 'enter' which is 'a starting point'; however, the word 'entrée' technically means 'a dish served as the main part of a meal'. But — and this is where it gets really confusing — it also means 'in a formal dinner, a light dish served before the main course'. Blame those pesky French!

Eating out is a relatively new idea for Australians. It became possible and fashionable around the turn of the twentieth century. We certainly had plenty of 'eating houses' in early Australia, but these were restaurants of necessity rather than convenience. The colonial cities had numerous taverns and cafés and the rural centres had shanties that served the pioneer equivalent of the counter lunch. We also had plenty of 'fast food' too, with saveloy sellers, pie men, and all manner of hot and cold foods sold by street hawkers.

Today, Australian life — particularly for city coastal dwellers — tends to be relaxed and the idea of buying cooked food seems to sit comfortably with most. The hugely successful 'throw another prawn on the barbie' campaign also touched the international market and reinforced our belief in 'God's own country' — and that included the tucker. Eating fish and chips and prawns by the beach is some people's idea of food heaven. I doubt if we view these takeaways as 'fast food', for that description seems to be reserved for the giant chain purveyors like McDonald's, KFC, Pizza Hut and Subway. These chains spread like wildfire and notch up staggeringly high local sales, which means a hell of a lot of Australians are eating a hell of a lot of their highly processed, over-promoted, under-nourishing food. We have been conditioned.

One of the realities of modern society is that there are now large numbers of single diners, and while some restaurants do cater for the lone diner, it still tends to have a 'lonely person' stigma. It is far better to purchase a decent takeaway and eat at home, relaxing with a good bottle of wine.

The term 'fast food' is of American origin; however, the good old meat pie was called 'the fast food of the sixteenth century' so the term is not totally new. Thankfully, we have not adopted the other American term of 'food to go' and the colloquial shout of 'and make it walk!'.

A man who can dominate a London dinner table can dominate the world.

(Oscar Wilde, 1854–1900)

After a good dinner, one can forgive anybody, even one's relatives.

(Oscar Wilde)

One morning, as I went to the freezer door, I asked my wife, 'What should I take out for dinner?' Without a moment's hesitation, she replied, 'Me'.

(Anonymous)

What will you have?
Cried the waiter,
Defiantly picking his nose.
Two hard-boiled eggs, you bastard,
You can't get your fingers in those.

(Reputedly by George Wallace senior)

CARPETBAG STEAK

The carpetbag steak is a popular dish in Australian restaurants. It is a prime beef fillet stuffed with half a dozen fresh oysters. Rich men were sometimes referred to as 'carpetbaggers' and one assumes this is where the association came for the name of the dish. Surprisingly, the dish is not well known in America or Britain.

CHIKO ROLL

An Australian fast food that appears to be a distant relative of the Chinese spring roll, and which is primarily sold in fish and chip shops. Ingredients include cabbage, carrot and minced meat, plus other mysterious substances, which are then deep-fried in batter. Its first commercial sighting appears to be 1951.

Q: What is worse than finding a mouse in your Chiko roll?
A: Half a mouse

CHINESE FOOD

Australians have been eating so-called Chinese food for a long time and much of it is a long way from real Chinese food. For a start we tend to have far more beef and lamb dishes and some extremely strange, brightly coloured sauces. Many Australians will remember the 1950s when they had to take their own saucepans and containers to the local Chinese restaurants, as there were no takeaway containers available. It was commonly referred to as 'going to the chows or chinks' — both derogatory references to Chinese.

CHIPS

For some reason Australians have stuck by the word 'chip' to mean potato slices. We are continually presented with fries or French fries but chips are ours. Large circular flats are called scallops as in the dressmaking cut of the same shape and name.

Chips (and fish) were traditionally sold in newspaper in most Australian shops. This little bit of our culinary heritage has changed in the past ten years and fish 'n' chips is now served in white butcher's paper which, apparently, is more hygienic. You certainly can't read blank paper.

I humbly dips my lid
I dips it dinky di
To the man who orders chips
When the menu says French fries.

(Clem Parkinson, Melbourne)

Australians also call the very thinly sliced commercial snack food 'potato chips' and, of late, new chip lines have been introduced including vegie chips, soy chips and rice chips. The potato chip, like so many other foods, has also been 'done over' and the shelves now carry chips with all sorts of peculiar flavourings including chilli chips, lime pepper chips, chicken chips, and cream cheese and onion chips.

COUNTER LUNCH

The hotel counter lunch is well known for its good value; however, when they were first introduced, in the nineteenth century, they were often offered free as an encouragement for drinkers. An 1890s hotel advertisement offered 'A Square Meal 6d, a Real Good Feed 1/– and a Perfect Gorge 1/6'. The counter lunch had virtually disappeared by the end of that century, reappearing during the Depression of the 1930s when the concept of a meal for a nominal amount seemed a recipe for good business. Newspaper reports show that threepenny counter lunches offered boiled mutton, German sausage, pickles, bread and cheese.

CURRY IN A HURRY

Australia's larger cities have seen the growth of small eat-in and take-out Pakistani and Indian establishments. Open late, these usually brightly painted shops offer a selection of North Indian dishes and savoury items. Most of the North Indian shops are actually owned and operated by Pakistanis rather than Indians. Tikka, samosa and pakora are popular with late night 'grab and run' diners.

DOGGY BAG

A twentieth-century Australian description of any food not consumed at a restaurant and then taken home in a container. One assumes that the leftovers are for the family dog, however this is not always the case.

DOUGHNUTS

The hole in the doughnut has been attributed to the Pennsylvania Dutch who punched holes in the original Dutch *olykoeks*. The hole has also been attributed to a New England sea captain, Hanson Gregory, who in 1847 punched holes in the dough because his mother's doughnuts were not cooked in the centre. Another story has it that the doughnut was created in New York where the dough was made in 'nuts' and was easier to cook in the middle if it had a hole. Yet another theory has it that the holes were created so the doughnuts could be transported on a pole and sold through the street markets. For those fascinated with this subject it should be mentioned that the first Krispy Kreme Donut rolled out (with a hole) in 1937. Commercial doughnuts came to Australia around the late 1940s.

FALAFEL

The falafel is known as 'the Middle Eastern hot dog' because of its popularity and the fact that it is found in Israel, Lebanon, Palestine, Turkey, Egypt, and just about everywhere else in the Middle East. With the increase in Middle Eastern migrants to Australia it is now a favoured takeaway here too. It is usually served in a pita pocketbread with the cooked chickpea paste known as hummus, or tahini sauce and tabouli salad. If you're lucky you will also add some of the fiery Yemenite condiment called zhug.

FAST FOOD

The American term 'fast food' has become part of the Australian colloquial language, implying any takeaway food. Since the emergence of giant international corporations like McDonald's, KFC, Burger King, Pizza Hut, etc, a body of urban myth has developed. One suspects that such myths are created and orally circulated as an attempt to control these multinational companies and their extreme advertising. Small wonder when one learns that something like 8000 McDonald's hamburgers are sold every minute and total sales now exceed 50 billion burgers. An Internet site offers that if all these Big Macs were lined-up they would circle the Earth nineteen times.

One myth has a mother discovering a complete cooked chicken head in her McChicken Wings, while another claims that the 'McDonald's 100% Beef' actually contains eyeballs and that the corporation is the world's largest purchaser of eyeballs.

Rats, mice, cockroaches, nuts and bolts and even Band Aids have reputedly been discovered in fast food products; however, these are usually urban myths and relate to people's fear of big business or the revenge factor.

The corporations also create their own myths, like the 'Colonel's secret herbs and spices' mix. It's said that only two people in the world know the recipe and they only know half each!

Colonel Sanders came to town
Riding on a chicken
Stuck his finger up its bum
And said 'it's finger lickin'

Marry, sir, 'tis an ill cook that cannot lick his own fingers. Therefore he that cannot lick his fingers goes not with me.

(*Romeo and Juliet*, William Shakespeare, 1564–1616)

FIRST RESTAURANT

Larousse Gastronomique pinpoints the world's first restaurant of the modern world as being in France.

Until the eighteenth century, the only places for ordinary people to eat out were inns and taverns. In about 1765, a Parisian 'bouillon seller' named Boulanger wrote on his sign: 'Boulanger sells restoratives fit for the gods', with an advertisement: 'Come unto me, all you whose stomachs are aching, and I will restore you.'

The world has been yelling '*Garçon!*' ever since!

FISH FINGERS

A fish finger is a piece of frozen white fish flesh shaped like a large chip, covered in breadcrumbs and then grilled or fried. It is another brainchild of Clarence Birdseye who led the frozen food generation of the 1920s. The first fish finger appeared in Australia in the 1950s. The French have a similar food they call *baton de poisson*. Presumably this is not as nasty as 'seafood extender' (whatever that is!).

FOOD COURTS

One of Australia's most popular fast food dining destinations is what is referred to as a food court. These are usually situated in large city building basements and suburban shopping centres. They offer a selection of fast food experiences covering a variety of international cuisine. One would imagine such places are a fast food hog's delight. Food is inexpensively priced and outlets share the central table and cleaning costs. Major brand fast food outlets are also included in such centres.

GOING TO THE GREEKS

Greek cafés played an important role in Australia's eating out tradition. Every country town worth its weight in taramasalata hosted a Greek café that served hamburgers, fish and chips, toasted sandwiches, and a range of Greek–Australian food. They were called names like The Paragon, Minerva, Acropolis and New Hellas, but to most Australians they were simply 'the Greeks'. Top of the menu was usually 'mixed grill with the lot'.

It was the Greeks who moved into the quintessential Australian tea-room café and milk bar of the 1950s and defiantly tried to save our Australian-style hamburger. You can occasionally find one of these delicacies with their real meat patties, fried onions and salad featuring beetroot slices but, sadly, the chain burgers seem to have won that battle. In the capital cities there were also Greek taverns where more exotic fare was dished up late at night along with somewhat illegal alcohol.

HAMBURGER

Lore has it that in the 1880s the Hamburg–America shipping line ran between America and Germany carrying Jewish migrants. When they ran out of fresh food they combined ground-up salted dry meat with breadcrumbs and onions, made it into a rissole and served it on a bread roll. One assumes there was no ham in the hamburger and that the name came from the name of the shipping company. The first recorded Australian hamburger was in the 1930s.

Q: Why was Noah never hungry?

A: Because he always had Ham in the house.

HARRY'S CAFÉ DE WHEELS

This is a Sydney meals-on-wheels institution that has moved into 'iconland'. It's famous for its 24-hour meat pies available in a variety of fillings, including mushy peas. The caravan outlet was established by Harry 'Tiger' Edwards after the 1930s Depression, near the gates of the Woolloomooloo naval base where it still stands today.

HOT DOG

It seems most of the world loves the idea of a frankfurter cradled in a bread roll and covered with mustard or tomato sauce. We adopted the American term 'hot dog' but we also called them 'Dagwood dogs' after a popular cartoon strip character.

The Spanish call them *perrito caliente*; the Italians, *cane caldo*; and the French refer to them as *chien chaud*. Germans call them *Heisser Hund*, and the Dutch know them as *worstjes*.

The noblest of all dogs is the hot dog; it feeds the hand that bites it.

HOT FOOD

Hot food in Australian can mean hot as in temperature but is more likely to refer to spicy food such as chilli or curry.

HOT POTATO CLUB

This was an unofficial club of regular travellers on the Manly steam ferry circa 1910. It was so named for the hot potatoes available on the journey, which were cooked in the boat's engine room.

PIE FLOATER

This popular fast food specific to Adelaide is basically a meat pie sitting on a bed of mashed peas and gravy. Sometimes the mush is poured over the pie. It is deliciously messy.

PIZZA

Considered a peasant's meal in Italy for centuries, modern pizza is attributed to baker Raffaele Esposito of Napoli (Naples) in the Italian region of Campania. In 1889, Esposito of Pizzeria di Pietro (now called Pizzeria Brandi) baked pizza especially for the visit of Italian King Umberto I and Queen Margherita.

Food historians also agree that an earlier version of pizza — resembling what today is called focaccia — was consumed by people living around the Mediterranean rim. Today's pizza, complete with pineapple pieces, boiled egg slices and other strange additions, has become a favourite with Australian diners.

The first Pizza Hut opened in Kansas in 1958 and the first Australian outlet for the chain opened in 1970.

ON TOP OF MY PIZZA
(Air: 'On Top of Old Smokey')

On top of my pizza
All covered with sauce
Could not find the mushrooms
I think they got lost

I looked in the closet
I looked in the sink
I looked in the cup that
Held my cola drink

I looked in the saucepan
Right under the lid
No matter where I looked
Those mushrooms stayed hid

Next time you make pizza
I'm begging you, please
Do not give me mushrooms
But just plain old cheese

PLUTO PUP

A rather disgusting fast food, which can still be found at fun parks and sideshow food alleys. Essentially a frankfurter on a stick, it is battered and deep-fried and then — as if that punishment wasn't enough — it is dipped in a heavy dousing of tomato sauce.

RAILWAY FOOD

Australian rail celebrated its 150th anniversary in 2005 and mention must be made of the railway food kiosks and restaurants that were such a feature of train travel. The grand railway stations, like Sydney Central and Melbourne's Flinders Street, all hosted large dining areas and, in most capital cities, white linen, sparkling silverware and predictable bain marie displayed food. The menu was interestingly predictable — oxtail soup, roast lamb and mint sauce, or corned beef and white sauce, tinned fruit salad and custard. Prices were acceptable, the service slightly eccentric and the clientele a mix of lonely, hurried businessmen, flustered country families and the occasional lost soul.

The railway refreshment room was another thing altogether and, for a new chum, a hysterical challenge. The country train guard would announce that the train would stop at Cootamundra or some other rural station 'for ten minutes only'. Seasoned travellers knew that it was a race against time and, once the train had stopped, they would sprint down the platform and order their sandwich, pie and beer. These were the days when trains didn't have dining cars and downing a beer at every stop became a feature of regional travel. The railway pie and sauce, usually referred to as a 'dog's eye with dead horse', was actually made in the railway catering kitchens in each state capital. They sold millions and they weren't half bad!

The following song, written in the 1950s and published in the *Queensland Centenary Pocket Songbook*, 1959, sums up the trials and tribulations of Australian railway refreshment rooms.

ON THE QUEENSLAND RAILWAY LINES

On the Queensland railway lines
There are stations where one dines;
Private individuals

293

Also run refreshment stalls.

Chorus
Bogan, Tungun, Rollingstone.
Mungar, Murgan, Marathone,
Guthalingra, Pinkenba,
Wanko, Yammaba—ha ha ha

Pies and coffee, baths and showers
Are supplied at Charters Towers;
At Mackay the rule prevails
Of restricting showers to males.

Males and females, high and dry,
Hang around at Durikai,
Boora-Mugga, Djarawong,
Giligulgul, Wonglepong.

Iron rations come in handy
On the way to Dirranbandi;
Passengers have died of hunger
During halts at Garradunga.

Let us toast, before we part,
Those who travel, stout of heart,
Drunk or sober, rain or shine,
On a Queensland railway line.

SANDWICH

The sandwich takes its name from John Montague, the fourth Earl of Sandwich (1718–92). Apparently the Earl was a rabid gambler and rather than leave the card table he asked for some cold roast beef between two slices of bread. This also had the added advantage of keeping his fingers free from grease.

There's a link to Australia, as it was Captain Cook who named the Sandwich Islands (Hawaiian Islands) after this very same man, who had been Lord of the Admiralty.

Sandwiches are the ultimate fast food and, understandably, we make them out of all manner of fillings. Sandwich bars are designed for the adventurous customer who simply has to point to a number of ingredients — no questions asked.

SAVELOYS

Saveloys were extremely popular in our capital cities from colonial days through to the 1940s when saveloy sellers hawked their brand of fast food through the streets. They carried small portable saveloy cookers, usually with a small heating device, strapped to their chests as they yelled their calls of 'All hot and steaming' with the more ribald ones offering 'What d'yer choke yer mother with? Hot saveloys!' It was common to give your stove a name like 'Spirit of England' or 'John Bull's Best'.

Frankfurters or red saveloys were not called hot dogs until after World War II and the commencement of the Americanisation of our language.

'Battered savs' were a popular Australian fast food: saveloys dipped in batter and fried. At some outside events, like the annual agricultural show or visiting circus, these battered savs were dipped in tomato sauce or melted cheese.

SHWARMA

A Middle Eastern sandwich similar to the *gyra* and usually made with spit-roasted lamb or chicken served with *fuul*, a paste made from fava beans.

SPRING ROLL

According to legend, spring rolls have their origins in the annual Chinese New Year celebration, called the Spring Festival. The first spring rolls featured fresh vegetables from the spring harvest; meat was added later. Today, spring rolls are a popular treat during Chinese New Year celebrations. Their gold colour symbolises wealth and prosperity for the coming year.

I'll drink to that!

Traditional toasts

Australians have an international reputation for being hard drinkers. We are referred to as — and we call ourselves — booze artists, winos, plonksters, groggers, piss artists, grog guzzlers, beer barons, and bloody good drinkers. We go on the ran-tan, to a booze-up, a piss-up, up to the boozer, or to the rubbity-dub. We get pissed as newts, shickered, full as a goog, blasted, full as ticks or pissed as a fart. We get home trying to avoid the booze bus and the blister and strife. Next day we recover with a stinker of a headache or a hangover from hell, and the only way to recover is to have a hair of the dog that took a bite out of you.

The word 'toast' is the standard English word used to mean a salute to somebody or something offered prior to consuming a drink. Considering the importance placed on alcohol in Australia's history it is no surprise that toasting emerged as a popular expression of folklore.

Sadly, toasting — like so many other social expressions born and bred in the pub such as singing, reciting and traditional yarn telling— has been almost annihilated by electronic entertainment and sound systems. It is hard to sing, let alone talk, in the modern hotel where television competes with video music screens, poker machines, electronic cash registers and insistent calls of 'number 68 to the snack bar, please'.

Early Australia inherited the toasting tradition from our British and Celtic ancestors but the art of toasting has a much longer history. As early as the sixth century BC, the Greeks were toasting the health of their friends for a highly practical reason — to assure them that the wine they were about to share wasn't poisoned. To spike the wine with poison had become a common means of ridding one's self of pesky wives, annoying friends, and political and social opponents. It's not difficult to see why sharing wine became a symbol of friendship with the host pouring wine from a common pitcher and drinking his glass before his guests. The Romans, impressed by the Greeks in general, and living in extremely Machiavellian times, adopted the custom with understandable enthusiasm.

By the 1700s, the custom had spread throughout Europe and especially among the upper class. Toasts were offered to a wide range of subjects and especially to beautiful women. A woman who was recipient of a number of such offerings was referred to as the 'toast of the town'.

By the 1800s, toasting was the proper thing to do and the lower and middle classes, eager to emulate the toffs, also raised their wooden and pewter mugs with toasts to their livestock, their friends and life itself. The penal settlement of Australia was controlled by a military governorship, and the primitive Government House hosted many dinners where toasts were raised to the King, the head of Royal Navy, the company, and the sundry guests. As the colony grew so spread the custom until, in the 1850s, toasts were raised to the wonderful discoveries of gold.

Today toasts are still very much a part of our lives, especially on those occasions where we celebrate anniversaries, birthdays, reunions, holidays and weddings. It seems as if most dinner parties, including gatherings of friends at restaurants, are accompanied by toasting. Most often it is a simple toast to all those present where everyone raises their glasses simultaneously after one person has 'proposed a toast' — usually a simple 'Here's to health!' or 'Here's to luck!' or even 'Here's to us!' If there is a newcomer or special visitor then the toast might be directed towards them. In recent years the toast has resulted in all people at the table then clinking their glasses with every other person — this is often troublesome with a large group. Recently a new version has appeared where the toaster clinks his or her glass and the table 'passes it on' so as to avoid the inevitable long arm. It is considered bad luck to not clink or, in the latter example, break the chain.

Special events call for special toasting custom. At a christening luncheon, toasts are offered to the baptised child first by the godparents, then by the parents, followed by the siblings and then any guests.

The father of the bride formally announces engagements with an appropriate toast. Usually the father of the groom responds. At the wedding reception, at which a meal is served, toasts are offered once all of the guests have been seated and have been served their drinks. At less formal affairs, toasts should be offered after everyone has gone through the receiving line and has been served a drink.

There have been some famous toasts in history. Humphrey Bogart's toast to Ingrid Bergman in *Casablanca* — 'Here's looking at you, kid' — must be somewhere at the top of that list. But who could go past Groucho Marx, who offered, 'I drink to your charm, your beauty and your brains — which gives you a rough idea of how hard up I am for a drink.'

Some Australian toasts are also simple rhymes that happen to have been used as toasts. Some are long but most are extremely short. Some are extracts from longer poems or songs. Many capture our unique sense of humour — our so-called 'dry' sense of humour.

Toasts, being a folklore expression, are passed on through oral transmission. That is, they are usually not learnt from a book but from repeated performance of friends. It is not uncommon for an individual to have his favourite and sometimes only toast that is repeated every time that person shares a drink … ad infinitum. It could possibly be a simple 'Here's mud in your eye' or even 'Cheers!' but the toast is always accepted in the spirit it is given.

BUBBLES

Bubbles in your drink mean you will have good financial fortune.

DRINK

He that goes to bed thirsty rises healthy.

THE DRINKER'S DREAM

Do you remember the summer of '63
That melted the rocks of the backcountry?
The year the sand fused into glass
And the sun burnt the gorge in Murchison Pass?

Well, I was there in that terrible heat,
Where borders of West and South Australia meet,
About 900 miles from Oonapelli,.
That was the time I met — Ned Kelly.

Out of the simmering, heat haze fog,
Strode Kelly, with arms loaded with grog,
'I'm Kelly alright!' he said to me,
'And I'm twice as dead as you'll ever be.'

'For 90 years I wandered this place,
In search of a suitable drinking mate.'
'You've found him!' I quickly said,
'So let's put some of these bottles to bed.'

We drank in the sun and talked of days
When men wore guts where they now wear stays,
Then came the thump of many feet,
As heavy boots thudded thru that stifling heat.

A line of men fractured the desert haze,
T'was old Paddy Hannan—Gawd spare me days!
Followed by Thunderbolt, Burke and Wills,
Ben Hall, Captain Moonlight and Saltbush Bill.

Each carried some grog — cold as a tomb,
So Ned and I moved, gave them some room,

To place the keg that was carried by Hall,
Fair in the centre, and on tap to all.

Then in strode Lawson and Ludwig Leichhardt,
Who said: 'Lassiter's coming, but it's OK to start,
I've invited some friends from the desert nearby,
And they're all decent blokes, here's dust in your eye!'

We were joined by a bright green kangaroo,
And an overweight wombat, who did a soft shoe,
A dignified dingo, with performing fleas,
And a soprano galah who squawked off-key.

And a sabre-toothed snake whistled 'Auld Lang Syne',
While a marsupial mouse, with his nose, twitched time.
We sat in the sun and we drank for a week,
In the finest company a man could keep.

I danced me a jig, for comic relief,
And in disturbing the dust found Lassiter's Reef.
There was copper and nickel and silver galore,
Diamonds the size of a knob on a door.

Rubies and sapphires — a fabulous haul,
And ten pounds of gold to each shovel full.
But none gave a thought to such meaningless wealth,
For each was contented unto himself.

After we'd drank for a year and a day,
The party broke up and we went our own ways,
I travelled south to the Nullarbor Plains,
And in two or three days was back home again.

But I said not a word of where I had been,
And never recounted the things I had seen,
But the experience taught me one important fact:

Never drink in the sun without wearing a hat!

(Collected from Bob Taylor, Rockhampton, NSW, 1990)

THE PRESERVATION OF THE AUSSIE MALE

The horse and mule live 30 years
And nothing know of wine and beers
The goat and sheep at 20 die
With never taste of scotch or rye
The cow drinks water by the ton
And at 18 years is mostly done
The dog at 16 cashes in
Without the aid of rum or gin
The cat in milk and water soaks
And then in 12 short years it croaks
The modest, sober, bone-dry hen
Lays eggs for nogs and dies at ten
All animals are strictly dry
They sinless live and quickly die
But sinful gin-full, rum-soaked men
Survive for three score years and ten
And some of us, the mighty few
Stay pickled till we're 92

(Collected from Bob Taylor, Rockhampton, September 1991)

WHY THE HELL DO WE DRINK?

We drink for joy and become miserable.
We drink for sociability and become argumentative.
We drink for sophistication and become obnoxious.
We drink to help us sleep and awake exhausted.
We drink for exhilaration and end up depressed.
We drink to gain confidence and become afraid.
We drink to make conversation and become incoherent.
We drink to diminish our problems and see them multiply.

DRINKING TOASTS

Here's to you as good as you are
Here's to 'em as bad as I am
And as good as you are and as bad as I am
I'm as good as you are as bad as I am.

I wish you health
I wish you wealth
I wish you gold in store
I wish you heaven when you die
I wish I could wish you more.

Here's to the turkey when you're hungry
Champagne when you're dry,
A pretty girl when you need her
And heaven when you die.

Merry met, and merry part,
I drink to thee with all my heart.

God made the vine
Was it a sin
That man made wine
To drown trouble in?

When God made Man, he made him out of string.
He had a little left, so He left a little thing.
When God made Woman, He made her out of lace.
He didn't have enough, so He left a little place.
Here's to God!

Here's to the life of the camel
Whose sexual desire is greater than anyone thinks.
One night in a moment of sexual madness
It tried to make love to the Sphinx.

But the Sphinx's posterior opening
Was clogged with the sands of the Nile,
Which accounts for the hump on the camel
And the Sphinx's inscrutable smile.

Here's to the tree of life
Long may it stand
It grows upon two rocks
Upon the Isle of Man
Here's to that little plant
That doth around it twine
It comes in flower every month
And bears fruit once in nine.

May God above send down a dove
With wings as sharp as razors
To cut the flamin' mongrel's throat
Who tried to cut our wages

There are many good reasons for drinking —
And one has just come into my head
If a man doesn't drink when he's living
How the hell can he drink when he's dead?

Selected sources

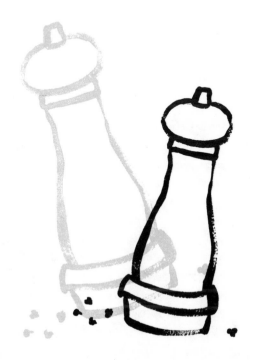

esearching a collection like this is a bit like making a stew out of what's available in the larder. Although much of the material was collected over the past forty years in my work as a folklorist, I also dipped into numerous newspapers, magazines, manuscripts, collections and books. I am grateful to the Mitchell Library in Sydney, the many people who have granted me oral history interviews since 1971 and to those keen researchers, food writers and cooks who have shared their wisdom and reminiscences. I am also grateful to the Queensland Sugar Corporation for their notes and statistics on the Australian sugar industry.

BIBLIOGRAPHY

Allen, Stewart Lee, *In the Devil's Garden,* Random House, New York, 2002

Anderson, Jean, *American Cookbook*, Clarkson Potter, 1997

Australian Journal, circa 1860–80s

Australian Women's Weekly, Sydney

Baker, Sidney J., *The Australian Language*, Currawong, Sydney, 1966

Blainey, G., *Black Kettle and Full Moon*, Penguin, Melbourne, 2003

Boswell, James, *Tour to the Hebrides,* London, 1785

Bryant, Max, *Bush Cooking,* Kangaroo Press, Sydney, 1988

Duyff, Roberta, *Food Folklore: Tales and truths about what we eat,* Chronimed Publishing, ND, USA

Dyson, Laurel Evelyn, *How to Cook a Galah,* Lothian, Melbourne, 2002

Fahey, Warren, *Classic Bush Yarns*, HarperCollins, Sydney, 2001,

— *Diggers' Song*, AMHP, Loftus, 1996,

— *How Mabel Laid the Table*, State Library of NSW Press, Sydney, 1992,

— *Ratbags & Rabblerousers*, Currency Books, Sydney, 2000

Fahey, Warren and Seal, Graham, *Old Bush Songs*, ABC Books, Sydney, 2005

First Australian Continental Cookery Book, Cosmopolitan, Melbourne, 1937

Green, Jonathan, *Consuming Passions*, Ballantyne, 1985

Hatfield, Jean, *Good Cheap Cooking*, Rigby, Adelaide, 1979

Harney, Bill, *Bill Harney's Cookbook*, Landsdowne, Melbourne, 1960

Hayes, Babette, *A Treasury of Australian Cooking*, Nelson, Sydney, 1962

Larousse Gastronomique, Hamlyn Books, London, 2001

Leach, Margaret, ed., *Funk and Wagnell's Standard Dictionary of Folklore*, 1950

McArthur, Kathleen, *Bread and Dripping Days*, Kangaroo Press, Kenthurst, 1981

Queensland Centenary Pocket Songbook, Edwards & Shaw, Sydney, 1959

Rudd, Steele, *On Our Selection*, published by **The Bulletin**, Sydney, 1902

Sorenson, Edward S., *Life in the Australian Backblocks*, Whitcombe and Tombs, Melbourne, 1911

Tannahill, R., *Food in History*, Crown, New York, 1988

Toussaint-Samat, *A History of Food*, Blackwell, USA, 1994

Webb, Mrs M., *The Doctor in the Kitchen*, London, 1935

ABOUT THE AUTHOR

Warren Fahey AM is a graduate of the Dingo University and School of Hard Knocks. He lives in Sydney where he collects, researches and writes about Australian folklore, produces records, cooks and occasionally sings bush ballads. He was awarded the Order of Australia in 1996, the Centenary Medal in 2003, and the CMAA Golden Gumleaf for Lifetime Achievement in 2004.

Warren Fahey can be contacted at wfahey@bigpond.net.au or Australian Folklore Unit, P.O. Box 262, Potts Point, NSW 2011. His website for Australian folklore is www.warrenfahey.com